SURVIVING HELL

SURVIVING HELL

SURRENDER ON CEBU

LTC WILLIAM D. MINER WITH LEWIS A. MINER

Based on the True Accounts of LTC William D. Miner

TURNER
PUBLISHING COMPANY

Turner Publishing Company

445 Park Avenue, 9th Floor
New York, NY 10022

200 4th Avenue North, Suite 950
Nashville, TN 37219

www.turnerpublishing.com

Surviving Hell: Surrender on Cebu

Previously published as *Surrender on Cebu: A POW's Diary - WWII* (2001) and
Surviving Hell: The Journey of a WWII POW in the Pacific 1942-1945 (2010).

Cover and book design: Kym Whitley

Library of Congress Cataloging-in-Publication Data

Miner, William D. (William Dilworth)
[Surrender on Cebu]
Surviving hell : surrender on Cebu / William D. Miner.
    pages cm
Originally published under title: Surrender on Cebu. 2001.
ISBN 978-1-59652-768-3
1. Miner, William D. (William Dilworth) 2. World War, 1939-1945--Prisoners and
prisons, Japanese. 3. Prisoners of war--United States--Biography. 4. Prisoners of war-
-Japan--Biography. I. Title.
D805.J3M545 2013
940.54'7252092--dc23
[B]
                                    2013002009

Printed in the United States of America
13 14 15 16 17 18 19—0 9 8 7 6 5 4 3 2 1

To my children and grandchildren:

This document contains a copy of the diary which I wrote during
World War II while I was a Japanese Prisoner of War.
I wrote and kept the diary at the risk of torture and death.
I am giving you a copy of this diary along with my personal accounts,
with the hope that you will keep it as a family heirloom
and give copies to your children and families.

Lovingly,
William Dilworth Miner (father and grandfather) 1994

"There are many books written by ex-POWs relating their terrible experiences during their captivity and I have quite a few of them, but this one, a diary of action, suffering and final freedom, is one of the best.

"The author—unlike most prewar personnel—made it a must to meet with Filipino civilians and thus was able to visit many sights seldom if ever seen by soldiers and officers on duty in the islands. He was a keen observer of people, places and events in Manila and other locations and his memory for names and ranks is excellent. To have been able to remember them in this book is most unusual."

—Jean Reldy, March 31, 2003

TABLE OF CONTENTS

FOREWORD

Surviving Hell is a story that has been waiting to be told; it is the story of Bill Miner during World War II. It is a series of accounts, from May 1941 to October 1945, describing his service on the island of Cebu and his subsequent capture and imprisonment by Japanese forces. It is a forceful and disturbing story that encompasses adventure, courage, persecution, death, and liberation. The effects of imprisonment for 39 months, with torture and deprivation being central to that imprisonment, are clearly marked. His ability to survive and transcend his war experiences and to go on to a substantial academic career and meaningful retirement are all enormous accomplishments.

"I am lucky," Bill Miner wrote. "People fell beside me and people were blown apart beside me. Everywhere I went as a prisoner, I tried to be aware of the situation and use it to the best of my ability in order to survive."

Bill Miner mentions at some length the people that he encountered during his tour of duty in the Philippines. These people were real, were factual. He introduces from time to time elements of individual personalities and what happened to them. I have endeavored to keep this journal intact, as much as possible, to clearly reflect what Bill Miner had in mind as he experienced the events that he narrates. Some accounts were written on Japanese toilet paper and were carried on his person at the risk of torture and death. A small, pocket-size memo pad was also used to tally the days of captivity and to record events.

In September 1945, Bill Miner reflected: "I have lost every close friend I had out here, have been through filth, destruction, near death many times, and lived under conditions that would warp men's souls. . . . "

—Lewis A. Miner

PREFACE

I would like to begin this third edition with the following letter:

LTC William Miner's letter,
written to his son Charles (Chuck) Miner,
in March 1975
(Edited)

Dear Chuck,

While you were home, just after you received notice of your appointment, you told me you were at the bottom of the ladder. That term "bottom of the ladder" always reminds me of an event in my life when I was at the bottom of the iron ladder and I didn't think I would ever make it to the top! How many times I was on the point of giving up and letting myself fall back to the bodies below me I cannot remember. Somehow I forced myself to hang on and take another step up the rungs to crawl out of the ship's hold!

It was on the prison ship *Oryoku Maru* which loaded 1,619 American prisoners in its hold on December 12 or 13, 1944. The ship left Manila Harbor the morning of the 14th, I think. We were under constant air attack by American carrier planes as we left. Its rudder being disabled, the ship gradually moved into Subic Bay (a few miles north of Manila). During the night, barges took the Japanese civilians off the ship and only the 1,619 POWs and a few guards remained aboard. The first two planes dived and bombed our ship, with a bomb striking the stern somewhere. The third dive bomber seemed directly above our open ship hold. It came screaming down at us and passed over and up. We waited in deathly silence for the bomb to fall. Out of that silence a nameless GI shouted, "Give them hell!" A second silence followed his voice and then the bomb exploded in our hold. It dropped through the open hatch, just missing the upper deck, forward side, and exploded about 20 feet away from me, blowing the side out of the ship and killing most of the 115 field officers. I was very fortunate in my location in several respects: first, the bomb fell away from me and not on me. Second, I was sheltered by the companionway (stairway) coming down from the deck to the floor of the hold (I had staggered down that stairway looking for a chance to get out quickly if the boat should sink). Instead of going back toward the side of the hold, I staged a fall and crawled under the stairway out of the way of men coming down. The guards let me stay rather than stop the men coming down (plus the area around me was soon filled up with closely packed men). I had more shelter and more air in that little triangular space under those steps than I would have had among the masses of men (where several men had their throats slit by bloodsuckers during the two previous nights).

When that bomb exploded, that heavy stairway sheltered me from falling beams, although an 8-inch square wooden beam hit its side and came to rest within six inches of my head. I was knocked cross-eyed silly for a while. The uninjured prisoners soon began to mill around and I was one of the first to start up those steps. (While those steps gave me some shelter during the first two days, they soon proved to be one of the filthiest places in the hold. The crap bucket details spilled the overflowing buckets on the steps. I got wet several times.) As we started up the steps, a Jap officer and several soldiers appeared at the top of the hold. The officer pointed his pistol at me and yelled something. I looked at him and at his gun and there was no doubt in my mind that he would kill me if I didn't get off the ladder. I moved back and went under the ladder. A big officer beside me sneered, "What's the matter? Are you afraid, Miner?" I answered, "Yes, I am!" "Well, let me go then." He got on the first step and I saw the Jap officer's pistol spout fire. I heard the thud of a bullet in the man beside me; he gasped twice and fell backward, shot through the heart, dead! The Jap officer emptied his pistol at others in the opening near me. Three Jap guards also fired into the hold. I just sank down under that ladder as far out of sight as possible and stayed there until after the Japs suddenly left. The ship tilted and was sinking!

Other prisoners then started up the stairway, which I had hastily vacated in the face of the pistol. I didn't try to get back on the stairway as the maddened men were screaming and throwing each other off the stairway in their effort to get out of the hold to the deck. I looked around and saw three men climbing "straight up" a steel ladder fastened to the side of the hold. The first one made it to the top and flopped onto the deck. The other two got part way up and fell off from exhaustion. The ladder was clear and I scrambled over the bodies to get to it. I put my hands on a rung and started to put my foot on the bottom rung, but I couldn't lift my foot that high. It wasn't until I stood on a pile of bodies that I got my foot on the high step. The way was clear above, but I could pull myself up from one rung to the next only with superhuman effort. Several times I almost gave up and let myself fall. But when I looked down at the bloody mess on the hold floor, I realized that if I didn't force myself to expend the effort, I would fall back to my death, since I wouldn't have the strength to get up the ladder again. I managed to move up a rung at a time. After what seemed an eternity, I finally made the last terrific upward surge and flopped over on the deck. After lying there to rest awhile, I got up to find a life preserver and swam ashore.

When you mentioned the bottom of the ladder, I thought again of standing in the hold and wondering if I could make it—one man had succeeded but two were at my feet having given up and fallen off. It was a long, long way up. . . .

Love,
Dad

ACKNOWLEDGMENTS

Without the time and effort of many people, this book would never have been possible.

Beginning with Clara Miner (Bill's wife) who, in the late 1940s, typed part of the original manuscript on frail onionskin paper, using the manual ribbon typewriter of those days.

I am under deep obligation to my brother, Charles and his wife Tiffany, for their review of the journal and for providing pictures and supporting documentation. My sincere thanks to my sister, Georgia, for providing the original diary, without which this book would not have been complete.

Special thanks to Bill Lair, John Jenkins, Robert Thielhelm, James Litton, Miriam Gremillion, Fred Baldassarre, Jean Reldy, Roy Moore, Bobby Stanford, and Xavier Aboitiz for their time, interest in, and devotion to this work.

I would be remiss not to thank my father for his perseverance in setting down the accounts as they occurred. Rarely does someone get to interact with a historical figure over a long period and be so profoundly influenced by his example. His courage and sacrifice were the inspiration for this book. It would have been a shame for these accounts to have been left on a shelf, moved from time to time and eventually discarded. As I put the final touches on each page, I am subtly reminded of the great sacrifices that he and his fellow soldiers made by the sounds of his grandchildren playing in the yard. On this day, no bombs are falling from the sky and no invading army threatens their well being. Thank you, Dad!

I would like to mention my children—Anthony, Andrew (US Armed Forces), Karilynn, and Kaleh Miner—for their support and interest. This book is for them and my brother's children—Sarah, Kristin, Cody, Tad, and generations to follow.

Finally, I would like to thank everyone who read the first and second editions. Thank you for your time, interest, and encouragement.

—Lewis A. Miner

PROLOGUE

The spring of 1941 was portentous of coming events. Already the war in Europe had reached critical stages. Germany had overrun all of Western Europe except Spain and Turkey. The former was pro-Axis while the latter was strictly neutral. The German forces in Russia had penetrated almost to Moscow and the battle of Stalingrad was fluctuating day by day. In Britain, the air arm was blitzing as wide a swath of destruction in a series of "Coventry Raids" as her ground troops were in Russia.

In the United States, Roosevelt was getting the Lend-Lease Program underway with much opposition. The Selective Service act of 1940 was slowly getting underway as well. Senators Burton K. Wheeler and Gerald Nye were gratifying their ego for prominence and sowing seeds of shame. They became leaders for a policy of Isolationism when they had the chance to be leaders of a "Cooperation for National Defense" movement. Any clear-thinking citizen could see what was in the air; why these men, supposedly leaders and statesmen, could be so blind I'll never understand. Those two men by their hindrance to national defense were responsible for more dead and wounded American soldiers than any other American at home or in the field. Soldiers were using trucks marked "Tanks" in Army training. They threw stones as substitutes for hand grenades. You know the rest of the story.

The public, in general, was doing a lot of wishful hoping and desperately shutting its ears and eyes to cold fact that the last remaining great power, the United States, would sooner or later be forced into the war. Americans have had such an easy life in the last two generations that they have developed the philosophical characteristic of shutting their minds to unpleasant situations and letting somebody else work the situation out for them, that is, until the situation gets personal, then they go into action.

On the Indiana University campus life was pretty sedate and untouched by the outside momentous events soon to affect the entire campus. A few of the men students were complaining because they would have to go into the Army via draft in June 1941.

Steven Skalsie, in 1941, when asked what he was going to do after graduation, replied he was going to work for a commercial company. The young man was an ROTC graduate, so I asked him what about going into the Army and being in on the ground floor, as a war was coming. "Hell!" he replied, "the war and the Army are the least of my worries."

Robert Schilling, 1941, when asked his opinion of the nearness of war, remarked that he "hoped to spend next Christmas at home."

Robert Irrnann, a graduate student in history, said, "I don't see how it can be avoided, but we can hope for the best."

Dennis Volonopolo, also a graduate student in history, said, "Let's worry about it if it comes."

In general, it seemed that the people (even the thinking people) were prone to shut their minds to the fact that war was inevitable. Instead of preparing for events that common sense and logic told them were inevitable and soon to come, they chose to prepare for the situation after the "horse had been stolen."

ONE

STUDENT DAYS AT INDIANA UNIVERSITY

FROM A MUCH MORE PERSONAL STANDPOINT, SPRING AND FINAL EXAMS WERE IN THE CAMPUS AIR BY MAY 15. ON RETURNING FROM classes at noon, Thursday, May 15, 1941, I found a letter from the War Department headquarters at Indianapolis informing me that I was being considered for duty in the Philippine Islands and to be prepared for immediate assignment.

This letter rather upset my daily schedule. I spent the afternoon informing my professors that likely I was leaving soon for the Philippines in spite of the fact that I was still in school.

I also had some civilian affairs that I would have to take care of if I were going away. It looked like (and felt like it, too) I was on the jump.

On Friday, May 16, I cut classes. I rose early, ate breakfast as soon as possible, and started to Indianapolis via hitchhiking. As I remember it, I made fair time and was soon in the city. Once there I went to the War Department office under Col. F. M. Armstrong, assisted by the Adj. Capt. Floyd Fix.

On meeting the colonel and showing him the letter the conversation went something like this.

Colonel: "First lieutenant and single, eh?"

"Yes sir, Colonel, just how definite is it that I will receive this assignment?"

Colonel: "Pretty certain. Captain, will you get the lieutenant's 201 file? You see, half of our reserves have already been ordered to active duty, many of them married men with children. We have the policy of not sending married men out of the continental limits of the U.S."

Capt. Fix appeared with my 201 file and another officer, a captain. The captain had volunteered for duty in the Philippines and apparently been turned down. The captain immediately started talking to Col. Armstrong as soon as he entered.

"Colonel," the captain said, "I thought I was being called to active duty and assigned to the Philippines. Now I receive this letter telling me I am not. What is the trouble?"

The colonel, "I am sorry, we can't use you."

"But sir, I was told by one of the staff of this headquarters that my name was on the list to go," the captain cried, "and what's more, I want to go and I volunteered for the detail!"

"I can't help that, captain," the colonel replied. "The cold turkey is that we are not sending any married men over to the Philippine Department now. You are married and have a family and that disqualified you for the PI Dept. We are sending only single men out there now. In spite of what some of my staff may have told you, you are not going. That's final!"

Turning to Capt. Fix, his adjutant, he said, "Fix, if this man's name is on the list to go, scratch it! Good day, Captain."

The colonel then picked up my 201 file and leafed through it murmuring, "Single, within the age limit, qualified, da da da. Capt. Fix, is this lieutenant's name on the list?"

"It is, colonel," responded the adjutant.

"Well, son," said the gray-haired colonel, "I guess you're one of them. It's a wonder we haven't called you before. If you hadn't been in school you would already be in the Army."

"Colonel," I said, "it's dead sure I am going?"

"I'm afraid it is," he smiled.

By this time I was wringing wet with sweat and the pit of my stomach felt like it was about to upset. I felt my fate was being decided before my eyes and within my hearing, yet I couldn't stop it for one second. How little did I realize standing there, that many, many times during the next four and a half years I was going to experience that same sick feeling in the pit of the stomach. Experience it so often that I would grow used to it. Nor did I expect later, time and time again, to watch unmoved a group of barbarian sadists decide my fate and thousands of others.

After being told I was certain to be shipped I left the colonel's office and hitchhiked over to New Castle, IN, to see H. G. Ingersoll and family. Hitchhiking was good in those days and I made good time. By noon I was out at the Ingersoll Steel Plant having lunch with Harold. After lunch I straightened up my business with him, I called on Victor Payne of the American Security Co. of New Castle. From Payne's I went over to the New Castle High School and visited Herbert Heller between classes. Herb was later Lt. (Sr. Gr.) Herbert Heller, USNR, in radar work, stationed on New Caledonia along with Robert Hamilton, who was a Seabee there.

Lt. Heller and I had quite a talk in those few minutes. We agreed that the trend of the times was straight toward war and we did not see how it could be avoided. To us we could not see how John Q. Public could be so indifferent to conditions concerning his welfare, but he was and still is after fighting the greatest war of our national history. Herb bid me a fond farewell and wished me the best of luck. I remember later in prison I often thought of our last talk and that I sure needed all the luck he could wish me.

By this time it was just about 3:00 P.M. and there was a 3:15 P.M. bus running from New Castle to Indianapolis. I wanted to take that bus, I remember, so I had to run for it because I stopped on the way out to see Miss Florence Smith whom I had dated in the past. She was busy when I walked into her classroom and I guess hesitated about talking to me during the class period because it would only increase the commotion I had already caused in the classroom. Realizing that she was waiting for the class to be dismissed at 3:00 P.M., I commandeered a sheet of paper from a nearby notebook, wrote a note, folded it up, and left it on the desk of the seat on which I was sitting. Then I left.

I arrived back at Bloomington about 7:00 P.M., worn out and dirty. On the way back to the dormitory I stopped at Westminster Inn to tell Miss Treva Rousch that I would be late for our date. On reaching my dormitory room I cleaned up and laid down on the bed for "just a minute." This was shortly after 7:00 P.M. When I awakened from the "minute's" relaxation, the clock said 11:30 P.M. Consternation reigned in my mind about a broken date. I thought the hour too late to make amends that evening, so went to bed. The next morning I made my peace with the young lady via phone.

The next morning I spent calling on my professors, Kohlmeger, Winther, Franzen, Thurston, Dean Smith, and the professor of economics. Everyone that I saw promised and did give the most cooperation that was possible. I was to report the next Thursday, May 22, at Fort Hayes, Columbus, OH. Each professor gave me a special exam on the next Monday or Tuesday, depending on when I could find time to take it. I had to take these exams without doing any reviewing as there was so little time to completely tie up all affairs in civilian life, pack my things, purchase some luggage, et cetera. May 19 and 20, Monday and Tuesday, I took exams in 15 hours of subjects. I drew a straight B in all those exams. I think my professors must have been prejudiced in my favor because such good grades without any traditional cramming and reviewing was not for the likes of me, for a Phi Beta Kappa perhaps, but not for the ordinary student.

On May 21, Dad and Mother came down to Indiana University bringing with them my youngest sister Ruth who was a senior at Knox College. I got to visit with them for about four hours on Wednesday. They departed taking all my worldly goods that I wasn't going to take into the Army with me. My other sister was in Chicago and I never got to see her until years later, after I returned from overseas. When my family drove away from

Indiana University on May 21, 1941, I was just leaving for two years. By that time in 1943 I was to have seen them again. The infinite little spark of life called man never dreams what the future may make reality. It was 54 months, four and a half years, before I saw my folks again. During that 54 months, I was to live more experiences than the ordinary man would ever dream of in his lifetime.

TWO

FORT HAYES

EARLY THURSDAY MORNING, MAY 22, 1941, I CLIMBED ABOARD THE BUS IN BLOOMINGTON, IN., EN ROUTE TO FORT HAYES IN COLUMBUS, OH. The trip was uneventful except for meeting Mrs. Floyd Fix, wife of Capt. Floyd Fix, stationed at Fort Hayes. In the following days I called on the captain in his office asking for pointers and advice about my coming trip.

I suppose my experiences at the reception center were similar to that of all incoming personnel: physical exams to be taken, forms to fill out, insurance to get, etc. We were issued no clothing as the post told us we would get all of that once we were at our post in the Philippines. Everything ran smoothly and we were soon through with our routine. The group slated for the Philippines was the only casual group around the post at that time and we were all reserve officers. We were assigned to companies for duty (in name only) and after a few days, we were aboard the trains for the West Coast port of San Francisco.

At this late date I don't recall whether I met the following men at Fort Hayes or on the train to San Francisco, yet they are the first of the men I knew who were later to be prisoners in the Philippines. Most of them never survived those hideous days.

About the first lad was 1st Lt. Jack McCoffrey of Logansport, IN; with him was 2nd Lt. Robert Emerson, also from Logansport. Jack was tall, slim, fair complected, wore a little mustache and looked extremely handsome. Better than that, he was excellent company. During those first few days, we struck up quite a friendship. He and Emerson were good friends. Jack, having no parents, lived in Emerson's home. He was a draftsman for one of the local Logansport companies.

Emerson was not quite 6 feet tall, reddish in complexion, red-headed and had a tendency to be heavyset. He must have weighed from 170 to 180 pounds. When he came to Davao Prison Camp 18 months later, he weighed 100 pounds less and looked like a ghost. Emerson also worked in Logansport and lived with his family. These two boys left for San Francisco via Logansport for a few days and then Chicago where they took the transcontinental train. After they left me in Fort Hayes, I didn't see them until they were on *President Pierce* sailing out of the Golden Gate.

1st Lt. William Nels was also at Fort Hayes with me. He was about 6 feet tall, slender, semi-bald, around 35 years of age. Bill was a schoolteacher by profession, a principal in some West Virginia high school. He was single and I believe all the family he had was a mother. I did not know him very well and after he got off the *President Pierce* in Manila, I remember seeing him only once when I ran into him at the Army and Navy Club in Manila. Nels was killed early in the war before things got really bad.

Another West Virginia boy was 1st Lt. Paul Schultz, also a schoolteacher. Paul was about 5'6" and didn't weigh over 150. He was slender and slightly built. I remember talking to him in Fort Hayes about the teaching profession. Three years later, while in Bilibid Prison in Manila, when we were waiting to be placed on the ill-fated *Oryoku Maru* in December 1944, I talked to him again. During that intervening time, while I was in the southern islands, he had seen service in Bataan, survived the Death March, dysentery while in Cabanatuan Prison, and a number of other things. Paul never survived the second bombing on that trip north.

There were about six or eight officers on the Santa Fe train from St.

Louis to Frisco. I don't remember their names with the exception of William F. O'Connor, 1st lieutenant, infantry, from Massachusetts. Bill and I got acquainted real well on that train "out." We were together all through our military careers from then on, until Bill went out on the Lasang detail, March 2, 1944, and I remained behind with the main Davao detail.

Bill O'Connor must have been about 5'8" or 9", very thin, with a tendency to be bald, and knew the Army thoroughly. He had been an enlisted man in Hawaii, a sergeant in a motor pool while holding a reserve commission. With the expansion of our armed forces, he had gone into active duty in the States and then was ordered out to the Philippines. Bill was to marry a nurse the next September and this was June and he was on the "way out." Out to the places where no more women were allowed and all Army wives and children were being sent home. He was pretty discouraged about having to leave his fiancée behind. Bill was a devout Catholic and the next Easter he was the only white man to go to a Filipino Easter service with me, just before all hell broke loose. O'Connor and I had long conversations on the train about the coming war. Both of us did not see how it could be avoided. I shall leave Bill for the moment and refer to him time and again later, as our trails crisscrossed the rest of his life.

At this point I shall drift away from the military passengers of this train trip to others more interesting.

One of the civilians was a high official of the Santa Fe Railroad. I wanted to know if he knew my Knox College friend, Tommy Willard, son of the Santa Fe executive in Chicago. Another was an ex-actress and dancer who had twin daughters. They were the idols of the entire train.

Finally, the most interesting were not Americans at all. They were Germans and the party consisted of a man, his wife, and two little boys. The man was part of the German Diplomatic Corps stationed in Washington, D.C., or New York. By this time the war in Europe had been on almost two years and of course our relations with Germany were becoming more strained as time went on. As a result he had been called home and was taking his family back via the long road home. The man was around 5'10", blonde, and rather flashy. He stayed mostly in their stateroom by himself, but his wife and family by day came out and occupied ordinary seats with the rest of the passengers. Once in a while the boys would get noisy. He would come out and speak very sharply to them and often to his wife in the same manner. Mostly he spoke in German, but sometimes he spoke in beautiful English with just a trace of an accent. He was distinctly unfriendly to all the rest of us.

His pretty wife was slender and good-looking, had a pleasing personality, spoke English with a delightful accent, and had plenty on the ball. She managed the two boys fairly well and spoke very sharply to them if they spoke German instead of English. I asked her why. She said it was a family policy that the children must speak the English language as long as they were in the U.S., else how would they learn to speak it properly? She was very friendly to everybody on the train (or tried to be).

The first day or two she didn't pay much attention to the soldiers in uniform, but as the trip progressed, she turned her attention more and more to us. Her husband was noticeably absent when she was conversing with one of us and it didn't take any brains for us to see that she was trying to pump us for whatever information she could get. Of course we knew nothing of military value at that time and it was no state secret as to where we were going. Some of our baggage was checked clear through to Manila. The last day before we arrived in Frisco, she had an hour's conversation with me. I found it mentally stimulating to parry her questions and leading statements by the same methods she was using. I had the satisfaction, at the end of the conversation, to know I had gained as much, or more information from her as she had gotten from me. Three days after I got off the train in San Francisco, and a day later, I saw them again at the baggage room in the railroad station. She told me then that they were taking the Japanese luxury liner *Tasuta Maru* for Tokyo about June 4, 1941. The next day, as a guest of Lt. Col. George B. Jones, MC (retired), I dined at an inn that was located on the San Francisco side of the Golden Gate Bridge. I watched that ship sail out of the bay and put out to sea. At the same time,

Mrs. Jones told me the morning paper had an article that said the Japanese liner had lain outside the harbor limit until it had assurance it could enter and leave with Japanese nationals. The captain was afraid he might be detained. It was possible that it would be the last Japanese ship to enter our ports for some time. I remember we speculated whether those Germans would ever reach their homeland.

Lt. Col. Jones showed me around San Francisco. He gave me some addresses in the Philippines and some tips on the customs in the Islands.

I didn't stay downtown, but moved into the Hostess House at Fort Mason, Port of Embarkation. While out there, I met several more officers slated for the Philippines. I shared my room with a chaplain, 1st Lt. Albert Talbot. He was a young Catholic priest being sent out for duty with troops in the Islands. He and I became quite close friends on the trip over. After he left the boat I don't recall seeing him again until around July 1944 when my group of American prisoners were moved from Davao up to Cabanatuan in Luzon. At this stage, Al was just a shadow of his former self, but still in good spirits and still doing his duties as chaplain.

The room directly across the hall from Chaplain Talbot's room and mine, in the Hostess House, was occupied by two tall Army nurses. The chaplain knew both of them. He introduced me to them as we met in the hall one morning. I talked for several minutes to the one whose name was Black. It turned out they were going over on our boat and I saw them several times aboard ship. I never saw Lt. Black, ANC, after she left the *Pierce*. She went to duty in the hospital on the Fortress of Corregidor and I heard about her from fellow prisoners in the early part of our imprisonment.

Fate moves in strange circles and makes life extremely interesting. You never know whom you will see or where. Five years later, lacking a month, as I write this tale, I met a Lt. Col. Harry Harding (he had also been a POW of the Japanese) in BOQ No. 5 at the Armored School, Fort Knox, KY. On the young colonel's desk was the photograph of a strikingly pretty Army nurse in full uniform. One look at the picture struck a familiar chord and I asked, "Your girlfriend, Harding?"

"Yes," he replied.

"I know her," I told him.

"You do?" he asked, looking startled.

"Yes! Her name is Black, Lt. Black. She is tall and dark and just as good looking as her picture."

"Where did you know her?" Harding inquired instantly.

"She went over on the boat with me, but I didn't know what had happened to her other than that she lived to be released."

While I was giving him this information, he dug up another picture, a large snapshot this time and showed it to me. It was Lt. Black all right and was so startlingly natural that it fairly took my breath away. I told Harding, and again he looked at me intently, whereupon I laughed again.

The first day I was at the Fort Mason Embarkation Office, I was standing in line, yes, the usual Army line, without which the Army wouldn't be the Army! The man immediately ahead of me wore captain's bars on his shoulders and during the tiresome wait, he stepped on my toe by accident.

"Pardon me," he said, quickly retreating from the injured member.

"I stand on it, too," I smiled, "so let's forget it."

"My name is Hughes, Joseph Hughes," he said, extending his hand by way of introduction. I looked at the man closely. I saw before me a well-built man about 5'9," round-faced, dark-haired and the dark stubble of a beard showing on his face giving him the appearance of being travel-worn and tired. Yet, despite that weariness, there was a spirit of friendliness gleaming in his eye. He had the bearing of a man who could take what life handed him. A few months later in the jungles of Bataan he was proving what sterling steel he was made of.

"Miner is the name," I replied as I shook hands with him. "Bill Miner. Are you also going out to the Philippines, Captain?"

"Yes, I am. I don't know what the detail is yet, but I'm definitely on the way. Where is your home, Lieutenant?"

"Illinois, Captain, 200 miles southwest of Chicago near the small town of Vermont. What part of the U.S. do you come from?"

"Near Boston," he replied. "I was an instructor in a military school not far outside the city. I have a wife and five children."

At that last remark I opened my eyes wide in surprise. "You look quite young to be so happily married, Captain," I said as a compliment.

There was pride in the captain's voice as he replied, "I am happily married, Lieutenant, and I wish I were just starting married life again instead of starting to the Orient. I would like to believe this situation would clear up, but common sense says it just can't clear up until our country steps in and clears it up. If you are just here to report in like myself, it won't take long and then, if you like, come upstairs with me. I know a captain in the Port Quartermaster Corps and we can go out for lunch. He will show us around and you can get an idea of the things just beginning."

We checked in and then looked up Joe's friend whose name I now forget, but the things I learned from him I didn't forget. This was June of 1941 and in that San Francisco Office of the Army Transport Service, I saw the signs of a great nation belatedly beginning to prepare for its own security. Troops and supplies were to be sent to Alaska, but there were no boats to take them, no roads after they reached Alaska, no facilities to take care of the men after they were landed, yet Alaska had to be fortified quickly. Just how quick that need was to become a battle reality we little realized then. The ATS was chartering commercial vessels as fast as it could to move supplies and men to Alaska, Hawaii, Philippines, Wake, etc.

"We need this, we need that," the ATS man said (listing a dozen items). "We just can't get them! Congress won't give them to us. It's going to cost us lives before this is over, perhaps your lives, and remember this, if you get caught out there without equipment, it's not the Army' s fault. It's the fault of Congress and the people!"

Hughes and I looked at each other in consternation. We had the feeling that the ATS man was barely scratching the surface of the actual conditions. I had that funny, sick feeling in my stomach again—the feeling I always get when I see my fate being decided and I am helpless to defend myself. As Hughes and I looked at each other, we saw the same question in each other's eyes. "Will I come back? Will we come back?" I personally felt like I was a pawn in a game of chess where the players were drunken fools who were deliberately playing with their eyes shut, because they were afraid to open their eyes and look at the board to see how bad the situation really was. I write this now while many of these same Congressmen have spent many months and countless millions of dollars trying to fix the blame of Pearl Harbor on someone in the Armed Forces. A simple child knows the answer, better all this time and money had been spent on how to prevent such an event from occurring again. After fighting two world wars, we still haven't learned to take care of ourselves. Less than a year after V-Day we don't have enough left of our Armed Forces to clean up the litter after a good Kansas cyclone. I am alive today. Major Joseph Hughes is dead. Dead of starvation after months of grim prison life. His heart-rending question in prison still rings in my ears: "Bill, why did Congress and our people ever let this country get caught so unprepared? I hope to God they learn this time!" Today I am back on American soil and the answer is, "Nobody has learned the lesson."

We left the ATS man after finishing lunch. I remember we were silent as we left. The very air of that office was filled with coming events and it took us an hour to shake off the spell of tragedy to come.

I met more officers at Fort Mason and by June 5, there were quite a few bound for the Philippines. Nobody was very happy and almost, without exception, we felt that we were going to have a grandstand seat on an oriental fracas. Just how grand it was going to be, we couldn't even dream.

THREE

AT SEA

A T 2:00 P.M. ON JUNE 5, 1941, THE *PRESIDENT PIERCE* PULLED AWAY FROM THE PIER IN SAN FRANCISCO BAY AND HEADED TOWARD THE Golden Gate. Its cargo was almost a thousand sad hearts. Of over 250 officers, there were six who came back on the *Storm King* with me. There were others, of course, but very, very few.

The *President Pierce* had about 800 casual troops, of which around 250 were officers, 150 were Air Corps lieutenants, most of them pilots. In addition, there were 13 Army nurses and about a score of civilians who were airplane technicians headed for China. Rumor had it that they were going out to join the Flying Tigers and keep their planes in the air. All these men lined the railings and decks of the ship as we slowly moved out of the harbor into the bay. Minute by minute the piers and shore objects grew smaller and faded away. New objects and familiar landmarks appeared, grew large, grew small, and disappeared. The Golden Gate Bridge drew near and soon was directly overhead. We could look up at the bottom of the roadway and see the great rivets and braces of the massive structure.

Soon they too faded away and the whole bridge span again became a comprehensive view growing smaller and smaller, fading as the ship left behind the United States, a land of beauty, quiet, and peace. Soon the coastline became an extended view lying low and dark on the horizon, its dark outline contrasted with rising and falling waves and clouds of white spray. The afternoon grew cloudy and gray. The sun became lost behind the clouds. The wind sprang up and grew into a small gale. The sea became rough. The air became very chilly as night settled around our ship as she rolled through the waves toward Hawaii. Then on to the Philippines where scenes of destruction, death, imprisonment, torture, and hate awaited us.

Jack McCoffrey joined me on the upper deck soon after we left the pier and we both watched as our ship departed. Jack, not having had the glimpse of the future through the eyes of the ATS officer, was in high spirits. He wanted to see the Philippines, Singapore, Indochina, China, and the East Indies. He was already straining at the leash to go. My sense of foreboding grew and it was with a heavy heart that I followed Jack below to our stateroom from our post of observation of our departure.

All my life I shall remember Jack McCoffrey as he stood at the railing looking west into the night. To me he was the spirit of American youth: clean-cut, vigorous, adventurous, dauntless, unafraid of life, and eager for the events of tomorrow.

As night came the ship began to roll pretty badly. I ate my dinner, but three hours later upchucked it all. Following that unpleasantness, I went to bed and slept well. The next morning I ate a moderate breakfast and felt half secure. By the end of the first 24 hours, I was back to normal and began to take an interest in the people and the happenings around me.

The staterooms were pretty crowded, four men where two should have been. In my cabin was 1st Lt. Harmon, MC and 1st Lt. James Pinnick from southern Indiana. Pinnick was a graduate of Indiana University Law School and had done some law practice. The third member's name I don't now recall, but I saw him after he left the boat in Manila.

Young Doc Harmon, as we called him, was stationed at Sternberg General Hospital in Manila. He contracted some strange malady and was sent home in October or November of 1941. I never did find out exactly what his trouble was; the Med Corps wouldn't talk about him.

Young Pinnick was a card. He had more energy than a bushel of kittens. In stature he was around 5'10", heavyset, but not fat, round-faced, dark-haired. He had a pleasant disposition, a ready wit, an easy laugh, was good company, and liked to smoke cigars. His favorite pastime on the boat was to lie on his bed, smoke cigars, and read. None of us had brought too many magazines along and by the evening of the third day out, Pinnick was lying on his bed smoking a long cigar and staring at the ceiling of the stateroom. Every once in a while he would blow smoke rings into the air. All of a sudden, he swung his feet off the bed saying, "Well, boys, I can't take this inactivity any longer. See you later!" He walked out of the room leaving us staring after him with open mouths.

"Yeah? Well, stay away from Charley's Steak House," I called after him as his footsteps retreated down the corridor.

Midnight came and we all went to bed. About 2:00 A.M. the lights suddenly came on and Pinnick stomped into the room. His white shirt was soaked—there wasn't a dry stitch in it; its front was stained with cigar ashes and its front pockets were bulging. Pinnick was without his cigar. We three rose upon our elbows and gawked at him in sleepy amazement.

In his left hand, he had a wad of greenbacks that he threw on his bed. Next, he emptied his shirt pockets of the same green stuff. From there, he started on his trouser pockets, emptying each with much ceremony. By this time all three of us were sitting up and pouring out a stream of questions. "What bank did you rob? Is there anything left in the vaults at Fort Knox? Lend me a thousand. Better give us a cut on that loot or we'll snitch on you."

"Boys," he said, "I got in a good crap game with the Air Corps. Those babies are plenty wild, but they aren't good!"

From there, he proceeded to his hip pockets which, we now observed, were also bulging. From them came more greenbacks. He had the biggest pile of crumpled greenbacks I had yet seen lying in the middle of that bed. We gathered around while he counted, "One, two, five, da da, da da 25, da da 50, 100, 150, 200, 250. Well, boys, that's quite a haul." He stood back looking at the piles of money. "Boy, does my back hurt," he said, rubbing it. "Hell," he exclaimed, tearing open his shirt and pulling out another bunch of greenbacks. "Let's see if there are any more!" he said as he felt his anatomy. He rubbed his watch pocket and then extracted more bills. These he also counted.

"Not bad for a night's entertainment?" he said as he totaled up about $275. He then stripped the pillowcase off his pillow, stuffed the money in it, tied a knot at the end and tossed it on the head of his bed for a pillow.

With that remark he undressed, took a shower, came back and said to us in general: "Now if you boys will let me, I'll catch up on my beauty sleep."

"Let you! Hell's bells!" young Doc came back at him. "Just who is keeping whom awake?" and threw a pillow at Pinnick.

Pinnick ducked, snapped out the light, and we heard him crawl into bed. A few minutes later he was snoring.

Pinnick slept most of the next day and the next evening he again lay on his bed after the evening meal. We looked at one another and waited. After he finished his cigar he got up, took off his tie and said, "Guess I had better go and give the Air Corps their revenge!"

We saw no more of him until long after midnight when he again came in loaded to the gills with greenbacks and wringing wet with sweat. This time Pinnick had around $200. He took the sum of $400 down to the safe next morning. When we got to Honolulu, a couple of days later, he cabled around $400 back to his wife, saying, "I don't have any use for it and she'll save it."

After two such nights he turned his attention to the slot machines. For a couple of days he sat in the barroom observing how the slot machines paid off; then, after the quarter machine had been played almost continuously for three hours he walked over and started playing, too. Before he quit he got the jackpot of about $27.50. Three days later he repeated his performance. By now he had the reputation of being "good" and he decided to find some other outlet for his excess energy for diplomatic reasons. Somebody had a law book that he borrowed to keep himself occupied.

Pinnick, I was told, was killed early in the war. I know he went to troop duty with a Philippine scout outfit, but I never saw him after he left the boat in Manila. I am afraid today his widow had good use for that $400 he sent home.

Col. William F. Sharp, later major general, in command of the Mindanao Force, was our troop commander aboard the *Pierce*. On his shipboard staff was Captain, later Major, Albert Kircher, Al for short; Major Knowles, then a warrant officer; Capt. Joe Hughes and naturally a few more whose names I don't remember.

There were four companies of enlisted men in the holds of the ship. On the second day out I was assigned to CO duty under Capt. Truesdale whom I shall mention later.

Another company commander was Capt. James (?) O'Donnovan. He was tall, dark, slender, and thin in figure and face, wore a very small black mustache and was very intelligent. I used to visit with him a lot and we became good friends. He had a lot of originality and used to debunk the international situation. Time and again he told me going over, "We are all dead heroes. There is no other way out!" When the war did come, he was a battalion commander in the 31st infantry and made a wonderful record for himself with his men. I am told he wore two guns and had several snipers to his credit. He died of dysentery while in prison shortly after the surrender.

Capt. Truesdale had another lieutenant to help with the company of casuals. He was 1st Lt. James Franz. Jimmy came from southern Indiana or Kentucky. I first met him at Fort Hayes, but it was not until our crossing that we really got acquainted. He was assigned to Fort McKinley when we reached the Philippines. Jimmy was another who did not survive the Luzon campaign.

Capt. Truesdale was married and in civilian life and had worked for the Bell Telephone Co. Upon reaching Manila he was assigned to the 31st

Infantry, as PX officer, in the Cuartel de España. This assignment he held until the war began. Then he was transferred to the Signal Corps and set out with, I believe, the Luzon forces. He lived through the campaign to become a prisoner and died of malnutrition and dysentery on board a prison ship to Japan in late 1942.

One of the most interesting friends I made on that boat trip over was a man named Capt. Albert J. Kircher. Kircher was heavyset, round-faced, wore a black mustache, had dark hair and dark eyes. His army branch was Field Artillery, but in civilian life he had been a mining engineer for British interests in Central American or northern South America. His versatility was remarkable and had a common sense about him that comes only from wide experience and a deep study of human races. Kircher's duty aboard ship was police officer; he did have a little activity once in a while. I got to know him through company duty. At this point, I'll drop him from the picture and pick him up again down in the southern island city of Cebu at the beginning of the war. I followed his career all throughout and he always took an exceptionally friendly interest in me.

To date I haven't mentioned the trials and tribulations of the trip. To us, it was just the bad beginning of a bad ending. Three days out of San Francisco, we entered the tropics and the ship began to warm up. Shortly after pulling out from Honolulu, the weather became really sweltering and the wind came from the east at the rate of about 16 knots. We didn't have a breath of air aboard the ship for days at a time. The smoke from the engines rose straight into the sky and soot fell straight down on us below. The ship's dining room was just above the overheated engine room, from the feel of it at least. Every meal in the room was stifling hot, but the evenings were the worst. We couldn't enter the dining room unless we had on a tie and a uniform blouse. Neither could we use summer civilian clothes and most of us had the heavy winter stateside uniform. Entering that dining room was torture, but we did have to eat. Certainly adapting our uniform to the climate would have been sensible, yet it wasn't done. Looking back, I remember those furnace evenings even more than the tortuous heat in the holds of some prison ships. Once I remarked, "God help us if a war breaks out. The rule book won't cover the situation!" It didn't! We had to make the rules as the situation demanded. To top things off, the ship was so over-crowded that we ran out of fresh water for all purposes except drinking. Even the salt-water showers were turned off part of the day. Laundry was quite a problem, too. When you added things up, the trip was unpleasant for everybody—officers and enlisted men alike. I went over on a luxury liner and I came back on an ordinary transport. The latter was much more enjoyable, being business-like and without unnecessary spit and polish.

Another friend I made was Air Corps 2nd Lt. Daniel Blase, who had just finished training when he was ordered overseas. His family and his fiancée had driven him out to San Francisco to see him off. Blase was as-signed to duty with the same company that I was executive officer for. We used to go as far forward as one could get and lean over the railing to watch the spray rise from the bow of the ship below us. This consumed hours of our time, just leaning over the railing and talking about everything under the sun. Sometimes we just leaned and looked at the sea. Occasionally, the ocean was so calm that it looked like deep blue oil gently stirring. There wasn't a ripple on its glassy surface. It amplified the meaning of the name "Pacific." The laundry woman on the ship said that in 35 crossings, this was her smoothest. Blase and I actually seemed at times to become part of this vastness. The only moving thing in that wilderness of water was the ship. Now and then flying fish would break the surface and skim over the water from a few feet to 150 yards. Going over we saw lots of fly-ing fish and there were many in the Islands before the war. After the fight-ing had been on for a year, I don't remember seeing many. Coming home across the Pacific many people made the remark, "There are no flying fish this trip." Somehow I wonder if our high explosive sea warfare might have been responsible?

Our first stop was a few hours layover in Honolulu. The famous Dia-mond Head is visible from way out at sea. Its appearance was barren like the coast of Southern California. As we drew near the port, the Royal Hawaiian and Moana Hotel on Waikiki Beach were pointed out. They were beautifully nestled in the palm-clad shore back of the narrow white beach. Yet somehow I felt a vague disappointment in the scenic beauty, the wildness, grandness and lushness that I expected were not there. My expectations weren't satisfied even when I went over the Pali. It wasn't until the Philippine Islands that the large white beaches, gentle seas, and tremendous forest giants (that I had expected to see) became a part of the scenery.

As the big liner drew up to a pier near the Aloha Tower, little Hawaiian boys swam out to meet the ship and dive for coins thrown to them from the decks. Those dark-skinned water wizards would dive for silver only. If someone tossed a penny, they ignored it. A band was playing on the pier and Hawaiian beauties decked with leis stood nearby waving to us and signing Aloha. Truly this was a tropical atmosphere.

The sun was setting, lighting up the sky to the west over the shoulders of the mountains. To the north, the Waialeale Mountains were standing dark and cloud-covered behind the city. Shore leave was at hand!

Six of us, among whom were Capt. Joe Hughes; a Capt. Genough, Dental Corps; Father Talbot; two other lieutenants, and I hired a taxi to see the city. It was filled with Navy men. We drove around the downtown part of Honolulu, dined at the Alexander Hotel, went to a series of native dances in a park not far from the YMCA and then took off for the Royal Hawaiian Hotel.

At the Royal Hawaiian, we drank Dole pineapple juice, looked around the place for atmosphere native to Hawaii. Instead, there was evidence of Dorothy Lamour. In the dining room by the beach sat two acquaintances I had made on the Santa Fe train from St. Louis to San Francisco. I stopped at their table to pass the time of day and then rejoined my friends.

The Moana Hotel was next on our list. Again we looked around and then passed on. We had not long to stay and we wanted to look at all the places of interest that we could. Late that night we ended up back at the Royal Hawaiian drinking pineapple juice. From there we went back to the ship.

There wasn't too much to do on board the ship going over. Some of the nurses had a fine time and several romances blossomed. There were only 13 of them and at least 250 officers.

Half of the latter were young Air Corps lieutenants and many of them single. The sundeck was the favorite place on the ship at all times because it was usually coolest there. At night some of the portable radios could reach commercial stations ashore and we used to congregate around the music and news broadcasts. Not far out of Honolulu, the sundeck became forbidden territory after sundown. It seems that the romancers liked the sundeck in the dark hours the same as the radio listeners and the lads who couldn't sleep because of overheated quarters, but lest the sundeck become the "sin deck," it became "off limits after sunset."

And so we sailed westward, ever westward. Each day saw us a little father out and each day was just a little warmer, each night a little sweatier and a little stickier. Each morning the red ball of a sun rose out of a clear sky behind us and each night that same red ball set in the seas ahead of us. Our ship was the only black thing on the surface of the deep blue sea.

Once or twice we met a ship. The captain chased all the men below and ran all the nurses up on the sundeck so the petticoats would fly in the wind and give the impression of our being only a passenger ship. On reaching Manila, we found out that the ship had been a British battleship, damaged by German bombs in the battle for Malta. She was on her way (supposedly) to Mare Island for repairs.

About the 16th day out we passed through the Japanese-mandated Marianas. The ship sailed just south of Agrihan Island, yet close enough we could see the squat red-roofed buildings nestling among the tall coconut palms. This island began to look something like what I had expected a tropical isle to look like. That morning the steward told us we were within "spitting distance" of Manila, within 1,000 miles.

Many hours and several hundred miles later, fairly early in the morning, it was whispered about that we should soon see land. By mid-morning, a low dark cloud appeared on the southern horizon. An hour or so later we could see that this was dark mountains. At midday we were within sight-seeing distance of the north shore of Samar and were passing numerous tiny islands. Even though small, some of them were mighty rugged and precipitous. One or two looked as though they rose a mile or more above the sea and most were heavily covered with vegetation. The mountains on the main shore of Samar were covered with a tremendously magnificent jungle forest. The scrawny brush on Oahu did not begin to compare with these forest giants!

As we stood and looked at those jungle-covered slopes, down the railing of the ship went a string of comments: "Unchanged for a hundred million years." "A new world, boys." "Pythons, fever, and dysentery." "One hell of a place to be." "Take me away from nature in the raw."

Little did we think less than six months later, these same fever-infested jungles were going to hide us, conceal us, give us food and water. And that, slightly later, we were going to eat those dreaded pythons and compare their white meat with the white meat of a chicken's breast in respect to taste and tenderness. Truly it was a new world. Very soon it was to be the scene of battle.

Late that afternoon we passed through San Bernardino Straits and as night fell proceeded up the west coast of southern Luzon. I was still at the rail looking at the dark line of the shore, the fires of the Filipino villages, the stars, listening to the strange new night sounds and smelling the strange tropical odors. Finally I went to bed; sometime the next morning we were to be in Manila.

Very late in the night or early in the morning, I woke up to the sound of low voices and extremely suffocating heat. The voices whispered, "Wake up, Joe, we're in." "Yeah, Joe, we're in Manila Harbor."

"The hell you say. You're sure? Yeah, you must be right, we're stopped and it's hellish hot. I wonder if old Dante ever knew anything like this."

I drifted back into an exhausted sickly sleep thinking, "Manila, I'm in Manila now. I wonder what it's like."

FOUR

TENDERFOOT IN THE ISLANDS

JUNE 24, 1941 DAWNED, A VERY HOT DAY WITH A BEAUTIFUL MANILA SUNRISE. BY DAYLIGHT THERE WAS FEVERISH ACTIVITY to repack and debark from the ship. We left the ship in alphabetical order by rank, and on the way down the gangplank, we were told the name of our assignment post. Our first solid footing in 19 days was the upper deck of Pier 7, at that time the largest in the world. We followed the ramps downstairs, located our baggage and went through customs inspection. Meanwhile, via word of mouth, word got around that representatives from the various department posts were to pick up the new men slated for their posts.

A Capt. Al Thayer located me and said where to take my baggage for transportation to my quarters. I was assigned to the 31st Infantry stationed at the Post of Manila. After getting my baggage and myself into the truck, I waited. Shortly afterward Capt. Fred Small of Denver, CO; Lt. Robert Emerson; Capt. Packham; Capt. O'Donnovan and several others, all assigned to the 31st Infantry, joined me. When the entire group was assembled, we were taken to the Army and Navy Club in Manila for lunch, after which we reported in to the headquarters of the 31st Infantry, Post of Manila.

The post was located at the Cuartel de España in the old Walled City area of Manila.

I was assigned to the Service Co. of the 31st Infantry, which was located in Santa Lucia barracks. These barracks nestled in a rectangular part of the old City Wall. This area had evidently been used by the Spanish as a soldiers' barracks and fortification point. The whole barracks area was built against the outside of the main city wall so that when one stood on the wall of the barracks he faced open ground on three sides and the outside of the main walls would be subject to gunfire or archery. At regular intervals these fortified areas jutted out from the main wall of the city. To get into this fortified area one had to pass through an arched gateway some 12 to 15 feet tall and about 15 feet thick. Those old Spaniards really believed in stone masses for security.

It was June 24 when I arrived in Manila. The next day I reported to my company and next my company commander, Capt. Robert Johnson and the other company officers consisting of Lt. Gordon Meyers of Wisconsin, 2nd Lt. James K. Smith from Georgia (or South Carolina), and 1st Lt. Charles Y. Garett from Kentucky.

During the next few days I met many other officers and men of the 31st Infantry. Garett ran into a Lt. Harold (?) Tuggle from Kentucky. Both Garett and Tuggle had gone to college together at Bowling Green, KY. When Tuggle and I got acquainted we found that he had been in college with a girl named Elizabeth Harrington whom I later knew as Dean of Girls in the high school of New Castle, IN. This small link of a mutual acquaintance established a firm friendship between us. Among the others that I became good friends with was 2nd Lt. Homer Martin from Kentucky, someone else who had, I believe, been in college at Bowling Green, KY. Another of the lads was a happy-go-lucky kid from North Dakota named Joseph Stienzland. Joe liked the west and always figured, even up to the last, on going back to the Big Horn country in Wyoming and owning a horse ranch.

Before we newcomers had gotten settled, we were thrown into a concentrated training course on tactics and small arms weapons; this was in preparation for the assignment of becoming instructors with the Philippine Army (PA). We arrived the last of June. The first of July Gen. Douglas MacArthur was made commander of the newly created US-AFFE (United States Armed Forces in the Far East) which was to consist of American and Philippine Army units. I will not go into the routine details of army life with the troops, but will pass on to more interesting personal experiences.

As was mentioned before, when in San Francisco, I got a dim impression of things to come. In Hawaii this foreboding was increased and after reaching Manila it was obvious within the first hundred hours that an ill wind was blowing. In less than a week I decided that the Philippines was no place for my money, so I made an allotment to my mother of every spare dollar not needed for living expenses. As a result, when the war did start, I had a total of $5 in the Manila banks, which I lost.

Everywhere that I have gone it has always been my idea that the inhabitants of a place furnish 90 percent of the interest. If you have friends and know interesting people, you can have a good time regardless of unpleasant surroundings. With this in mind, I gathered addresses of people in the Philippines before leaving the States and on the way out.

When my father had been in college at Macomb, IL, during the early part of the century, there had been six Filipino boys attending. At least two of these six had risen high in the life of the Philippines. One was Dr. Camilo Osias. The other was Dr. Francisco Benitez, then dean of education at the University of the Philippines. Dean Benitez and his family remained quite loyal to the Philippine Commonwealth and the U.S. all through the Japanese occupation. He and his family survived the siege of Manila in early 1945. When the Americans retook the Philippines, Dean Benitez became the director of the Bureau of Education under President Osemeña. Because of lack of transportation, I didn't get to see Dean Benitez in late 1945 when I was in Manila, but he did answer my letter.

Shortly after my arrival in Manila I called upon Dean Benitez and his family in their home on the outskirts of the city. He had a charming wife and family and a very beautiful home. The visit was both enjoyable and enlightening. From what he told me of the various people, dialects, and languages, I knew the Philippines was going to be extremely interesting. He too had something to say on the imperialistic tendencies of Japan and the increasingly arrogant attitude of the Japanese people living in the vicinity. I saw Dean Benitez several times before I left for the Visayan islands.

Another person on my list to look up was a Miss Lenora Jones, sister of Miss Maude Jones, English professor at the University of Indiana. Miss Lenora Jones had been a teacher in the islands for several years so she knew people and places.

Harold Ingersoll of the Ingersoll Steel and Disc Co. had given me a letter of introduction to their company representative in Manila, Spike Wilson. Spike was an old-timer. He had come out to the islands in the Spanish-American War and had stayed after it was over. Spike was a member of the Elks Club in Manila and had a great many contacts that proved exceedingly entertaining.

The most permanent civilian friend was accidentally made through Miss Lenora Jones. This man was another teacher, L. W. Jacobs. Milwaukee was his home originally. Jacobs had been in the islands 17 years by the time I met him and was exceedingly well educated. He had traveled through Burma, Saigon, Indochina, Dutch East Indies, been to all the great cities of China near the coast or within sailing distance on the large rivers of China, and had studied at the Imperial University in Tokyo, Japan.

Jacobs was well versed in oriental arts and goods. He knew good silver work from India or bronze from Japan. One glance at an Oriental rug was enough to tell him whether or not it was authentic. He knew good ivory or jade when he saw it, or wood carving from Bali. Not only did he recognize genuine articles, but had at his fingertips the history and background of these things and the designs on them. Jacobs was also quite an authority on Philippine customs and weaving. Personally he was likable; mentally he was stimulating and the amount of knowledge he had was tremendous.

In these few weeks, I undoubtedly saw more of the "real Manila" than many people who had lived there for years. I rarely went to a nightclub. A nightclub is a nightclub whether you find it in New York, Chicago, San Francisco, Honolulu, Manila, or Shanghai. Jacobs would meet me when off duty, and we would go off to some native part of the city and penetrate into its heart and see life which I didn't even dream existed.

Once, we saw a Chinese measuring raw gold stolen from a mine near Baguio and smuggled into Manila. One other night he took me into the shop of a Chinese merchant and called for the proprietor himself. From the depths of the interior came an ancient and stately Chinese man in a silken kimono. Ceremoniously they greeted one another and then Jacobs told the old merchant I would like to see some of his treasures. We went through the dirtiest storehouse I ever saw into a storeroom that was fixed up into living quarters. There, from some gorgeous mahogany chests were brought some silks, jade statues, and some old ivory carvings. These were museum pieces, even my unpracticed eye could tell that.

We went through Chinatown, to the Japanese area, to all the old stately cathedrals of Manila. To the Tondo district, to the Yangco Market area, which was filled with every type of Philippine ware, to Gandara Street or Thieves Row where you could find everything from Cleopatra's girdle or Brunhild's sash to Caesar's ghost. There were things hundreds of years old and up to modern vintage and there was a price on everything. Jacobs said that if some of the old established shops did not have what you wanted, just describe what it was you wished, and they would name a date for you to come and get it regardless of what it was—a diamond from India or a slave girl from China.

He took me to an ancient part of the city where the streets had been paved with headstones from ancient graves and you could still see the dialect inscriptions on the stones.

Another time we went to an ancient part of the city to a Chinese house where the door knocker was the most exquisite bronze feminine hand I have ever seen. The fingers were long, slender, tapered, and gracefully curved. The hand swung from the forefinger and the wrist was the base of the knocker. The old Chinese had refused to place a price on it; it wasn't to be sold.

I could go on and on for hours about our excursions around the city of Manila. Everywhere we went I was introduced as a special friend of Jacobs and if I ever went back to one of these places, I called for the person in charge to whom Jacobs had introduced me. If I desired to buy anything, my personal check was accepted without question and I was shown nothing but worthwhile, genuine goods.

I went to the Union Protestant Church while in Manila. Rev. Walter Felley Brooks, I believe, was the pastor; several nationalities of white people went there. One member was an American Negro. Everywhere were interesting people, interesting things, and interesting friends. I was out to get as broad an experience as possible. The oldtimers were glad to find somebody showing appreciation for something other than the conventional tourist lines.

Old Manila, with its sights, its smells, its contrasts, its magnificent Dewey Boulevard and Taft Avenue, was vastly different from the Tondo slums (Lake Shore Drive versus Maxwell or Halstead Streets in Chicago); its mixture of races both occidental and oriental; its mixture of cultures, atmosphere, and backgrounds was quite a place. There was hardly a race or religion on the face of the earth that wasn't represented in the city. One had only to look and recognize in order to find Chinese, Japanese, Javanese (Malinese?), Burmese, Korean, Russian, Polynesian, Dutch, British, French Portuguese, Spanish, Indian (East), and any other race you can think of. There was the modern occidental part of the city. There were the various Oriental areas and then there was the old Spanish walled city. Its magnificent cathedrals and homes were surrounded by narrow streets and filth. There, little naked Filipino boys ran around the streets and held up their hands crying, "Give me a penny, Joe." It wasn't safe at night to walk down the sidewalks of the walled city. Like many of the European medieval towns, the second stories of the shops and houses extended out over the street. Unless one walked a chalk line down the exact center of the thoroughfare, you were apt to be drenched by someone emptying his night can out the window on you. Even with all precautions, you were not safe from splattering. Robbery and murder were not uncommon. There were certain areas where we always went in groups, of at least three, for safety's sake.

Time passed quickly; the days were filled with duty or outside interests. One event shows how ironical things can be. Back at Indiana University, I had a roommate named James F. Coffee, 2nd Lieutenant, FA Reserves. Jim gave me the merry ha ha about being sent to the Philippines. Six weeks later Lt. Coffee walked down the gangplank in Manila.

I didn't get to greet him when he arrived because I was on a reconnaissance trip in Bataan. However, I did send him a letter via courier that was delivered to him personally. Two weeks later, about August 15, I tried to visit him at his post in Fort Stotsenberg. I missed him then, and after we were taken prisoner, reports about him were vague and uncertain. After sifting through what news I could get, I gathered he was a prisoner and had been taken to Japan early in the war, sometime late in 1942. Many months later, over three years to be exact, when I was liberated and back in the 29th Replacement Center near Manila, I was walking from the orderly room to my tent when I found myself face to face with Jim. Our reunion was like that of long separated brothers. We were both going home and happy.

Toward the last of August 1941, all the people from the various forts in the Philippines who were slated to go out to the Philippine Army as instructors (at its various posts and camps) were assembled in the theater of the Post of Manila. They were briefed as to their assignments and the location of their respective posts. I drew an army camp at Calape on the island of Bohol, which is the first sizable island west of Leyte. I was the only American officer assigned there and I was to be assisted by an American corporal, Curtis Sizemore, of the 31st Infantry and a Philippine Scout, Sgt. Jose Bosco of the 26th Cavalry. That's all my orders told me, not a thing about where it was, how to get there, or what to take with me. This last was important because in some areas, a white man had to make his own food and the means to prepare it. Therefore, I went up to the major who was putting out the dope and said, "Major, where is the island of Bohol?"

"It's one of the southern islands not far from Cebu."

"What installations are at this camp; what am I to expect?"

"I don't know. Our maps show that there is an army post located there, and that's all I can tell you about it."

I was completely nonplussed. Here was the boy from the big headquarters and he didn't know anything about it! It was just a spot on the map.

"This can't happen to me," my comprehension cried, but cold logic piped up the next moment, "But it is. That spot on the map, no matter where it is, is where you are going to live for the next three months at least." It was as though a stone wall had hit me on the head. It wasn't until the noon meal that my numbed brain started to function. This was just the beginning. Many times later I would say to myself, "This can't happen to me, but it is! Now what in the hell are you going to do about it? Are you going to go to hell, or are you coming out of it?" The answer always was: "I'm coming out of it!"

The cogs began to whir. If the Army couldn't tell me where it was sending me, perhaps my friend Jacobs could. If he himself couldn't tell me, he would know someone who could. We had been relieved from company duty to get ready for our new assignments. I took off. This was the first step. I located Jacobs at lunch in the Oriente Hotel where he lived.

"Jacobs," I said, "I have been ordered to take charge of an array training post at Calape, Bohol. The Army can't tell me the first thing about it! Can you give me some idea about the place and what to expect?"

"Yes, I can! I did some archeological work on the island one time. It's a Visayan island between Cebu and Leyte. I don't remember the town of Calape very well except I have been through it and it must have a population of at least 5,000 inhabitants. The Visayans are a friendly people and I think you will grow to like them. You certainly get to know the real life and culture of the Filipino people. In fact, I rather envy you having the chance to go to the province of Bohol. It is far enough south that it has an even climate, no hot dry season or cold, damp, rainy season—very nice weather, a nice climate all told."

"What should I take in the way of equipment?"

"Everything—canned food, oil stove, Coleman lantern, cooking utensils, etc. You might have to live in a nipa hut. Before you go, I'll give you the address of a friend named Dart Williams who is the provincial superintendent of schools for Bohol. Dart is a handsome, friendly man and we call him 'God's gift to the women!'"

Before I left I got that address and later I did look up Dart. We became good friends and before this war was over, Dart became quite active in the guerrillas.

I left Jacobs and went about my preparations. As a result of his advice, I knew where I was going, what possible routes, what to expect when I arrived and what to take in the way of equipment for living conditions. Once there I did live in a nipa hut and cooked my own food, etc., but I didn't suffer.

On August 28, 1941, I boarded the inter-island luxury liner, *Mayon*, bound for Tagbilaran, Bohol, via Cebu City where I was to leave the luxury liner and take a local ferry going from Cebu City to Tagbilaran, Bohol, for a five-hour trip.

We went via Iloilo, the provincial capital of the island province of Panay. Jacobs had given me the address of Mr. and Mrs. C. M. Hodges in Iloilo City. The Hodges were extremely wealthy and were formerly from Lubbock, TX. Since the ship stopped at Iloilo for several hours, I planned to look up the Hodges.

The *Mayon* was filled with Filipino soldiers and officers who lived or worked around Manila and were reporting to their various posts for duty. Talk about overloading, Filipinos slept in corridors, in the lifeboats and all over the ship. My baggage had been put on board by the Army and it was all mixed up with other baggage on the deck. Passengers were sitting on it, tramping on it, and otherwise abusing it. By this time I had learned that the flash of money flying through the air does wonders. I flipped a silver coin high a couple of times and then approached a deckhand who was watching with glistening eyes.

"Hello, Joe!"

"Where's number one stevedore boy?" I asked and flipped the silver coin where he could catch it, which he neatly did.

"I go get him, sir," he replied and disappeared in the mass of passengers. I stuck my hand back in my pocket, pulled out another silver coin and started flipping it.

Shortly the Filipino deckhand returned with another man whose bearing revealed some authority.

I flipped the second coin to the Filipino deckhand, reached in my pocket for several more and started jingling when I spoke to "number one boy."

"Señor, I have four pieces of baggage in that pile which I want to have placed inside where they will not get wet and where I can have you get them quickly when we reach Cebu. Do you know of a place to stow them?"

"Yes, sir, I know just the place, sir," and I tossed him a coin. He whistled to a couple of other deckhands and they retrieved my baggage as I pointed them out. The number one boy placed them in a little room just below deck that had one bunk. "They will be safe here, sir. This is my bunk. Any time you want them, we can get them quickly."

I rewarded all for their work and left them happy. Later, in Cebu, the number one boy took care of my baggage very efficiently.

Early the next day, we arrived in Iloilo. I went ashore, located the Hodges, and was taken on a sightseeing tour all around the small city.

The boat left late that same afternoon and went over to Pulupandan, Negros Occidental. The next port of call after Pulupandan was Cebu City where we arrived about 1600 on August 28, 1941. After checking my bags on the ferry, I started out to see that city and a man in business there by the name of K. L. Morrison.

Morrison was vice-president and treasurer for the importing firm of

Erlanger and Gallenger in the Philippines. The Cebu office was under his charge and I found him at his work. He lay that aside, visited with me, and then phoned his wife. Mrs. Morrison drove down and took me on a tour of the city.

Cebu City is about the oldest spot in the white man's history of the Philippines. Magellan landed there and he was killed on Mactan Island, which lies in the harbor of Cebu City. I was shown the oldest street in the Philippine Islands. It was an old-world-looking passageway, narrow, cobble-stoned; the second stories of massive stone dwellings on each side extended out over the street. The walls of these dwellings were solid for the height of the first story. The upstairs had iron-grilled windows. It had a typical medieval atmosphere all through. Like Manila, Cebu City had a beautiful occidental area and then a large nipa-hut area where the majority of the Filipinos lived. The total population was about 150,000. Besides the Spanish, the white colony numbered only about 70, consisting mostly of American and British. There were a few Dutch, Portuguese, Germans, etc., all of them representatives of commercial firms, generally of their respective countries. After this quick tour of the city, I went back to board the ferry for the island of Bohol. The family gave me a standing invitation to make the Morrison home my headquarters at any future date I might happen to be in Cebu.

By the time I returned, the ferry was about ready to sail. On it were Corp. Curtis Sizemore and the scout sergeant Jose Bosco. I had never seen these two individuals before, so it was with a sharp eye that I scrutinized them both. I liked what I saw.

The Filipino scout sergeant knew the language, had been raised on Bohol, and, in general, knew his way around. He decided he could take a smaller boat and arrive at Calape ahead of me. Once there he would look for a place to locate the three of us until we could get permanently settled. I sent him on ahead and then went above to see the other American officers who were going to be on the island of Bohol with me for the next three months. There were six of them, all strangers except one.

I walked out on to the upper deck of the little ferry where the six American officers were watching our withdrawal from the pier into the harbor. The first form I laid eyes on was the tall thin figure of Capt. Bill O'Connor. Was I glad to see him and he me! We were friends meeting in a far away, strange land. O'Connor then introduced me to the following officers: Capt. Paul D. Wood, who was to be in charge of the Officer School in Tubigon, Bohol. Wood was a West Point man.

First Lt. Duane L. Casper was from Walla Walla, WA. Casper was one of Wood's assistants. Capt. Hoyt, another West Point man and second in command of the Tubigon School; Lt. Pratt, whom we soon named Donald Duck because he talked all the time and in a very hoarse voice. Last was 1st Lt. Gordon Utke from the Dakotas. Utke had been in the islands for a year or so and was married to Col. Carter's daughter. Utke, although stationed at the Tubigon Cadre, was not part of the school. He was the instructor for the machine gun company of the 81st Infantry, Philippine Army, stationed there.

There we were, eight American officers who were stationed on the island of Bohol for the next three months: six officers at the Cadre School at Tubigon; Capt. O'Connor at Tagbilaran Cadre with two rifle companies; and myself, in charge of one rifle company and a battalion headquarters unit at Calape. We all looked at each other with the friendly eyes of pilgrims in a foreign land and headed for the unknown. We all felt it was to be quite an adventure ahead of us.

It was five hours from Cebu to Tagbilaran. Our little ferry skirted around several sandbars and coral reefs, which were only a few feet in height. Several were a few inches above the smooth surface of the "blue to green" sea. Flying fish frequently broke the calm surface of the water. The bow of the boat was low and we got some excellent views of the little fish.

At other times we went between narrow passes or defiles between small, but heavily forested islands. Coconut palms and mangrove trees extended clear out into the seawater in many of these narrow lanes of water. At other places, we saw wide, sandy beaches fringed at the rear by thick growths of tall coconut palms. To me there was more charm possessed by these beaches than the famous Waikiki Beach in Honolulu.

Most of us stood at the bow railing watching the described scenery. Lt. Casper, however, was an exception. Casper sat at a table on the lower deck drinking warm beer (there was no ice in these waters or on this type of boat, nor was there drinking water) and writing postcards. He said the post cards were to help him catch up on his correspondence. Considering that we did not know how much time we would have in the future for such chores, I thought his policy a good one and followed suit.

E. L. Morrison had telegraphed Dart Williams of Tagbilaran, Bohol, that I was arriving that evening and would he please meet me at the dock. About 1700 our ferry rounded the palm-fringed coast of Bohol and pulled into a large bay. As the boat approached the dock, I stood on the bow deck and saw one lone white man standing beside a black Packard sedan, observing our approach. There was a look of bewilderment on his face as he counted eight American officers in uniform plus two noncoms, instead of one lone American lieutenant.

We docked. I stepped ashore and inquired if he was Williams. He was. Then followed introductions all around. In the end, Williams took us all out to the PA cadre where we found a maintenance crew. Of course they didn't know we were coming, but we managed to get them to send transportation down to the pier and get our baggage. Williams having delivered us, left, promising to see me later. There was a lot of confusion and he undoubtedly was glad to escape.

Our group took inventory of the situation and surroundings and then we took over, Capt. Wood in command. The first thing to do was to get some chow, as it was late. Taking the cadre truck, we all piled in and went back downtown. Tagbilaran is built around a square that contains the vendors' market booths on market days. It was almost 2100 by that time and not a single eating place appeared open. Finally, one of the Filipinos directed us to a Chinaman's restaurant. We stopped at that building and looked at it in consternation. There were some wooden steps leading up to the second story where a weather-beaten sign said "Restaurant" in English. The building itself was square, supported by four pillars about 10 feet high. The floor was on top of these four pillars. The walls were of woven sawali (pronounced *sawa-lee*) with nipa palm thatching for a roof. Underneath that house were two pens made of woven bamboo. In one were two razorback pigs (these razorbacks would "out-razorback" our Arkansas variety) and a flock of droopy chickens. It smelled worse than the Chicago Stockyards in mid-August. If this were a restaurant, we were angels! But it was a restaurant and we weren't angels. The Chinaman came down the stairs dressed in dirty white trousers and an undershirt. We had to eat, so we told him we wanted "American chow outta cans." Could he fix? I think everyone of us chimed in saying we wanted American chow. He gravely listened to us all with an inscrutable face and then said. "Okay, me fix" and motioned us to follow him.

We trailed up the stairs and sat down at a long table with benches beside it for seats and waited. Sights and smells were prevalent. Pretty soon the odor of cooking drifted into the room from behind a movable panel. Shortly afterward a comely looking Chinese girl, gaudily dressed in calico, began bringing out the dishes of soup. The dishes were dirty and greasy. The soup was hot, greasy, had eggshells and pinfeathers in it. Not many of us ate much of our soup.

Next the Chinese girl brought out a platter of rice with some pieces of boiled chicken in it. She then proceeded to take each dish of our uneaten soup and threw it through a hole in the floor. The pigs awoke immediately and started an awful squealing. Dish after dish was emptied and the empty dish placed in front of us. The Chinaman then passed the platter of rice and chicken to Capt. Wood. The captain gingerly took a little of the rice and chicken and passed it on to O'Connor. When it came to Capt. Hoyt he made some remark about still being seasick from the trip down. The platter passed from hand to hand, nobody taking more than a few small spoons of the rice and chicken. I was no different from the rest.

Not one of us dreamed that less than a year later, every single one of us would have eaten that entire platter of rice, at a single sitting, declaring all the while that it was a "feast fit for a king."

We ate what we were going to of the rice and chicken. Then we told the Chinaman we wanted some fruit for dessert. He brought out two (quart) cans of Queen Anne cherries and opened them right at the table. He passed the cans to us and we passed them around. When an almost empty can reached Wood, he just ate out of the can, remarking, "If any of you boys want to do the same, just tell him so," and pointed at the China-man. I think everyone of us called for an individual can of cherries and ate out of the cans. The Chinaman's eyes bugged out. You could almost see the thoughts flashing in his face about the uncouth, barbaric Americans who wouldn't eat rice and ate cherries out of a can.

By this time, the only kerosene lamp was about to flicker out and several of the boys were exceedingly squirmy. I was, too. I thought I felt things crawling on my legs. I reached down and picked something off my leg. It squashed between my thumb and forefinger. I looked at in in the flickering lamplight. It had been a bug and it had a characteristic odor I was soon to become well acquainted with. Yes, it was a squashed bedbug with its pungent odor of almonds.

We left immediately and once we got outside of that filthy, stinking place we felt like we had a new lease on life. Every one of us was scared stiff we were going to get dysentery from that meal!

We drove back to the cadre and started looking for places to sleep. We all had our bedrolls, but nobody had thought to bring along any twine to hang our mosquito nets with. As a result we spent the entire night slapping mosquitoes. Slap! Slap! Slap! What a night it was. I think every mosquito on the island of Bohol entered that room, took a bite out of us and flew out to make way for another. I never heard such cursing in all my life. In the morning Wood's face was so welted and swollen from mosquito bites that I hardly recognized him.

The next morning we tore open somebody's box of canned chow and got some canned goods for breakfast. After that we went to our various post locations via the cadre truck. My post at Calape was on the road to Tubigon where Wood and his six officers were going. They dropped me off on the way.

Calape, Bohol, was a strange new place to me, yet I was lucky. I walked into a good barracks on a level parade ground. It had running water, electric lights, flush toilets, and bunks enough for all the men I was to have in my camp. O'Connor at Tagbilaran had the same facilities I had, but only for a quarter of the number of men he was to have. Capt. Wood was even worse off than O'Connor.

What I didn't have was a typewriter for all the army paperwork that had to be done, paper for it, field manuals for training programs, and equipment of any type for training soldiers. That barracks was absolutely barren of any equipment except one small desk, some built-in brick stoves, and the heavy iron cauldrons for boiling rice in. There were no facilities for washing mess gear or even heating water.

With the cadre buildings were five Philippine Army regular soldiers who were the caretakers. Through them I gained knowledge of the PA system of contracting locally for needed food and supplies. This I did. I had five days grace before my troops arrived to scare up the minimum necessities to start my camp with. There wasn't even a stick of wood to build a fire around that place. I used quite a bit of my own money in order to be able to function when the time came. It was a great life. There was so much to do that I didn't have a chance to think.

Calape, Bohol, was a friendly little Filipino city 41 kilometers north of the provincial capital, Tagbilaran. It lay on the west coast between the mountains and the sea. About two miles east of it, the mountains rose sharply to the height of about 1,400 feet. Once you were on the mountain slopes you ran into thick jungle. Though jungle-covered, the mountains had numerous trails. There were valleys on the other side of the coast range which were heavily populated. To the west of the town lay a sizable bay sheltered from the open sea between Bohol and Cebu by Pacijan Island.

My camp lay on the north side of Calape. Its grounds consisted of a level grassy plot of about five acres. It was surrounded on all but the town side by small coconut plantations. These plantations were small, very close together, and very numerous. To the casual observer they appeared to be one continuous plantation stretching for miles. The trees were very thick and about 80 feet tall. To the west side of my camp, about a mile away, lay the sea. Between the camp and the bay lay coconut plantations, rice paddies, and mangrove swamps. Farther away to both north and south lay beautiful sandy beaches with beautiful tall palms growing right out of the sand. In some places the white sandy beaches were 100 yards wide. At other places the coconut palms had been planted in the sand clear to the roller's edge. My camp was on the edge of a grassy meadow that lay in the midst of a forest of coconut palms. A white crushed coral road ran through the forest and past my camp.

Capt. Wood left me at my cadre barracks. I watched his group disappear in the coconut forest and turned to look at my surroundings.

Sgt. Bosco came out of a house in a nearby coconut grove.

Sgt. Bosco, saluting, said, "Good morning, sir. I hope the lieutenant had a good trip yesterday."

"Yes, Sergeant, we had a wonderful trip." I glanced at Sizemore as I said this and he grinned in a sickly manner.

"Everything is all hunky-dory, Lieutenant."

"How's that, Sergeant?"

"I contracted for a house for the lieutenant and Corp. Sizemore, a *lavandera* to wash the uniforms, and a cook who can cook American chow!"

"Hells bells, Sergeant. How did you do all of that?"

"It's easy, Lieutenant, if you know the methods."

"Where's the house?"

"There, sir," he said, pointing to a large spacious-looking nipa hut across the road. It was sheltered by coconut palms and the bottom floor stood on four slender pillars 12 feet above the ground. At the back, under the house, I could see a pen with a pig in it!

"And the *lavandera*, Sergeant, where will she live?"

"There, sir," pointing to a small nipa shack 100 yards from my dwelling. It was so poor-looking that it wasn't built high enough to have the usual pig pen. Again I looked at Sizemore whose face was a study of mixed emotions.

"And the cook, Sergeant? When does he come to begin work?"

"Very soon, Lieutenant. In time for noon chow." I tried to conceal my feelings at this stage. This sergeant was a "hot potato" and right on the ball. He had me all fixed up one way or another. He either had me fixed up in fine shape or he had me in a hell of a mess.

"Well, Sergeant, how soon will the people move out of the house and I can move in?"

"Already, sir, they have moved. Last night they went to live with their son." I sat down on my bedroll, took off my cap and wiped my forehead. This boy was too much for me; he had all the answers.

(Weakly) "That's a very big house, Sergeant, and we don't have any furniture."

(Quickly) "Oh, but, sir, that is hunky-dory. I knew the lieutenant had his bedroll, so I contracted for the furniture, too."

"But, Sergeant, won't this be pretty expensive?"

"Fifteen pesos a month, sir. It is really a very nice house, sir." The sergeant looked very worried at this remark.

"Fifteen pesos," I muttered in amazement. "That's $7.50 gold. I'd give a lot more than $7.50 for a roof over my head in this country."

I didn't want to live in the barracks with the Filipino soldiers.

"Sergeant, I guess you have taken care of everything. I am sure glad you are the scout detailed with me. Can my cook speak English and cook American chow?"

"Yes, sir. Lieutenant. He lived in Hawaii 15 years and worked for the Army."

By this time I decided I was lucky. This Filipino sergeant was plenty bright, he had been around white men and knew what they wanted. He certainly had been a quick worker here and he had the air of one who knew his stuff.

"Okay, Sergeant. You go get the cook and better get me a houseboy, too."

"His son is the houseboy, sir."

"Get them here on the double; I want to get settled before tonight."

"Yes, sir!" He saluted and scuttled off into the coconut palms.

I turned to Sizemore and said, "Well! Can you beat that?" I was flabbergasted.

"No, Lieutenant I can't. I didn't know there were Pinos like that."

I got up and walked for a few minutes, looking around and thinking. Here was a new situation; so far I was master of it. The sergeant's manner had been that he expected me to expect of him what he had accomplished. I wasn't going to change that attitude. Here was a horse that wanted to travel and I might as well travel as far as I could while moving was good. I decided the best policy was to express a desire or wish to the sergeant and then shut up and watch what happened until I got my feet on the ground and knew what the score was. It worked!

In a few minutes the sergeant came out of the coconut trees on the double. Ten feet behind him dog-trotted a middle-aged Filipino man in a dirty white undershirt and white duck pants and 50 feet behind the man, on the run, was a boy about 12 years of age. These two were cook and houseboy, respectively.

"Lieutenant, this is Alejandro, your cook, and his son Pablo, your houseboy."

"Alejandro, I am glad you and Pablo are going to work for me. Right now, move this baggage over to my house," I said, pointing to the house I was to occupy. "Sergeant, have a couple of the soldiers here bring over those two iron bedsteads from the cadre office. We don't want to sleep on the floor."

I won't go into the task of housecleaning around the kitchen. The extent, quality, and type of filth were in accordance with the rest of the things I have mentioned in regard to sanitation. Strange to say, but circumstances alter opinions. One year later if I could have walked into that house I would have said, "Isn't this the height of luxury and sanitation?" That house, on looking back, was about 900 percent more sanitary than the places where we lived in Japanese prisons. This first day I got my quarters cleaned up and in order, we even got the kerosene stove and Coleman lantern working before nightfall.

In a day or two I was able to get the houseowners to remove their pig and a big two-wheeled cart. In a few days more, the swine odor began to disappear. The cook and the houseboy lived in their own home which was not far away and came to work early each morning.

While all these glittering generalities were taking place, small individual events were happening which concerned me. One in particular that I remember occurred one morning shortly after 7:00. I was in the toilet sitting on the stool when a loud banging occurred at the front door of my quarters.

"Wait a few minutes and I will be there," I said, expecting it to be one of my orderlies. The knocking sounded again, louder this time. "All right, damn it, I will be there, but you will have to wait until I am through here."

Upon my finishing that sentence, the door opened and I heard somebody come in. At that sound, I reached for my gun which I always kept near me, cocked it, got off the stool and moved towards the door with the gun leveled. As I reached the door Filipino Col. David was advancing across the center of my living room. Behind him were other Filipinos. At the sight of me, with a leveled gun in my right hand and holding up my pants with my left hand, the whole group stopped.

"Colonel, when people come into my house they identify themselves first. I have already shot at one thief in the night and I never know when to expect another. I came out here prepared to use this gun and I find you and your friends. Don't you think you should have told me who you were before you came in and eliminated this danger?" With that I put the safety on my gun and returned it to my holster.

"But the Vice-President of the Philippines, Señor Osmeña, is coming here to stay, so I brought him right in."

"The Vice-President of the Philippines is certainly welcome to occupy my quarters with me and I will do everything I can to make him comfortable. You, sir, were most unwise to bring him into this place without warning me of your identity. Won't you bring him in, sir?"

"This is the Vice-President," he said, pointing to the man in the doorway behind him.

I looked at the calm face of the elderly Filipino standing in the doorway of my quarters. Sure enough, it was Vice-President Osmeña! Behind him stood various members of his staff and some soldiers carrying their baggage.

"Won't you come in, sir, and share my poor quarters?" I then started to pull up my pants and stuff in my shirttail. Talk about being caught with your pants down—I certainly was in this case, and by no other than the Vice-President of the Philippines!

"You will pardon my appearance, Mr. Vice-President. I was not expecting visitors at this hour of the morning. I don't usually greet my guests with a .45 in my hand. However, someday I do expect to have some guests on which I will use the weapon. Breakfast should be ready in about 15 minutes. Won't you join me?"

"We are sorry to have frightened you, Captain, and we really had no chance to give you warning of our coming."

With that speech, the stern face of the old man relaxed into a smile and he stepped forward with outstretched hand to shake hands with me. I saluted him and then shook hands with him. When he moved forward, the rest of the group moved in and they deposited their baggage on the floor inside the door.

On September 1, 1941, most of my quota of 140 troops came in from Tagbilaran. They brought with them their equipment in the way of blankets, uniforms, canteens, and mess kits. They didn't have any weapons. Those were yet to come.

Out of the regular PA crew of five men, one could run a mess after a manner, another could do the clerical work if he had a typewriter (I borrowed one from the local Provincial High School), another knew how to operate a diesel engine for lights, etc. Under these men, I had to assign soldiers to learn the duty from the ground up. It was a hard job selecting men capable of doing these jobs because they demanded some education in reading, writing, and arithmetic. After examining these men, I decided that if a man had completed the third grade, he was well educated!

Those first two days were a nightmare. The lads couldn't understand me and I couldn't understand them. There were men from several different islands. Often a different island meant a different tribe and a different dialect spoken. Both the commissioned and non-commissioned officers, in most cases, had been assigned their commission and rates through the influence of political connections and not through their qualifications for the detail. To give an order he spoke to a member of his squad in Tagalog who understood him, who in turn translated the command in English to a third member of the squad. This third member then translated the command from English to Visayan for the remainder of the squad. This command had to pass from the noncom through two interpreters before his squad could understand the order. With their knowledge of languages the percentage of error was practically 100 percent. To begin with, that noncom could not understand me. He gave his order by watching what the other squads did. The whole setup seemed to run backwards. I had to sift all these things out for myself.

What about the Filipino officers, you ask? They were pretty bewildered. All were young, inexperienced, afraid they would do something wrong, unable to fully understand English or to translate English to their troops. Those first few days I told them to watch and I didn't work them too heavily. Slowly they gained confidence and grew used to assuming command.

Cpl. Sizemore was just as badly off as I in the language difficulties. He practically sweated blood daily. Each night he was exhausted. My savior through all of this chaos was Sgt. Bosco. He could speak several dialects and he knew the training routine backwards, forward, and sideways. For hours at a time he would keep five or six officers busy with their troops. These officers had to learn with their men. He could teach them their administration work at night. Each night, after the troop duty was over and the troops fed, the corporal, the sergeant and I held night classes for the officers and noncoms. The classes were on the mistakes of the day and the training for the next day.

I had to know everything, oversee everything, be everywhere at once, and try to keep the officers and the men in good spirits. All of them were like a group of children; most of them had never been away from home and family before and they got homesick. Many of them had never had so many clothes before. The uniforms were ill fitting and the shoes were hot tennis shoes that didn't fit. We gave them 10 minutes rest out of each hour. When they would fall in at the end of the rest period 75 percent of them were barefooted and carrying their shoes. They were like a bunch of children; you got the most out of them when you had them laughing and pulling with you.

The training was a 13-week basic training schedule worked up at Fort Benning, GA, calling for 44 hours training a week. We had to break this master schedule down into a daily schedule for each week. The authorities of the headquarters in Cebu City demanded that the training schedule should list the training manual and the paragraphs in the training manual concerning the training for each hour of the day. If our daily schedule said that at 2:45 P.M. we should be in the field simulating advance by infiltration, woe be to us if we were not doing that at 2:45 P.M. Often those troops were in the mud and water because there was a tropical downpour at that time of day. They had only one change of clothes and these were usually wet and dirty. Those rains didn't last long, as a rule. If we had been permitted to take our 4:00 P.M. subject, which was an inside lecture, while it rained, and then resume the 2:45 training subject when the rain was over, the troops would not have been so miserable. They would have gotten 100 percent more out of the training with half the effort. In the first place, a Fort Benning training schedule should have been revised before being used in the Philippines. It didn't have a word about jungle fighting and, in the second place, we weren't permitted to use it sensibly. Orders were orders.

I arose at 6:00 A.M. and turned in around midnight after conducting night schools and later doing my paperwork. The corporal and the sergeant had pretty much the same schedule. I watched them grow thin and tired. It was killing work. Looking back I wonder if I wasn't too conscientious about my duty for my own good. I had to see to two training schedules, a battalion headquarters, and a rifle company, to daily take care of the camp supplies, administration, and sanitation. This last was not easy. You don't get a race to give up personal habits and customs just because you induct them in an Army, put them into clothes, and call them soldiers. It was a great life if you didn't weaken. I pushed my assistants and drove the Filipinos those first few weeks. The last, poor devils, were just like lost children that didn't know what to do. The rapidity of advance, demanded by the master schedule, kept them in a complete state of bewilderment. I never had more willing students though.

The whole setup was a vicious circle and somehow I felt I must fit the training more to the Filipino psychology.

One of the men I later knew in prison, Maj. Campbell Snyder of Louisiana, often recited a piece of poetry which I think covered the situation fairly well; quoting from dim memory:

It is not good for the Occidental fair
To hurry the Easterner mild,
For the brown man smiles,
And the white man riles,
And it wears the white man down.
The end of the fight is a tombstone white,
Which bears the inscription:
Here lies a fool
Who tried to hurry the East.

By the end of the first two weeks the officers were beginning to feel more at home with their men.

At the end of the two weeks I called a council of all my Filipino officers. All could understand English more or less. We held a conference, exchanged views on the training schedule, equipment, language difficulties, etc. When I had gotten as many ideas as possible, I dismissed them with the promise to have some alterations pertaining to the training for them Monday. Then I gave the whole camp weekend leave.

Monday morning, I presented the Filipino officers a plan with the following points:

1. Teach the troops what was expected of them by observation.
2. Substitute explanation for demonstration.
3. Use the native dialects whenever possible.
4. Gather the best-educated men into a demonstration team.
5. Lead the troops themselves.

That was to be my contribution to the camp that Monday morning in the middle of September 1941.

What about the contribution of the troops? That was conspicuous by its omission. To be exact, "by their omission." Two-thirds of the entire camp had taken leave. All knew that they would have to be back by midnight Sunday. Came time to fall in at 0700 Monday morning, the troops fell in and great gaps appeared in the ranks. The sergeants reported one by one to their platoon leaders.

"Sir, 10 men absent."

"Sir, men absent."

"Sir, men absent."

The company commander reported to the battalion CO. The results were appalling, more than a third of the camp was AWOL. By this time the face of every man in camp was on me. The platoon lieutenants were so scared that they were almost white. The company commander was visibly trembling and the battalion commander seemed to have lost his tongue and couldn't talk enough to make his report.

I was fit to be tied. I was so astonished that I was speechless. I didn't know what to say and the men couldn't have understood me if I had started sulfur fumes rolling toward them. I just stood and looked them up and down and after three minutes or so of silence, I turned my back on the whole scene and wrote a letter in long hand. After about 10 minutes the battalion CO tiptoed in and asked what he should do. I laid down my pen and walked over to the door. The men were still standing at attention while the officers were standing in a sickly group. Cpl. Sizemore and Sgt. Bosco were just outside the office door discreetly saying nothing, yet on quick call.

"Sergeant, Corporal," I called in a funny voice.

"Yes, sir," they answered in unison and saluted.

"Explain our new lesson plan to the officers, explain the lesson subjects and get under way with the Filipino officers instructing the platoons." I returned their salutes and again walked inside. I heard their voices start the program as I finished my letter. I then called an orderly and had him personally take this letter to the post office. This was a personal letter addressed to Col. Theodore Sledge, CO, 8th Military Area, Cebu City, Cebu. (It asked for field manuals.)

I then left the office and went to my quarters across the street. Once there I sat down on my bunk and laughed! This wasn't the American Army; the more I thought about it the funnier it got and I started laughing. I had a good laugh when I remembered the consternation in those faces. After an hour or so I returned to the training ground to see how things were going. I still held my silence. A few of the late soldiers came into camp from off the bus as it went by. I told the battalion CO to put all AWOL men in fatigue clothes and have them start to work on various police details around camp. I don't know what those Filipino officers told those men, but it was pretty rough from the sound.

At noon the corporal and sergeant told me things had gone well with the training that morning and that I had them all guessing what I was going to do about the situation. I just sat tight, ignored the situation, and observed reactions. I decided by the time the day was over and as long as I kept silent, the more they would toe the line. That I did. As those men who were AWOL returned, they were put to work cleaning up the camp. They cleaned up a lot that day. At retreat most of the men had returned and the next morning none were AWOL. Tuesday I carried on the regular training hours. At retreat I ordered all the men who had been AWOL to fall in at 6:00 P.M. They lined up at 6:00 P.M. and I looked them over. Pausing in front of a private who could speak English, I said, "Why were you AWOL?"

"Sir, I went to see my family."

"Why did you not return by midnight?"

"Sir, I could not."

"Why not?"

"Sir, the lieutenant said I could go visit my family. He signed my pass. I take the boat to Cebu City. I take the provincial bus to Santander. I take banca to Siquejor Island. I get home Sunday morning and I stay with my family all day and all night. Monday morning I take banca back to Santander. I come back to camp last night!"

I said nothing more. I knew family ties were very close, a lot closer in some ways than ours. I went on down the line. All of them had gone home or to see some relative at some place too remote for the time. The fact that all had returned after only a short visit showed that they did not intend to desert. I gave them an hour of grounds police and dismissed them. Privately I had decided to dismiss the whole episode and nothing more was said on my part. As a result the extra fatigue had disgraced the AWOL boys in the eyes of the rest of the camp and I had my camp looking real neat and tidy. When the district inspector came around later in the week, my camp was rated excellent and the best on the island. The Filipinos thought the district commander had come around to investigate the AWOLs. I didn't disillusion them. The whole episode was a stumper at the moment; but it resulted in establishing me more securely in charge of the camp.

On such a detail, with different races that way, you have to feel your way around and it is best not to be hasty. Study the people involved and bend their psychology to attain the ends you desire. More and more I applied this to my training and I found things becoming more organized.

I don't remember the names of all the Filipino officers. The ones that I do remember include 1st Lt. Valentin Velasco, who was right on the ball. I am not sure that he didn't know more about the Army than I since he was a Philippine regular. He was invaluable during those first weeks in getting the camp organized. Somewhere he had been in training with American troops and he would cushion the occidental and oriental differences between myself and the troops. Ricardo Estrella was my supply officer. He was a likable chap and very helpful. His name was Spanish—translated into English, it meant Richard Star. Estrella was a reservist and a Philippine government employee in civilian life. He had charge of the National Forestry Office in Cebu City, Cebu. He also was familiar with white men.

Lt. Ignacio Javier was the commander of troops. He was young and with not much experience in handling men at the time. He improved as time went along. His father worked for the Shell Oil Co. in Cebu City.

Lt. Jose Momonana was another of the young officers. He likewise was young and an Army career man. He came from Luzon and was a Tagalog. Momonana didn't know too much about white men and he had a very violent temper, which made it hard to get along with him. He was either all for something or all against it. There was no medium road for him.

The last I remember was 1st Lt. Perfecto Mabugat. As far as I became concerned his name should have been Imperfect and not Perfecto. Velasco was transferred to the district headquarters in Cebu City to take the job that Mabugat had. Mabugat was sent to my camp, which made the two just trade places. Mabugat was as bad as Velasco was good. He was a regular in the PA and his branch was infantry. He was a licensed physician who evidently had gotten through medical school somewhere, but didn't make a good living so he joined the Army. My troubles really began when he appeared. The four previous years he had been a battalion commander and commanding officer of this Calape Camp. In fact, I lived in his house and it still bore his wooden nameplate. Now, instead of being the big dog in a little puddle, he was just another Filipino lieutenant under an American officer. This was quite a social comedown for him and he resented my presence very much. He was quite well known socially among the townspeople and it galled him not to be the CO in their presence. He was unreliable and inefficient.

The training went merrily on. The rifles were old Enfields, which had long been obsolete for the U.S. Army. When it came to grenades, there were none to be had. I taught the soldiers to use stones in their throwing exercises. At first I made them use the U.S. way of heaving a grenade, then upon experimentation I found they could throw it twice as far in their natural way. Training regulations or no training regulations, in the heat of a battle those Filipinos would forget the white man's method and revert to their own. Better to get the idea across to them what the grenade would do if they pulled the pin and threw it in whatever manner they could throw it farthest.

In the jungle training those boys were very good; they were right at home and with plenty of ingenuity. They took to the art of camouflage with no difficulty. They weren't such good shots though. They were afraid of the recoil of that rifle. With no more time and ammunition than we had, I never did get some of those boys over shutting their eyes and jerking the gun when they fired. One lad in the rapid-fire exercise shut his eyes and fired his whole five shots before he opened them again. Where those bullets went I have no idea, except that they didn't go into the target!

The first firing exercise was held in a farmer's valley cornfield. When the second firing exercise was due, the cornfield was planted and we could not use it. Accordingly, I had to search in the foothills until I found a suitable place for a range and then get the owner's permission for using it. Once the permission was gained, I had to build a whole new setup, pits for safety, frames for the targets, rope, cloth, paste, etc.—all had to be bought. I paid for these out of my own pocket. As a result of that practice, those boys riddled a farmer's banana plantation by their overshoots. The trees were so riddled with bullets that they died. I paid for two in order to do away with any possible hard feelings.

Those were long, hard, exhausting days. I was often too exhausted at night to anymore than take off my shoes until I woke up late sometime in the night, when I would undress and go to bed properly.

Col. Theodore Sledge was the CO of the 8th Military District, which was composed of the islands of Cebu and Bohol. Every once in a while, Col. Sledge would ship his car over on the ferry and take a night boat to Bohol. Then he would make a personal tour and inspection of the camps at Tagbilaran, Calape, and Tubigon. On one trip he brought Col. Callahan (or Monahan) from department headquarters in Manila. They had dinner with me. I was always glad to see these inspectors because they often were the only white men I would see for days or even weeks at a time. Col. Sharp, later Maj. Gen. Sharp, CO of the southern islands, stopped very briefly one afternoon. He found me out in the field with the troops.

After I got the camp started, I received a 1 1/2-ton truck and a station wagon for camp use in getting supplies and transporting the soldiers to and from the boats when they went on leave. Because supplies were so short, often the three camps had to lend each other equipment. I managed to visit the other camps now and then and exchange ideas and notes. Sanitation was the chief problem we had in common. The flies were incubating in the latrines, around the kitchens, and in the water ditches in the camps. Capt. Woods was having his hands full with his school. In the school there were quite a number of field officers and they resented the strict discipline of the school. In our sense of the word, it wasn't strict discipline, but in comparison with what they were used to, it was strict. It took all of Paul D's diplomacy to keep everybody on good terms.

I went down to O'Connor's camp one day for supplies at the small depot there. I found Bill in a blue mood. I only needed to use the stock phrase, "Well, how are things going?" to set him off.

"Going? Why, things are going to hell! Do you know what I am doing? I'm building houses (latrines to you)! I was in the First World War and all I did there was build houses and clean stables. I later served in Hawaii and all I did there was wash and grease cars. Now I come to the Philippines and what do I do? I build more houses. No wonder this Army is going to hell when all it does is build houses!"

He paused and lit a cigarette. I noticed his hands shook as if he had the palsy. I looked at the man sharply to note that his face was haggard, his eyes sunken, and that he had lost about 20 pounds.

"Whoa there, oldtimer, take it easy. You have been working too hard. It's noon time now; how about knocking off and let's go eat?"

"Okay, I just got a house rented and a couple of Filipino girls to take care of it and cook."

"I thought you stayed here at the barracks and ate at the mess here."

"I did for about 15 days, but I couldn't stand it. I didn't have one single minute's privacy. The Filipinos were always bothering me even when I was in bed. The food was mostly rice and it was very unappetizing. One day they had some soup, which smelled so rotten so I investigated the kitchen. The cooks had a hog for that day and they had made soup out of the entrails. The whole mess was rotten. I became very sick at my stomach and vomited. After that I couldn't eat at the mess there without getting sick from the thought of that stinking mess! Now I have a good mess, but I have lost my appetite."

I ate with O'Connor and he did have a good mess considering the situation and location. O'Connor had been at that camp about a month and most of that time he hadn't been able to eat. It was no wonder the man was a wreck physically. The next time I saw Col. Sledge I told him something ought to be done about Bill as he was in pretty bad shape. The colonel looked the situation over and made his own opinion about Bill. Shortly afterwards, Bill was transferred to the district headquarters in Cebu City. There he got back on his feet somewhat as he now lived like a white man.

The man who took O'Connor's place was 1st Lt. Myron Sharp. Myron, like the rest of us, had his troubles.

The Army camps were fairly free from disease. There was some malaria, dysentery, and typhoid. I lost one man, Sgt. Delata from the island of Cebu. I gave blood for a transfusion for him but even then he died. O'Connor helped me out with that mess. He took the body to Cebu while I went to the hospital exhausted. I stayed there three days and was very fortunate to be able to have a hospital to go to.

The hospital was a Presbyterian Mission Hospital in Tagbilaran, Bohol. It had been established by a missionary physician named Graham before the turn of the century. The old Dr. Graham was dead, but his daughter, Miss Graham, still lived there and carried on her father's missionary work. Three Filipino doctors carried on the medical end of it. Living with Miss Graham at that time were two young middle-aged missionaries, Mr. and Mrs. Joseph Livesey. The Japanese had just recently run them out of Korea. I saw them several times while on Bohol and got to be quite friendly with them. I asked them a lot of questions about the Japanese and their answers were not what I liked to hear. During the war, I believe, Miss Graham and the Liveseys lived with the natives all the time. I heard they got through the war alive.

Around October 1, 1941, I spent a weekend in Cebu City. Cebu was the second city in size in the Philippine Islands and the metropolis of the southern islands, having about 150,000 population. To make the trip I drove 15 kilometers to the small port of Tubigon and took an inter-island ferry to Cebu, about three hours away. When I speak of a ferry here, I don't mean the flat-ended boats you find in our bays and harbors. I mean a sharp-bowed, often sea-going boat of 75 to 100 feet long. It was built to carry cargo and passengers, cargo below the water line and passengers on the two decks above the water line.

This boat was packed with soldiers and civilians going to Cebu. Filipinos were perched on the railing, rigging, steps, everywhere. There were very few benches or seats aboard. I wondered if we were going to have to stand for the next few hours. This was all new and strange to me so I was content just to stand at the railing and watch.

As the boat drew away from the pier, some of the deckhands began to shove people aside, and set up canvas cots on the deck. As fast as the cots were set up people sat and lay down on them, sometimes a whole family of several children all settled themselves on one cot. The people who were standing disappeared as if by magic. Soon everybody was lying down except a few leaning against the rail. Most of the people went to sleep. I got a cot in the scramble, sat in it awhile and then moved around some to see what was going on. I wandered up to the pilothouse and there I found Lts. Casper, Herr, Pratt, Utke, and Capt. Hoyt. I joined the group. From the pilothouse or compass deck we watched the small islands slip by. The large island of Bohol sank into the green sea and its mountains dimmed in the purple haze. The dim island of Cebu became more distinct as we approached. Several times our ship altered course as it went by a sand bar or a coral reef, which rose a few inches out of the sea. I enjoyed the trip immensely and I enjoyed the company of my fellow Americans more.

Before leaving Calape, I had sent a telegram to K. L. Morrison, manager of the Cebu branch of Erlanger and Gallager, that I was coming over. He replied that his car would be waiting for me. As the ferry drew into the harbor of Cebu I took a keen interest in all the harbor activity and in trying to locate Morrison's dark Buick sedan. There were several inter-island boats in the harbor—the *Mayon*, the *Elcano* and one or two more were there—the first two, fast passenger boats, were heading for the ports of Manila, Iloilo, Cebu, Zamboanga, and lesser ports. The others were more cargo boats than passenger. Their chief cargo was copra, hemp, rice, etc. There were all sorts of bancas, fishing boats and quite a number of Japanese fishing boats. The latter were better equipped than the Filipino boats. Our little ferry sailed in and out among the various craft and finally approached a pier and slid alongside. It anchored and the mad scramble began as the Filipinos went down the gangplank. I remained on deck to watch and to see if I could locate the dark sedan. I didn't. By and by a well-dressed Filipino attracted my attention by shouting, "Lieutenant!" and pointing toward a group of cars. I recognized him as Morrison's chauffeur, Adolpho. I waved in reply and went to get my baggage. On leaving the boys, I made plans to see them later in the evening.

Morrison's Buick and chauffeur were at my disposal until late in the afternoon. Immediately I reported in at the 8th Military Headquarters to see what the latest dope was. I talked a short time with my CO, Col. Sledge, and met his assistant, Capt. Roy D. Gregory. Gregory was a West Point man and before coming to the southern islands he had been stationed at Fort McKinley with Philippine Scout troops. Originally he had come from a small town not far from Decatur, IL, which is the home of Millikin University. We had several mutual acquaintances we found out during the course of our conversation. The fact that we came from the same part of the country was enough to make us friends, let alone the fact that we were similar in character and had similar likes and dislikes. Roy was a pretty quiet fellow but he had plenty of gray matter upstairs. He made a wonderful record for himself during the war and rose to the rank of lieutenant colonel. Many a day later, in prison, we worked side by side in the Davao rice fields, on the logging detail, or the farm, or some other backbreaking, heartrending work. I can still see him in my mind's eye standing in a rice paddy, covered with mud, wearing a battered old Filipino hat with a hole in the crown and a g-string. There was a quiet grin on his face and a twinkle of dry humor in his eye, even when the going was the hardest. His is one of the pictures that will live with me to the end of my days.

From the headquarters I went downtown shopping for cooking utensils and canned food. I found some wonderful candied yams, had a haircut, shampoo, and shave. From there I went out to Morrison's house for a shower and back downtown to meet Morrison. The first thing we did was to find a *botica* (drug store to you) and get some ice cream and cokes. (I had been living on boiled water for the last month and bathing out of a five-gallon gasoline can.)

I spent the evening with Morrison, his wife, Buster, and little boy, Kenneth. They had a beautiful home out on the lower slopes of the mountains, looking to the mountains and over the city. Their home was quite palatial and very, very comfortable.

I didn't realize how much I had missed ice water, easy chairs, screens from mosquitoes, the latest magazines, electric lights, and a large nice soft bed. It was the first time in five weeks I had relaxed enough to think about all these luxuries. Yes, that shave, haircut, and shampoo were first-class luxuries. Anybody who has really been around would agree with me that it is only the softies who take even those ordinary things for granted.

Later that evening K. L. took me to the only air-cooled theater in town and I almost froze. After that we went out to the Country Club where I met several other Army men whom I had heard of, but hadn't met till then.

1st Lt. Russell Cracraft was one of the first of these Army men I met at the Club. I don't remember where he came from, but he had charge of a PA camp in Argao, Cebu, which was directly across the strait from my camp. Like myself, he was out all alone.

The second lad I met resembled myself in stature and build. To make things more confusing his name was Miner and it was spelled like mine. He was 1st Lt. John S. Miner from Pomona and Laguna Beach, CA. John was called Jack part of the time and "Buck" at other times. I was called Bill and often we were mixed up, both of us being called "Buck" at times. We tried to figure out if we were any relation to each other. We finally gave it up as a bad job, but both of us always suspected that we were distantly related. Never at any time yet have I come across somebody with my name who was not distantly related to me somehow. Jack was in charge of a camp near Medellian, at the northern end of the island of Cebu.

Another lad was 1st Lt. Robert P. Chrisman from Los Angeles. Chrisman, along with Jack Miner, was one of the few who had been able to bring their own cars with them. Chrisman was stationed at a PA camp right at the edge of Cebu and had his mess and quarters with the head-quarters in Cebu.

2nd Lt. Dick McKawn was another who was stationed in the PA camp in Cebu. I don't remember much about his background, but I dimly recall that he was an orphan and lived somewhere in the bay region of San Francisco.

At the Cebu camp was a 2nd Lt. Howard Humphreys, who claimed two homes. One was in the Virgin Islands where his parents lived. His father was a Navy officer, I believe. The other was his legal address, which he gave as McLean County near Bloomington, IL. Later I found out he owned 335 acres of the finest cornbelt land in the U.S. and had a fiancée standing by. He will appear from time to time in my accounts until he died in faraway Moji, Japan.

About this time I met a Maj. Howard J. Edmands, who was a Philippine Scout officer and had been in the islands for years. He knew the islands well and the natives, too. His wife Jane was back in the States somewhere and his daughter Shirley was attending Knox College, from which I graduated five years before. Edmands had lived a colorful life up to the time I met him and he lived an even more colorful one after the war broke out, until he died, a prisoner on the white sand dunes of the beach of San Fernando, La Union, Luzon.

At another time at the headquarters of the Southern Forces, I met a young Capt. William L. Robinson. He was West Point 1937 and seemed to be right on the ball at the time. During the war, before the surrender, he rose to be a lieutenant colonel on Gen. Sharp's staff. Later, in prison, he was one of the administrative officers in the Davao colony. I never got to know him very well as he never went out on work details, that I know of. On board the ship taking the Southern Island prisoners from Bugo, Mindanao to Davao, he was slapped in the face by the Nips. Later, in prison when his eyes went bad, it was rumored that the Nips had injured one of the optical nerves. Later, one half of the people in the camp had their eyes go bad, so it was generally attributed to malnutrition.

Also in General (then Col.) Sharp's office, I met a Capt. William Halloway, cook, an Englishman by birth. Sometimes he was called Dash Cook. His branch was the adjutant general's department, as I remember. He became a lieutenant colonel on Gen. Sharp's staff. There were some who made fun of him in various ways, but when it came to the final stand I will eagerly say that he showed himself a hero during the second bombing of our prison ship, on the trip from Manila to Moji, Japan. He should be awarded a citation for his efforts and the service he rendered the wounded during and after that bombing and strafing. When most people were huddling in groups on the floor of the hold, he was up asking everybody who could spare a rag, torn undershirt, handkerchief, etc., to let him have it for the wounded. If someone had a rag he would wade through the blood, torn bodies, the dead and debris to get it and then he would take it to a wounded soldier. He did that for others regardless of danger to himself and he did not husband his strength while doing his good deed. Often to stir around and exhaust oneself proved fatal because there was no food to restore one's strength. Col. Halloway, cook, died of exhaustion and malnutrition a few days after we landed in Moji. I wonder how many people are now alive because of his efforts. It's people like him and his deed that make me proud that I am an American. Time and again I saw little deeds of kindness turn the tide of a man's life.

In this same headquarters I met Sgt. Iphraim Iglewitz, who had been stationed in Corregidor under Lt. Col. Clair M. Conzelman of Barrie, VT. I first knew Iglewitz and later in prison I became very close friends with Col. Conselman. Iglewitz was very helpful in some of my administrative work.

Another officer that I met at this headquarters was Col. Braddock, MC. Col. Braddock was a gentleman and a scholar. He was an active physician and surgeon and regardless of the occasion, he was always courteous. I remembered the first time he spoke to me he used the word "Sir." I was just a 1st lieutenant and he was a colonel. Before that conversation was over, I understood why he was so well-liked by those around him. Years later in Mukden prison I saw him give his spare clothes away, in the face of an approaching semi-Arctic winter, to American soldiers with far less than he. I am glad to acknowledge receiving a woolen blouse from him. I saw Col. Braddock several times before the war.

Each time I was in Cebu I called to see Col. Sharp. Sometimes I saw the colonel and sometimes I didn't. Since he was the CO of the Southern Islands he was often out on inspection somewhere. I think he visited my camp twice.

A little later than this, about the middle of October 1941, there were at least two other officers who came to Cebu and I got to know them before the war.

The first was 1st Lt. Lyles G. Hardin from Rock Hill, SC. Hardin's father had been a minister and died when he was still young. His mother was then Dean of Women, not far from Rock Hill. Jardin was about six feet one and weighed over 200 pounds, had a wonderful disposition and a keen sense of humor. We soon nicknamed him "Tiny" and "Tiny" he remained to us until he went down on the prison ship. Tiny was stationed in Argao, Cebu, with Lt. Cracraft.

The second was 2nd Lt. Lee Johnson of Scotland Neck, NC. This Lee Johnson should not be confused with Maj. Lee Johnson who was an older man. Johnson had a southern accent so thick you could cut it in slices and butter your bread with it. He was in charge of guarding military supplies on Mactan Island in the harbor of Cebu.

Another officer I met about this time was 1st Lt. Calin B. Whitehurst. One of the first things he did was to show me a picture of his wife Rose. Whitehurst was in the 8th District Headquarters with Capt. Gregory and Col. Sledge before the war started.

Prior to the war, it was usually at some social gathering in Cebu City on a weekend when all these officers would get together. Not all I have mentioned were together any one time. It took two or three weekends in Cebu before I met them all. I remember the first weekend there because it was my first return to civilization after living in what was a foreign land for a month. I had a good visit with my old company commander, Capt. Robert Johnston, who was then Col. Sharp's S-4, and Capt. Al Kircher who was the engineer for Col. Sharp's staff.

In addition to these Army men, I met quite a number of civilians, both Spanish and American. Of the first was Eduardo Aboitiz whose family owned the La Naviera Filipinas Steamship Co., and some of his friends. Among the civilians were Capt. and Mrs. C. J. Martin, manager of Cebu Stevedoring Co.; Mr. William Ogan, owner of bus lines on Cebu and Bohol and who had been a soldier in the Spanish-American War; Mr. William Noble, son of Fredrick Noble, both of Standard Oil in the Philippines. Mr. and Mrs. Self, Mr. and Mrs. Miller, Mr. and Mrs. Edward

Short of the Goodyear Rubber Co.; Mr. Dave Offleck of Proctor and Gamble; Dr. Hawks of the U.S. Public Health Service and others.

There was a dance at the night club that night and I met several Spanish girls: Maria Theresa Aboitiz; Carmen Godinez; Ester Moro, daughter of the Cebu harbor master; Sofia Pastor. About midnight, the Morrisons and I left the Club and returned to their residence.

That night I slept in a real honest-to-goodness bed, the first since I had left the States some three months before. Since that time I had slept on army cots or less. It was a wonderful feeling to be between clean white sheets in a wide bed—a bed so large that it would be large for two; large enough you didn't feel cramped by the mosquito net around it and there was a light at the head! I felt like a white man again and read myself to sleep with a two-month-old magazine, new to us out there in the Orient.

The weekend was over far too soon. By noon the next day, I was back on the ferry to Tubigon. Col. Sledge and his adjutant, Perfecto Mabugat, who was later to be transferred to my camp and of whom I have spoken elsewhere, were aboard. Col. Sledge was going over on an inspection tour of the Bohol camps. I visited with him all the way over, mostly catching up on the trend of things concerning our training and the world situation. He, like myself, was wondering how many days of peace we had left. Things were looking black for Russia.

I resumed my schedule of training on return from Cebu. A few days later a memorandum came from the Southern Headquarters to the effect that at the end of the first six weeks training, a party for the troops would be held. This was more grief, but orders were orders. Theoretically, we were supposed to persuade the community to throw the party for the troops. Well, that was the American way, not the Filipino way. I was already out of pocket for expenses and I just dug down some more. I assessed every officer in camp, the scout sergeant, the corporal, and myself 10 pesos each. I appointed Lt. Estrella chairman of the party committee and told him, "Take over."

The Filipinos under Lt. Estrella decided they wanted to throw a dance and serve ice cream for refreshment. This was growing interesting. The boys would have to have girls if they danced. Problem was, how to get the girls? You don't just invite the girls and they come. The Filipino priest frowned on dancing in Calape so I had to pay a personal call on the Father, inviting him to attend our Army dance in order to get his blessing for the party. The same thing for the major in order to get more community support, then the school teachers of the high school where the girls were and via the teachers send invitations to the duennas of the girls. As it turned out, the duennas were often the whole family: papa, mama, and all the children. By this time, I was tearing my hair. Oh, for the good old American way of living. If you wanted to take a girl to a dance you simply called her and the two of you went out to your dance! Right then and there I decided if I ever courted a girl, I was going to do it in the U.S.A. I went through the same procedure at another nearby town. Give me a few more years of this and I would become a first-rate politician. I had to agree to furnish transportation for town dignitaries and many of the girls, plus duennas. Hiring an orchestra was the smallest and simplest item. Finally there was the ice cream for refreshment. I had to send Lt. Estrella to Cebu City to arrange to have that especially packed and sent over by boat to Tubigon the day of the party. He met the boat to receive it. This had to be well taken care of since ice cream melts, particularly in the tropics, and you have it out in the province about as often as you find a chicken with a mouth full of teeth. I really believe the ice cream was about the most important item of the evening to those boys.

The party was a success. There were enough girls for the boys to dance with, around 80 with various members of their families. All in all, there must have been 250 guests, only 80 of whom entertained the soldiers. The rest were, shall we say, the "overhead." Where those girls got their dresses and why they had them, I don't know. These weren't the south sea island girls I was used to seeing under a palm tree or in a nipa hut. Everyone came in an up-to-date American dress. Some wore long formals and others wore conventional dresses appropriate for evening wear. I could have easily imagined myself back in a high school gym at a community party as far as those girls were concerned. They danced American or Spanish dances, except for special numbers, to American or Spanish tunes. I was learning things. From the dance floor, I let my eyes wander to the townspeople on the sidelines. Men and women and a few young children in colorful Filipino and Filipina garb. The old hillman, who was squatting on his haunches, was wearing a pair of dark shorts and a pink flowered embroidered tunic (so thin you could see through it). He was bare legged, barefooted, and he was chewing betel nut. His wife was standing beside him in a long embroidered dress of some strange thick material unfamiliar to me. I wondered which one of those dusky beauties on the dance floor was their daughter. In contrast to this couple was the mayor of Calape and his wife. Both were in up-to-date white American clothes (he in a white suit and she in a white formal). This was truly a land of contrasts; south sea island and occidental cultures were mixing here. To me the native dances were more interesting than our own. Shortly before midnight we served the ice cream which, luckily, was still nice and solid. Everybody was served. The party then ended and I sent the girls and their duennas home, the dignitaries, and finally the orchestra. I turned in about 2:30 A.M., a physical wreck. It may have been fun for the soldiers, but it was work to me! About 4:00 A.M. one of my lieutenants woke me up to tell me the truck taking the orchestra back to Tagbilaran had turned over. There was no rest for the weary. I had to go see about it. Luckily nobody was killed and I was able to get the truck repaired so it would run again.

There are always some amusing things about any detail if one has a sense of humor. I made an inspection of the grounds one day about two months after the camp began. There was too much paper around the Guard House rooms, so I gathered it up as evidence when I jumped somebody. Returning to the office, I sat down at my desk and idly looked at the scraps. On one of the pieces, in pencil, I found a perfect gem of a love letter written to some Filipina girl by one of the soldiers. It ran something like this:

Guard House

This date

Señorita Meo:

Today you have walked past the guardhouse so many times that I fell in love with you. You look so pretty with the hibiscus in your dark hair. You don't know my name, but you will when you read this letter and *"poco"* Jose will give it to you when you return. I will meet you tonight under the palm tree near this place.

I remember thinking that the Americans didn't have anything on the Filipinos. The way of a man with a maid is the same regardless of the land or the language.

There is a custom of the Filipinos that I like very much. In the day time you can walk through the streets of the towns and hardly anybody speaks to you. Yet when evening comes, a feeling of friendliness floats through the air. The work clothes disappear and the evening or holiday clothes appear. The older people sit around their houses, but the younger people stroll through the streets or under the palm or banana trees. Whenever you meet them on the street singly or in a group, or if you pass a house surrounded by middle-aged or elderly people, the greeting is sure to come, "Good evening, sir," or *"Buenos noches, señor."* You reply with a similar greeting. If you show any inclination to visit, they will invite you to a seat and bring out some coconut milk, beer, or tuba (native liquor made of fermented coconut palm sap). The white man has made his reputation with the islanders—the reputation of drinking constantly.

In some places the funeral custom of the Filipinos is quite different from ours. We mourn our dead indefinitely. In the Philippines they have the funeral and mourn the dead. After a short period of mourning, two days or two weeks, the family and friends dress up in their best and have a party celebrating the new life the recently deceased has entered into. This is a happy occasion. After the celebration is over they then act like normal people without sorrow in the family.

Some interesting things happened in the field in the line of training. We had a series of night marches. One night I had the troops start down the road. Knowing that some didn't want to go, I was making a check on who was in camp. The camp was deserted except for the guard detail, so I took off down the road through town after the troops. About 100 yards from camp I ran into two Filipino soldiers carrying their canteens.

"Where in the hell have you been? Don't you know you are supposed to be on the march?"

"Yes, sir, er, but, sire, we have been to fill our canteens!"

"Couldn't you fill them at the water faucet at the barracks?"

"But, sire, my friend had the canteens."

"Sire, we left the 'cuan' at the house of his friend last night. We went to get them tonight and did not get back before this!"

About this time I began to smell something besides a rat. "Let me see those canteens!" and snatched them away before the surprised soldier knew what was happening. I unscrewed the cap of a canteen and took an incautious sniff. That full breath made me sneeze so hard I lost my cap and one of the Filipinos snickered.

"What in the devil do you have in there?"

"*Tuba*, sir," he answered, quivering.

"Hell, I thought it was TNT the way it knocked my hat off," I muttered, too astonished to do other than pick up my hat.

"Officer of the Day, Lt. Gonzaga!" I shouted.

"Yes, sire, coming!" answered Gonzaga from the guard house.

"Put these men in the guard house." I then emptied both canteens (2 quarts of *tuba)* and handed the canteens back to their owners.

This episode resulted in such a delay that I had to commandeer a *caromata* driver and his pony to trot three miles down the road to catch up with the troops.

Another time we were having a night problem up in the jungle-covered mountains. To get up to the foot of the mountains we had been following ridge tops. Traveling these ridge tops under a full tropical moon is an experience few people could have and ever forget. The night air is soft and balmy and often on the breezes floats the rich, sweet perfume of the night-blooming cereus. That perfume itself is unforgettable. The moon overhead pales the stars in its brilliance. Small, fleecy, white clouds float gently over it now and then, momentarily dimming its brilliance. At times we walked under palm trees or thick tropical ferns, in other places we passed through small areas of jungle. Other places the ridge was so sharp that it was barren and we could look for miles in all directions. With the brilliant moon we could distinguish the different shades of green in the forests below, at times we saw night-blooming flowers and in areas of the forest there were flocks of lightning bugs (fireflies) flicking their little lights on and off. Off to the west below us was a low even forest of coconut trees, a strip of white sandy beach, beyond that the deep dark blue, almost black arm of the sea and miles away, rising out of the sea in a black broken line was the island of Cebu. Behind us to the east rose the nearby jungle-covered mountains. On either side of us running parallel were deep ravines and other ridges running from the mountains to the sea. They were spotted with the deep dark green of the jungle.

We were having a rest stop on the high, bare top of a ridge where we could enjoy the beauty of the night. I lay on my stomach, my chin cupped in my hands, drinking in the beauty of the night. Suddenly I felt something icy cold crawling up my pants leg. I stood up and stomped. From out of that pant's leg tumbled a centipede nine inches long and bigger around than my thumb. It was coal black and started to wiggle away. I cursed and stomped on it. Then I lay down again after looking over the ground carefully.

At this time one of my Filipino officers came and asked if the soldiers could sing. I consented, so the soldiers sang their native songs there above the moonlit jungles. One sergeant had a very melodious voice.

"Sergeant, you have a very good voice and sing well."

"Thank you, sir. Would the lieutenant like me to sing a song for him?"

"Yes, indeed."

The sergeant spoke to some soldiers in the dialect. To my astonishment, in almost perfect English, he sang the American song, "I Understand," to the background humming by his companions. This blending of cultures continued to amaze me. Each time I found something new.

I had another exhibit by the soldiers. This time it was pure Filipino art. One afternoon after a day's heavy training in the jungle, we came back to the edge of a coconut plantation where it was so pleasant that I gave the company a rest period. The soldiers started to sing. To break the monotony, I had one of the officers break them into two groups and started some competition. From singing it went to other things and finally to what I would call "bolo fencing." Up to that time, I thought I had seen some fancy fencing. These lads took a bayonet in each hand and started some intricate knife work. They were so fast and came so close to each other that I stopped the use of bayonets and made them use straight sticks. Those boys went to work then and really outdid themselves. Right then and there I made a mental note never to get within reach of one of those knives. What I saw there convinced me that the boys in the "Three Musketeers" were amateurs compared with the best of these lads of mine. I learned something new about my men.

Another amusing incident occurred in my camp office. A Filipino soldier, who for obvious reasons I shall call Joe, walked into my office and saluted.

"Sire, Lieutenant, may I use the *cuan?*" he asked, pointing to the typewriter (remind me to explain this word *cuan.)* Joe lived on Luzon, had a wife and several children, and was well set in the Army for a career.

"Sure, here's some paper." Joe sat down and starting clicking on the machine. I was curious because the boys didn't usually come in and ask to use the machine. I noted that he took the usual number of carbon paper. As he typed I got more and more curious. He would type a few words, think a bit, type some more, etc. He wasn't running true to form. Joe finished, took the original and the first carbon copy, tore them up and threw them away. This was too much for me. As he covered up the machine, I asked him, "Joe, what in the devil are you up to?"

He looked startled and then sheepish, but made no move to show it to me.

"Here, let me see that, you rascal!" and grinned at him to take the sharpness out of the words.

"Just a *cuan*, sire," and grinned weakly as he handed it to me. I looked at the carbon copy. It was a letter in the following form of military correspondence:

Subject: Marriage

To: Commanding General of the Army, Manila, PI

Paragraph No. 1. The undersigned was a . . . in the Army, so many years of service, drew such and such pay, was single, etc.

Paragraph No. 2. Under A.R. dash dash dash a soldier of his standing was qualified to marry.

Paragraph No. 3. Request the undersigned to be granted permission to marry Miss . . .

"What the hell, Joe, you're married!" I exclaimed, looking at him in amazement.

"Oh, but, sire, my wife, she is in Luzon and I must have a girlfriend here."

"But, Joe, you don't need this to get a girlfriend, do you?"

"But, sire, she is a school teacher and she wants to get married. I got one wife already, sire, and she is very good. I don't want two wives. I just want a girlfriend here."

"Well?"

"Sire, I take this carbon copy to give to my girlfriend. I tell her only the commanding general in Manila can give me permission to marry. I tell her it will take three months for the answer to come from Manila. We move to Carmen one month. I give her this letter and it makes things okay with her."

I was too nonplussed to do anything but try to hide a grin. Talk about a wolf. I made it a policy never to interfere with the private lives of my troops except to help them.

Joe took the letter to his pretty schoolteacher and the following night her friends gave her a betrothal party.

I mentioned the word *"cuan."* It is a most versatile word. It is of Spanish origin and the Filipinos use it to fill in when they lack a word, regardless of the language. It's used in every dialect I came in contact with and can mean anything under the sun. It's pronounced *"Quon."* I have had it used four times in one sentence and it meant a different thing each time. For example, by one Filipino in my office, "I put the *cuan* on the *cuan,* and Jose is getting the *cuan,* and Federico has the *cuan."* This was accompanied by various gestures. When I got it all boiled down, it meant simply this, "I put the typewriter on the table, Jose is getting the paper, and Federico has the cover!"

It was a merry life trying to comprehend a dozen languages.

Toward the first of November, I made another one of my visits to Cebu City. It stands out in my memory for two different things. One, my first meeting with a little man named V. R. Brown and, second, it was my last free vacation or day off for almost exactly four years, 1941–1946.

I again went to Tubigon and took the little ferry over to Cebu City. The Morrison car met me and at the Morrison home during dinner I met Dr. V. R. Brown. We called him Doc because he had three Ph.D.s from various parts of the world. These doctorates came from the University of New Zealand, University of Peru at Lima, and the Royal Academy at Madrid, Spain. Knowledge was, as he expressed it, his "stock in trade." Doc had traveled all over the world, not as a tourist but as a scientist. He was at home in the East Indies, South America, and, at the outbreak of the war, he had been doing some forestry research in Rio Muni or Spanish Guinea in Central Africa. Somehow or another he got a car and drove clear across equatorial Africa to the Indian Ocean, took a boat for India, and from there he got to the Philippines. He was then in Cebu teaching English when I met him. He was "good" in any subject from Shakespeare to chemistry. Before the surrender came, he was making hand grenades for the Army. I have met many people with knowledge galore stored in their heads, but few who had a practical application of all their knowledge. Doc was practical to the last degree. When we were imprisoned by the Japanese it was Doc Brown more than anybody else who upheld the morale of all of us. He took over the prison kitchen and made "food out of nothing." We owe Doc for making the unpalatable food edible.

The other highlight of that visit was the picnic Sunday. Maria Teresa, her cousin, Sofia Pastor, and Ester Moro were the girls. Edward Aboitiz, Lts. Gordon Utke, Howard Humphrey, Herr, and myself were the boys. The girls took us out to the country home of the Aboitizes, which nestled under the coconut palms on Liloan Beach, north of Cebu City. There they served a complete picnic of both Spanish and American foods. Later we went banca riding. I was in one with Ester Moro and ventured out to where the rollers were fully eight feet between the crest and the pit. We got swamped. I remember how she laughed and instructed me how to assist her to empty the water from the banca. Once emptied, we climbed in, she took the paddle, and we continued on our way over the waves.

On November 23, 1941, all the elements of the 81st Infantry were assembled in the 81st Division cantonment at Carmen, Bohol. Some of the other elements of the 81st were there at that time. The concentration brought the following Americans together: Capt. Colin B. Whitehurst; Lts. Melvin Herr, and Duane Casper of Walla Walla, WA; Richard Cook, Rotert H. Pratt; Eldon McKown; Gordon Utke; William F. O'Connor; Howard Humphreys; John S. Miner; Robert P. Chrisman; Joseph Stensland; Russell H. Cracraft; Lyes G. Hardin; and Capts. Roy D. Gregory and Charles Hoyt. In addition to the above were Sgt. Pizonka, Cpl. Curtis L. Sizemore, and Cpl. Smith. Also Capt. Jack Fritts of Galesburg, IL, and Col. Woodbrige were present with an FA unit. There were a few others who arrived a little later after I left on a special mission to Cebu.

Comparing those first few days in the division cantonment with what I heard about similar areas in the States, I am convinced that the States areas were picnics. I never saw more flies in my life except once later on a prison ship. This area was quite large in its building area. The buildings were all new and hundreds of natives were still working in the area. The sanitation was such that you had to watch where you stepped or you had to wash your shoes.

The American officers were assigned in advisory capacity to the various units even down to the companies. Stensland, Utke, John S. Miner, Cracraft, Hardin, and I were all battalion advisers. The others were placed at key points around the division. Lt. McKown was division supply officer. Pratt was the transportation officer and I don't remember the posts or who was assigned to them.

There is an old saying that nothing remains the same very long in the Army. That was certainly true in those days. I had just gotten things semi-organized in my battalion when I was called into division headquarters one morning at 0715.

"Miner, in 20 minutes Col. Woodbridge is going down to Tagbilaran. You are to accompany him that far and then take the boat for Cebu. Once in Cebu you will receive two more battalions, receive their equipment, and take them back to Tagbilaran. I will have transportation awaiting you at Tagbilaran on your return. Whom do you want to help you?"

"Lt. Stensland, sir."

"All right. I'll get hold of Stensland and inform him. You go get your bedroll."

Saluting, "Yes, sir," I then walked out. I double-timed to my quarters and started furiously rolling my bed.

Sure enough, in 20 minutes Col. Woodbridge sounded his horn outside my quarters. Stensland was already in. After dumping my bedroll on a fender, I climbed in the car and we started for Tagbilaran.

The drive down to Tagbilaran was very beautiful in jungle-mountain scenery. Some of the canyons were deep and sheer and the streams at their bottoms were white and rushing. I remember thinking, "I would hate to have to walk through those jungle-covered mountains." In just a few short months afterwards I was "thanking God" for similar jungle-covered mountains in which to find concealment from the Japanese.

Joe and I arrived in Tagbilaran in time to sail on the noon boat for Cebu City. This was a quiet five-hour cruise. We were the only Americans on the boat and there were practically no Filipinos on board. I remember how we loathed the steamed rice dinner with burned chicken soup, yet in just a few days the war was to start; this was around November 28 or 29.

On arriving in Cebu, Joe and I took a taxi out to the district headquarters at Lahug Field and reported in. Once there we found the troops would not arrive for 36 hours. We then took off for a day's rest.

I called on the Morrisons that evening and had another wonderful visit. The next morning I went down to the Southern Islands Headquarters to see Col. Braddock, Force doctor and surgeon, about some stomach infection I had had for a number of weeks. After examining me thoroughly he decided to send me to Sternberg Hospital in Manila for observation and treatment. We were afraid of appendicitis. This was Friday morning; on Sunday night one of the interisland boats, the *Elcano,* would leave for Manila. He told me to be ready to sail on it. On the way out I ran into Capt. Al Kircher. I told him the latest developments about myself.

Kircher said, "Bill, stop down at La Noviera Filipinas Steamship Co. office and tell Don Ramon Aboitiz to put you in the same cabin with me. I have to return to Luzon to an engineering detail in Gen. MacArthur's headquarters in USAFFE (U.S. Armed Forces in the Far East). This I did, glad to have him for company.

The next two days were just routine checking of troops and equipment. Again our chief difficulties arose from the lack of comprehension of English on the part of a Filipino. Here is just one episode of the day: I got a Filipino corporal to run an errand for me.

"Corporal, take this note over to Lt. Stensland, the American lieutenant in building number 15. To get to building 15 take this road (pointing), go down to the second street, turn left, and it is the second building on the right. There is a big black number 15 on the front of it. Now tell me what you are going to do."

"Sir, I am going to get somebody who can understand English."

By this time I knew never to be surprised at what would happen. You'd send someone after a book and he would bring you his neighbor's hat. I finally sent a sergeant who was familiar with the post to deliver the note to Joe.

By Sunday night at 7:00 I had helped Joe Stensland and Capt. Roy Gregory get all the troops on the boat and it sailed away. Two hours later, thoroughly exhausted, I was aboard the *Elcano* standing beside Al Kircher. We watched (from the deck railing) the busy turmoil below us as the ship's crew cast away the moorings and we put out to sea. We remained silent at the railing as we watched the harbor slip away from us and the shores of Mactan Island slide past us. The lights of Cebu City faded and were lost behind the palms on the shore. The ship rapidly passed the beacon light on the northern tip of Mactan Island (where Magellan was killed) and then turned north. When we turned north we left Mactan behind, glided into the open sea, and were struck by the full force of the low, rising, tropical full moon. The night was almost as light as day. After a few minutes of drinking in the beauty of the night, the calm, dark, flashing seas, and the purple mountain peaks of Cebu behind us, we left the railing and Al took me over by the captain's cabin. There, he introduced me to Capt. Aranda, the ship's captain and a beautiful Spanish girl named Romana Corominas. Señorita Corominas' family was part owner of the boat and the steamship line. The four of us fell to talking.

The next morning Kircher and I spent the time sitting on the main deck talking.

Kircher said, "We're sitting on a bubble out here, a bubble called peace, which in turn is sitting on a base of TNT and there's little yellow b . . . playing with a lighted match and the fuse to the whole setup. One of these days soon the whole thing is going to burst under us and we'll never know exactly what happened! (This was December 2, 1941.) The entire world will be in the fracas. As things now stand there is only one major power on the face of the earth that is not at war. That is the U.S. We can't stay out of it; it's impossible, regardless what the fools at home think about living in isolationism. We have got to get in the war and win it if we expect to preserve our way of living. All of Europe has been conquered, but Russia who has her back to the wall and is almost exhausted. She has got to be given a breather and more equipment. The British don't have what it takes. They lack the resources in material, their ordinary cockney soldier is underfed, undernourished, and doesn't have the physical lasting qualities that it takes to overcome the crack German armies. The British lost most of their equipment at Dunkirk. We will have to re-supply it to them or they will fall whenever Hitler decides to invade England. I tell you, Bill, we sit here in the cool, calm luxury of the sea breezes, but the calm is the calm before the storm—a storm such as the human race has never seen before will sweep across the face of the entire earth. It's going to make the fracas in Europe to date look small; the U.S. is going to play the major role in it. The days of peace are over and the war is at hand. It's near, far nearer than most people realize."

I sat in silence trying to imagine such chaotic events and wondering how soon the tragedy would strike. Little did I dream that before the week was out, the bubble would have exploded and we would be in the midst of war. Many, many times later at war and in prison I thought how literally Al Kircher had hit the nail on the head. I never knew him to be wrong in his common sense, matter of fact, or judgment.

The rest of the morning I spent visiting with the few other passengers aboard. Of these were a man and wife, Americans, both extremely tall and refined-looking, who lived in Manila. They had been on a short business trip to the southern Philippines. He was the U.S. Steel representative in the Philippines. I asked her one time why she hadn't gone home while she could. Her reply was that she decided to stay with her husband and "risk it." She hadn't long to wait.

Kircher and I were eating lunch in the dining room about 1300. Kircher said, "I wonder what the trouble is? The engines just shut down, the ship is losing speed and the breeze is fading out."

Looking out the window, I said, "You're right, and there's a big island right off our starboard." I walked over to the doorway and out over the deck to the railing. There I stared at a tall peak rising out of the sea about a quarter of a mile away. It rose steeply from the water line to its pinnacle top. I took a good look and returned to our table.

"It's a fair-sized island with a sheer jungle-clad peak rising in its middle. It must be a mile high. I'd hate to have to climb that baby."

"I hope we don't lie here long or it will be hot and we're short on water, according to the captain. Let's go see what the trouble is when we finish lunch."

On finishing our lunch we went up on the bridge to see Capt. Aranda. We found him perspiring freely and cursing his luck.

"What's the delay, Captain?" asked Kircher.

"A broken tooth on one of the drive shaft gears and we can't turn the engine over without danger of tearing up the whole gear assembly. I have just radioed our Maila office for help. It will be 12 or 14 hours before a tug can arrive to tow us."

"Well, that isn't too bad, is it?" asked Kircher.

"We are very close to that rocky shore there (pointing to the breakers less than a quarter of a mile away). We have a fishtail wind and if it settles down to a steady blow from our port side it will cause us to drift right on to the rocks. It's too deep to anchor here off Sibuyan Island."

"That will be my first time for such an experience, so let's hope the wind turns in our favor. Come on, Bill, let's get in the shade and get what breeze we can. It's too hot up here."

Kircher and I found a couple of deck chairs, moved them into the shade on the starboard side of the deck and relaxed in them with our feet on the rail. We watched the breakers a short distance away to our front and tried to keep cool. By and by I fell asleep. When I awoke there was a cool, steady breeze blowing in my face. The island with the mountain was definitely farther away than when I fell asleep. Time and nature had solved another problem that involved me. Before many months I was to find that time and nature were great friends of mine.

Time passed swiftly. After dinner there was a gorgeous sunset, the sun sinking into an island-infested sea far off to the west. As the sun set, a full moon became brighter in the eastern sky. Soon the whole world was again bathed in brilliant white moonlight. Sibuyan Island stood stark and dark in the sky.

To our south and west was a dark silver sea bordered on the low horizon, in the west by dark, low islands.

I climbed up on the sundeck. Near the wheelhouse were Kircher and Capt. Aranda. Several feet away seated near the railing, with an empty chair beside her, was Ramona Corominas. This was sweet! Here was a charming *señorita* all alone on the sundeck of a ship afloat on a calm sea. Overhead was a lover's moon bringing out the beauty of the nearby forested island and the surrounding sea. Clearly, it was a night for romance and there was no competition! I pulled a deck chair near Ramona, sat down and put my feet on the railing beside hers.

About 2:00 A.M. Wednesday morning, I was awakened by a shout coming through my porthole. I arose and looked out. There was a tugboat coming alongside via the aid of a searchlight. I dressed and hurried topside to watch the tug toss us a line and slowly get the ship under way. After a loss of about 14 hours, we resumed our journey in tow at the rate of about seven knots an hour instead of our usual 15. This delay caused us to arrive in Manila about 2000 Thursday night instead of noon that day. The next two days were slow but enjoyable, a repetition of Monday night and Tuesday. Thursday night I bade the U.S. Steel couple good luck. I met Ramona's sister, Curly, and said "adieu" to her as we watched the unloading of the ship's cargo.

Kircher and I slept aboard that night.

The next morning I arose late and found a note from Kircher saying he was going after transportation for us and our baggage.

I went down to the dining room for breakfast and there, to my amazement, was Morrie Cleland of Cebu City, the diesel engineer of the La Naviera Steamship Co. I had seen Morrie at the club the evening I had boarded the *Elcano* in Cebu. Here he had arrived in Manila ahead of me via boat and was on hand to take care of the ship's repairs.

This was getting to be a small world after all. I sat down and we had ham and eggs together. After a short visit, I took off to finish my packing. Al Kircher arrived shortly with an Army truck; we loaded our baggage and shoved off—he, for Mac Arthur's headquarters; I for Sternberg General Hospital. I left him downtown on the Escolta Street to make some purchases and he was later to bring my baggage to Sternberg Hospital. It was Friday morning, December 5, 1941. After taking care of some business affairs, I reported in at Sternberg Hospital. On being assigned to a ward, I relaxed and took it easy while I looked over the patients in the surrounding beds.

I heard a voice from the other end of the room. "Hello, Miner! What do they have you in here for?"

Recognizing the individual, I replied, "Hello, yourself! What do they have you in here for, Magers?"

"Malaria. I picked up the bug shortly after we landed."

"I just can't understand it! Here you are, a 2nd lieutenant in the Air Corps with malaria. I thought they kept you guys so far up in the air all the time that you never had a chance to come in contact with the ground maladies."

"They can't do it without some planes! I've been over here five months and the planes we're supposed to have haven't arrived yet. We were told when we sailed in June that they were on the way. Somebody is asleep at home. Who is holding up the works, Congress or the public in general? It looks to me like Tojo is going to take over pretty soon. One of our boys was up a week ago and he swears he saw some Nip planes over northern Luzon. He says we sure as hell don't have any like them, so they couldn't be ours."

"Hold on here and give me a chance to get my breath before you start taking it completely away! Who else is in here that I know?"

"None of the boys that came over on our boat. Remember that pretty, blond, good-looking nurse that came over on the boat with us? She is here on duty in this ward. You'll see her when they make the rounds."

With that, Lt. Magers went back to his bed and I started to unpack what little I would need for a protracted stay.

"Can I help you with that, Lieutenant?" came a voice from my back across an empty bed. I turned around to meet the friendly smile of a slender, dark, young lieutenant.

"My name is Montoya," he continued and walked around to meet me with an outstretched hand. We shook hands.

"I hardly think I need any help, but I am glad to meet you. Where are you from?"

"Santa Fe, New Mexico, and it's a mighty fine place to be from!"

"No doubt it is. I imagine the least you could say against it is that the climate is a lot cooler! What are you in for, malaria?"

"No, not malaria. I hurt my back some time ago and it hasn't cleared up so they sent me in here to give it a rest." He grinned and so did I.

"Well, are you?"

"Sort of. At least I have caught up on my sleep."

By the end of the afternoon I had met all the men in my ward and had found out that my recent CO, Col. Theodore Sledge, was in a nearby ward. I paid him a short visit and returned to my ward in time for the evening rounds by the doctor.

The longer I live the smaller the world becomes. I sat on my bed and waited for the doctor and the nurse. In they walked, after a short delay. The first in, carrying the chart was the good-looking blonde nurse. I recognized her as one of the 13 nurses who had come over on the boat with me. The doctor who followed was tall, slender, and familiar looking. He stopped in front of my bed.

"Hello, Miner, when did you come to town? I thought you went to the Southern Islands?"

"Fancy seeing you here. I had forgotten that Bill [Harold] Bertrand worked here. I always thought he spent his time over at Santa Monica Courts drinking Cokes." Bill grinned and the nurse smiled. "Seriously, though, Doc. I have a pain in my tummy, so they sent me up for observation and treatment."

"Hard to say just now what the trouble is. You'll likely spend Christmas here because we'll give you a complete checkup."

Bill Bertrand and I had become friends in the Santa Monica Courts where both of us had lived a few months before. I saw him briefly the next day or two as he went about his duties at Sternberg Hospital. Before I had a good visit with him the war had started and I was on my way back to the Southern Islands. I never saw Bill again until October 1944 when I found him working in the Bilibid Prison Hospital. I came upon him going through his wards one day shortly after I arrived. He was part of the hospital detail and I was part of a large group of prisoners waiting to be shipped to Japan. Bill was much thinner then, but he still had his good sense of humor and his same flashing smile for his patients. He had practically no medicine or equipment to work with, and as I watched him I saw that often all he could give his patients was his flashing smile. On observing some of the live skeletons, I imagine this last thing was often pretty hard to do. Bill was still a member of the hospital detail when I left aboard the *Oryoku Maru*. Six weeks later he was rescued and taken back to the U.S.

The next two days were uneventful. On Saturday, December 6, Col. Carrol came through making an inspection. He told me to put my pajama top on because I might be seen from the outside. This burned me up. Which was more important, the patients' comfort or the possibility that some Filipino might look into the hospital window? There is only one sensible answer, the patient's comfort. The next day was Sunday, December 7. I went to church in the morning and in the afternoon Al Kircher came to see me. The two of us visited all afternoon with Col. Sledge. Things were calm in the hospital that evening and night.

After darkness settled, a beautiful tropical full moon bloomed in the night from behind the nearby palm trees. The soft night breezes blew over us as we sat on the porch of the ward.

Everything was quiet and peaceful in Sternberg Hospital.

A few minutes to 0600 on Monday morning, December 8, 1941, everybody was quietly sleeping. Two or three minutes to six a woman's shrill voice pealed through the ward. "My God, get up! Pearl Harbor has been bombed!" There stood our blonde ward nurse. Every man in the ward roused up and stared at her and the men around her. The voice had awakened them and the ringing words slowly penetrated through the minds of some. Others had been sleeping too soundly to do more than stare stupidly. Muttering followed.

"Oh yeah?"

"The hell you say."

"If you want to wake us, you at least don't have to do this to us, do you?"

"No kidding?"

"Will you say that again, Nurse?"

"Did you say what I think you said?"

"Will you guys shut up. I want some sleep!"

The nurse said, "Pearl Harbor has been bombed!" She looked frightened.

"Will somebody turn on a radio? Tony [Antonio Montoya], turn on your radio! We'll find out if it's true."

Tony jumped out of bed and almost lost his oversized pajamas. I started to laugh at him. He grabbed his receding pants and pulled them up while he turned on the radio. It began to sputter. He found a station over which an excited babble of voices could dimly be heard. Suddenly the voice of Don Bell (Clarence Biliel, Manager and announcer at radio station KZRH), local Manila radio commentator, burst out startlingly clear.

" . . . most distressing incident has occurred. News just now flashed from Hawaii says Pearl Harbor has just been bombed. As yet we have no details about this, but indications are that the news is true. As soon as we get the details, we will broadcast them, so just stand by for the details any moment . . . "

No one was asleep any longer. All were out of bed in various disarray, huddled around the nurse, Tony, and Tony's little radio. There was a breathless hush in the ward and the men looked from face to face trying to realize just what the future meant, as Don Bell's voice ceased. Some looked white and sick, others stunned and uncomprehending. Somebody relaxed and said, "Well, boys, this is it!"

Nobody said anything for a minute, then I heard Magers mutter, "Damn it, we don't have any planes, not enough, not near enough! I feel like a fish in the rain barrel."

The radio announcer, Don Bell, said, "We have a little news now." (There was a general scurry back to Tony's radio.) "It seems that early this morning a large number of strange planes suddenly attacked Pearl Harbor. We haven't heard yet as to where they came from, but reliable sources think they came from Japan. Just how much damage they did at Pearl Harbor we don't know. All reports are very vague . . . "

"It won't be long now," said Tony. "I am going to pack and get ready to go back to my unit. It's those damned Nips, I'll bet. They'll be here before the day is out!"

Tony was right.

The ward went to breakfast about 0700 and was back by 0800. There were continuous news flashes coming in over the radio. They were not much, but if one would assimilate and sift them, a trend could be seen. Something dire had happened at Pearl Harbor; it had caught our forces by surprise, our Air and Naval forces had suffered badly, and finally we could expect an attack on the Philippine Islands at any moment. That was the gist of it. Shortly after 0800 the music suddenly stopped. It was interrupted, and Don Bell came on the air.

"We have just had word from Baguio that they are under a bombing attack up there. Before we could get any of the details our source of communication quit on us."

The boys in the ward, huddled around the radio, looked at each other. One lieutenant said, "That's getting close. They may be down here to bomb the harbor pretty soon. I am going to ask to go back to my unit."

For the next hour or so the radio kept bringing intermittent news flashes about the current situation in the Philippines, Hawaii, and the U.S.

We knew definitely that the Japs had attacked us in Hawaii, around Pearl Harbor, and in the Philippines. Just what other points in between we did not know at that time.

Sometime after 1000, word came over the radio via Don Bell. "Our Army Forces are now undergoing a heavy air attack at Clark Field and Fort Stotsenburg. There seems to be a large number of enemy bombers concentrating on our airfields and we can expect some of them any moment at Nichols Field [5-10 kilometers from Manila]. Everybody should stand by in case the city should be attacked."

Shortly after that, the radio quit giving new details as it received them. It became more vague and confused. It didn't follow up the threads it had started to spin in the early morning. The censorship was beginning to function, leaving people up in the air as to what really was happening. I will never forget those first few hours of the war. Everything was in confusion it seemed. In the matter of a few hours our entire civilization out there had to change from peacetime routine to defensive war conditions. The war was a surprise to most people and the realization that we were at war and under attack left many people mentally stunned. This, in turn, left them helpless and confused, particularly the latter. The streets of the city became filled with native *carromatas* full of worldly goods of people trying to get out of Manila. When an air raid alarm sounded, the people just disappeared from the streets. Where they went, I never could decide.

Inside the hospital, there was a lull in routine activity. The doctors and nurses disappeared shortly after breakfast and it was almost noon before we saw them again. The rumor got around that they were being briefed as to their new wartime organization within the hospital.

Meantime, we in the ward hung around the radios eagerly listening to every scrap of news that came from them.

About an hour after the news came over the radio that Clark Field was being bombed, news flashed through the hospital that the airfield was completely destroyed, with tremendous losses. Some of the doctors and nurses were going up to help take care of the wounded and the dead, of which there were so many the hospitals there could not take care of them. They were taking some ambulances and buses up to bring back the overflow of wounded who could travel. This, as countless other rumors were proved, was not quite as bad as it sounded. I think they failed to injure one or two percent of our Air Force and there were some survivors of the attack. It was perfectly true, though, that there were so many dead and wounded that the Clark Field and Stotsenburg hospitals could not take care of them. When the buses and ambulances returned, they brought men who should never have been moved, but it was either bring them or leave them outdoors exposed to the elements.

Col. Sledge, Lt. Tony Montoya, and I stood by the gateway and watched the Clark Field convoy roll away from the hospital.

Col. Sledge said, "I hope it gets there safely without an air attack."

"I hope so, too, Colonel; those boys up there must need help pretty badly," said Lt. Montoya.

If I remember correctly, there was another air attack somewhere in Luzon that afternoon. The radio reports were very vague and nobody could make out many details. The only thing that seemed certain was that there was a war on and we were on the receiving end of it. Two or three of the patients of the hospital had gone down to some of the various headquarters to see if they could find out how things were going and how much damage had been done to our forces in Hawaii. The general feeling was that catastrophe had hit and shaken the very foundation of our defense. A great many wondered if Hawaii was to be the initial invasion point and the Philippines bypassed. All of us feared that the harbor of Manila would be bombed before the day was over. Toward the middle of the afternoon, somebody came in with some news from MacArthur's headquarters. This news was that the real news was so bad that it wasn't being put out even at the headquarters. Only two or three men were supposed to know and they were supposed to be sworn to secrecy. To make a long story short, "Things were in a hell of a mess!"

During the day the city of Manila had several air alarms. No plane came over the city, but there were, undoubtedly, hostile planes not very far away. To my memory, Nichols Field had not yet been bombed. During the first day, the crowds on the city streets would fluctuate greatly. The streets would be filled with people and then the air raid siren would sound and the people would suddenly scurry for cover.

The evening meal was over before dark because the city was going into an absolute blackout. At the hour just before dark, I was out on the ward porch, which faces the street and looks across into the park in Manila. There were several field officers sitting there, among them Col. Sledge, discussing the situation in hushed voices. At this time, Capt. Al Kircher came out onto the ward porch and inquired for me. He had some of my baggage with him. He was mobbed when he was recognized as not being a patient of the hospital. He carried a gas mask and wore a .45 caliber. Questions were poured on him.

"How many raids on Clark Field? Did any Army planes survive the raid?"

"What was the truth about Hawaii and Pearl Harbor?"

"Was there any truth that 3,000 men had died in the Pearl Harbor raid this morning?"

"Was there help on the way?"

"What were Congress and the War Department doing?"

Of course these were all questions the captain could not answer. I sat back and listened. I felt that I was very young and had a lot to learn. This was a new game to me and I could perhaps learn something if I just listened and observed older and wiser men. Yet, at the same time, I noted from the type of questions they asked that they were no better off than I, that on some of the questions, my answers were just as good as theirs. The time had come for common sense and straight thinking. Originality was at a premium.

Sometime around 2100, Al rose to go. I went to the gate with him. Just before we parted I said, "Al, everything you have told me about this situation has come true. Now just between us, what is your personal opinion about what happened in Hawaii and what is in store for us here?"

"Bill, that would be hard to say. A wire came into headquarters this morning. Only two or three people know what it said. I have no idea what it was, but it apparently is such bad news the men are sworn to secrecy. It's got to be bad news, Bill. Japan has jumped us. The nature and psychology of the nation is such that they were sure of themselves when they started. This wasn't a cat-and-mouse game. Japan is the tiger and our forces in Hawaii the mouse. Therefore, Japan used a tremendous force when she hit us. She hit us on Sunday morning when everybody was still in bed drunk from the Saturday night parties. God! She must have struck us an awful blow. She must have hit our airfields with the same devastating effect she did Clark Field. She must have found half our Navy in Pearl Harbor and sunk it. You ask me what I think—I think we caught hell in Hawaii worse than we did here. They caught our forces on Sunday morning with their pants down and shot the ass off of them. If the Navy is as bad off as I think it is, it will be a year before we can replace our losses. By that time, Japan will have conquered all the world she wants, like ending up with the East Indies and Australia. Boy, we are left out here in the middle of the ocean and a tidal wave is soon going to sweep over this place that is worse than we ever dared to dream. Today when they caught our air force on the ground at Clark Field, the Japanese gained almost complete air superiority. All we have left are a few fighters based in Nichols Field and a few other odd planes. Any time the Japs desire to come in now, they can. Their bombers can knock out our Asiatic Fleet at will and then their transports can steam into the Philippines at will. We are soon going to be attacked on all sides and there will be no help from the States. We don't have the planes, ships, men or other equipment to save these islands. The U.S. has been caught asleep and the lives of the American sons and many of the Filipinos will be the price for this unpreparedness. Every time you see a man die out here due to the Japanese just remember that it is because the American public would rather drink cocktails and play bridge when it should be thinking of its security. You are now going to see what the price is for our national pastime. We may last a few months, but not longer than that. It won't be possible for our men to last. If you ever wanted to see adventure you are going to have your chance. Within a few days the Nip Air Force will destroy Nichols Field, our Navy out here and then walk in. We haven't seen anything yet, but it is coming. You had better go to bed now and get some sleep. There won't be many more nights, if any, that you can sleep uninterrupted. [How right he was!] Good night, Miner. When do you leave here?"

"I leave the hospital tomorrow morning in order to make room for incoming wounded. Then I am going to try to get a boat back to my troops in the Southern Islands."

"It may take several days to get a boat out. Do you have a place to stay? If not, come over and stay with me."

"Thanks, Al. I'll bring my stuff over when I leave tomorrow. Good night and many thanks for coming down." With that, Capt. Kircher set off through the dark Manila streets and I returned to sit beside Col. Sledge.

"It's been coming, boy, it's been coming. Wasn't that what we tried to tell those Philippine Army troops you had on Bohol?"

"That's right, sir. Only it came quicker than I thought it would."

"Do you have a place picked out to go to in case of an air raid? If you haven't, that curb along the side of the street is as good protection as there is here."

"I hope we don't have to use it soon. I think I shall turn in and get some sleep while things are quiet."

With that I left the colonel still sitting in his chair on the ward porch. Soon I was asleep due to unused-to mental strain. Sometime after midnight I was awakened by the sound of the air raid sirens. All of us got out of bed and got more or less dressed. A few minutes later we heard airplane motors in the north. That was the signal for us to leave the ward for the more open parts of the hospital grounds. I went down to the ward porch and found Col. Sledge and some other officers. As the motors of planes increased their roar, we heard explosions off to the north. That was the signal for us to leave the porch. Col. Sledge and I went across the lawn and sat down on the street curb where it would only take an instant for us to lie down in the shelter of the curb.

It was a beautiful night. The moon was high and full, its brightness dimming out all but the large stars. There were no lights in the city, but because of the bright moon, the buildings stood out with more clarity than they did on a rainy day. The streets were pathways of white light bordered by glistening palms, which cast their dark shadows along the sides of the streets and around the buildings. The moonlight was bright enough to read a newspaper by. To us huddled down there listening to the planes overhead, it seemed like they were coming straight over us. In the moonlight the Pasig River, a few hundred feet away, showed up against the dark of the ground like the white center stripe on a tar highway. The enemy planes had only to follow the river down to where it joined the sea and they knew where the heart of the city was. As the motors drew overhead, we flattened out on the street and waited until the planes had passed, far enough beyond us for any bombs they might drop to land on us. Then we sat up and breathed a sigh of relief. We were safe for the moment although we did not know for how long. As things remained quiet, we gradually drew back into the hospital edges where we could sit and lean against the building. There we waited for the two siren blasts that would tell us all was clear.

Sometime around 0200 or 0230 there was a commotion outside the main gate of the hospital.

"The ambulances and buses have returned from Clark Field. They are full of dead and wounded."

"Stand back. Make room so they can get in. *MAKE ROOM!*"

There was a general rush of patients to the area where the transportation was driving into the open courtyard.

"Get back, damn you! Make room, so we can attend to the wounded. We don't have room to get the litters off the ambulances."

Right then began my education in blood and broken bodies. The characteristic stench was drifting over the hospital area. This was just the primary course for the heavy stuff to come later.

"Will 10 patients volunteer to carry litters with wounded on them from the ambulances to the hospital?" I was in front, so I stepped forward to the open door of an ambulance. There the sight that met my eyes I'll never forget.

On the floor of the ambulance was a stretcher and on it was an almost naked figure of a man. His clothes had been shot and torn away until they lay in streamers. One leg had a very bloody bandage around it, the other had several dark spots in it that looked like holes. A pool of blood had soaked into the stretcher under the legs. A little farther up were more dark bloody spots on the white flesh of the thighs. Around his middle was more red blood-soaked bandage which was dripping; one hand and arm was bound to a bamboo piece to act as a splint; around his forehead was another bloody bandage. By the laws of nature, this man should have been dead judging from his looks, yet he had survived a trip of more than 100 kilometers over bumpy roads.

Seated along the side of the ambulance were other drooping figures swathed in bloodstained bandages and splints. In the dim light they looked like ghastly apparitions from out of this world. I still think that man on the stretcher was almost out of this world. I didn't recognize any of these men, they were too ghostly. The first scene made a big impression on me, yet the time was to come before long when I was to see far worse and become so used to it that I regarded it as commonplace and part of the game we were playing.

I took hold of one side of the stretcher, another man the other and slowly we drew the moaning, bleeding man from that ambulance until all but the opposite end of the stretcher had cleared the end of the ambulance. Then two more caught the opposite end of the stretcher and we, slowly and carefully, made our way through the crowd until we had him inside a ward where the corpsmen and a nurse took over.

On the way out we passed other stretchers being brought in. Their burdens were just as ghastly as the one we had brought in. Less severely wounded were being helped into empty beds nearby. The odor of raw flesh and fresh blood became prevalent through the hospital.

Everywhere there was an empty bed a wounded man was put in it. There were more wounded than the hospital could take care of. I don't remember how many wounded came down that night. I have a vague impression there were at least 80. Some died on the way down and some died shortly after they arrived.

During all this time the air raid was still on and we had to work under blackout conditions. Flashlights were used to see our way inside the hospital corridors. After placing our litter with the wounded man in the ward, I went back to help some more. This time I found an Air Corps lieutenant, HuGay by name, whom I helped under the guidance of a nurse to a bed in a ward adjacent to mine. She told me to stay with him while she went after some bandages. HuGay was in pain, although he tried to make light of his wounds.

"Do you have a cigarette, pal? I lost mine."

"Looks like you damn near lost more than your shirt, Buddy." My cigarettes were somewhat crushed, as I had put my hand on them as I helped him through the door. Finding a match nearby, I lit the cigarette and passed it to him, holding the still-lighted match so that its light shown in his face.

He looked drawn and haggard and there was agony in his eyes. His breath came in irregular gasps and his sentences were irregular while the words were broken.

"Did they hit you down here?"

"On the outskirts perhaps, but not in the city. The hospital is unimpaired and can easily take care of you."

"That's good. They took us by surprise and we lost practically everything. Most of our planes burned on the ground." (Here he knotted up and groaned.) "It was a close call for me. They got me in the ankle and on the arm."

"Did you manage to save any planes?"

"Only a few. Not enough to do anything with." He groaned again.

I said nothing more. There was nothing I could say. There was no use in my saying empty, useless words trying to assure him into false security. We would both know I was lying. His cigarette burned out. I lit another for him and one for myself. We smoked in silence until the nurse returned. "Relax now and I'll see if we can fix you up. Where are you hurt?" asked the nurse.

"My ankle and my upper arm. They got me both places."

"Will you hold the flashlight for me while I clean him up and put on the bandages?" she asked me.

"Sure, I'll be glad to. Will another light help? Yours is pretty dim."

"Yes, if you have one. Let's see his ankle."

I turned both flashlights on the ankles. One was large and swollen with a small blue hole on one side of it. I couldn't see the other side to tell if the object had passed clear through it. I didn't ask any questions for obvious reasons.

"Not too bad. Now turn the lights on the arm."

I obeyed. The shirt sleeve was in tatters and stiff with blood. There was a large piece of it stuck in the middle of a three-inch circle of raw muscle on the biceps. The nurse gave this a tiny jerk and it came loose. HuGay groaned and went limp. I thought for a moment he had fainted. Then he rallied.

"There are a few more fragments of shirt we must get out or it will become infected. This will hurt a little, but you can take it, soldier." Then she took a pair of forceps from among her things and one by one pulled the pieces of cloth out. HuGay squirmed. I could hear his teeth as he ground them together to keep from crying out. Finally the ordeal was over.

"You can relax now, lieutenant. This isn't how the book says to do it, but it gives you a clean wound. A few more hours and it would be infected. Tomorrow there will be more wounded coming in. It is best we clean your wounds at once."

She then poured some solution over the wound to wash it out. The wound was now raw and red. The room stunk of raw "beef" and fresh blood, which completely obliterated the smell of drugs prevalent in the hospital. HuGay retched at his stomach.

"It's about over, soldier. You have a clean wound that should be free of infection. You are one of the luckier ones. Now for a bandage, son."

The nurse continued to doctor and bandage the arm. Soon she was through. Then she said, "Now, let's fix up your ankle."

She asked me to take off his shoes and socks so she wouldn't get her hands dirty. I obeyed and she went to work cleaning up the wounded ankle. She bathed and then bandaged it. Soon she was ready to go.

"You are all right now, Lieutenant. I'll give you something so you will go to sleep and rest."

"Thanks for doing me up. Is there a cigarette left for the nurse?"

"Yes, there's plenty, enough for all of us." We smoked our cigarettes in silence and darkness.

"Good night now, Lieutenant. I'll see you tomorrow." Looking at me, she said, "Let's go."

I followed her out into and down the corridor.

"Thanks for holding the flashlights. It would have been hard without you. Just think, this mess is only the beginning: much much worse is yet to come, I'm afraid. I must go now and see if there are more yet to care for. You had better get some sleep, if you can."

"Good night, Nurse, I wish I could do more."

She walked down the dark corridor and out of my life. I never saw her again that I know of. I only saw her face in the shadows cast by the flashlights. Her face was grim and tight and her hair was disarranged. I would not know her in the good daylight. As the weeks went by, and report on report told of the mounting casualty lists in Bataan and Corregidor, I often thought of her as one of those heroic nurses who were the angels of mercy to our wounded and weary soldiers. Those angels, who day and night with pitifully inadequate medicine and facilities, willingly gave their service, strength, and courage to our men. I can still see her there in the blacked-out hospital room working over this lieutenant. Her face was grim, she was hurting him and she knew it, but she went on, her movements swift and sure. I think tearing those pieces of cloth out of that wound hurt her as much as it did HuGay. Those nurses had a tremendous job on their hands and they did it heroically.

I went back to my ward, although the all-clear siren had not sounded. I was exhausted from nervous strain. Flopping on my bunk, I fell into a troubled sleep. The war was on and I was right in the middle of it. GOD HELP US ALL.

The next morning we all awoke early and listened to the radio again. " . . . during the night Nichols Field was bombed. Not much damage resulted. Feverish preparations are being made against future attacks . . . " The radio told of attacks elsewhere in the Pacific. " . . . not much more has been learned about the details of Pearl Harbor. It seems that our forces have really been hit hard there . . . "

We all had breakfast hunched around the dining room table talking in hushed voices. Some of the people didn't have very good appetites. I'm afraid I was one.

After breakfast I went back to my ward and packed. I had decided to try to get back to my unit in the Southern Islands while it was possible. If it were still possible. As soon as I was packed, I left my baggage under the care of the blonde nurse, Sally Durett, I believe that's what her name was. Then I took off for the Port Area and Fort Santiago. The latter was the headquarters of the PI Department. There I presented my orders for my return to the Southern Islands and they cut some new ones sending me to Wright, Samar, as my unit had left its cantonment area at Carmen, Bohol. There they told me I would be lucky to find a single boat going south. After waiting an hour for my orders to be cut, I received them.

While waiting that hour I tried to see what was going on there at the headquarters of the Philippine Department. Everybody was extremely nervous and nobody seemed to know much of anything. A great many of the desks were vacant. There was little or no activity among the civilian employees. Most of them were just sitting around talking in hushed tones. Only when somebody like myself came in and wanted something short and simple done, was there any activity. Everybody seemed to be waiting for something, a bombing raid most likely.

As soon as I received my orders I took off for the headquarters of the Port Area. There I was informed that all sea traffic was at a standstill. I was told to go down to Pier No. 7, then the largest pier in the world, when an ammunition boat might be going south soon.

Over to Pier 7 I went. I found one ship alongside and they were loading bombs on it. I walked into the office and recognized Lt. Rothblatt from Chicago, standing before a major's desk.

"Hello, Bill, what do you know?"

"Not a damn thing, except we are in a hell of a shape!"

Rothblatt and I had gotten to be good friends in Santa Monica Courts on Dewey Boulevard when we both lived there. I hadn't seen him since I went south.

"Can I help you?"

"Can you tell me whom to see about finding some transportation south to Cebu at least?"

"See the major here. He has charge of all the shipping going out. This boat alongside is going south with some cargo in a day or two, I think. I have to hurry back to my post now. I don't like to be away too long and the major is delayed for some reason. Look me up if you think I can help you."

"Many thanks, pal. I'll wait here for the major. Good luck if I don't see you again."

"Good luck, Bill. I don't envy your trip on this boat." With that he walked out the door waving to me.

I lost track of Rothblatt after that for several months. Later, in February or March, while in the Censor's office in Cebu looking over some radio messages from Bataan, brought in by a P-40 pilot, I saw one from Rothblatt to his parents in Chicago. It stated he was still all right. I sent it on via RCA. Later I believe an answer came back via RCA and I tried to send it on up to Bataan via a P-40 pilot. I don't know if he ever received it. About two years later, in August 1944, after I had moved as a prisoner from Mindanao to Cabanatuan, Luzon, I ran across Rothblatt working in a rice paddy adjacent to mine. Later that night in prison camp we got together and talked over old times. Shortly after that the Japanese started moving American POWs to Japan. Rothblatt was on either the October 10 boat, which was torpedoed and sunk with only seven survivors or he was on the *Oryoku Maru* with me and died on the trip north. I think it was the latter; and that he died in early January 1945.

I waited a few minutes longer until the major returned to his desk.

"What can I do for you, Lieutenant?"

"I have orders to go to Wright, Samar, to rejoin my unit. The QM HQ sent me over to see you about a possible ship going south as far as Cebu City. Have you anything?"

"The ship outside that we are loading with ammunition and bombs is going south in a few days. You can go on it. It's the only thing I know of now that will be going."

"Hmmm. That's hot cargo! I sure won't rest easy on that!"

"Only the Devil himself would rest easy on that ship. Sorry."

I took off. I had done all I knew to do at the moment. I found a taxi in front of the QM office and hired him to take me downtown to the Philippine Trust Company Bank. On arriving downtown, I found I couldn't get within a quarter of a block of the bank door. There was a run on the downtown branch of the Philippine Trust Bank and they had closed their doors. I couldn't get in to cash a $10 check. I told my taxi driver to take me back to the hospital. Once at the hospital, I went in to talk to Col. Sledge. I found him in the company of a Lt. Col. Connally.

"Well, what do you know, boy?"

"Nothing of general interest. I found a ride back to Cebu City on an ammunition boat in a few days."

"Ammunition boat! Can't you find anything better than that?"

"No, sir. The QM HQ told me I was lucky to find that. There is only one boat scheduled to leave the harbor for the Southern Islands. There is a run on the Philippine Trust Co. Bank downtown. I couldn't get near the doors which were locked."

"I am going out to Fort McKinley in less than half an hour. If you need some money, I can fix it up so the Philippine Trust Company branch bank will cash your check," said Connally.

"Thanks, Colonel. I'll go out with you as I need some expense money in order to get back to my post in the Southern Islands."

"A staff car will be here in a few minutes to take me back to my regiment at Fort McKinley. You can ride out with me."

Shortly Lt. Col. Connally's staff car did arrive and I accompanied him out to Fort McKinley where he took me to the bank and fixed it so I could get some money. Thanking the colonel, I left him.

"Good luck, Colonel. I hope this doesn't last too long."

"Good luck to you, lad, on your boat trip. Bon Voyage!" I never saw the colonel again and I never have found out what happened to him. I remember him as a kindly gentleman who went out of his way to do a stranger a good turn when times were trying.

I left the colonel at the bank door and walked over to a taxi, which I hired to take me to Manila. Winding in and out through the streets of Fort McKinley, rounding one corner my taxi almost ran into a formation of scout MPs. In charge of this group was an American officer. I recognized him as Lt. Jack McCoffrey from Logansport, IN, who had come over on the boat with me.

"Stop, driver, I want to talk to that American officer back there."

"Yes, sire!"

Stepping out of the cab, I greeted him, "Hello, Jack. This is a surprise to see you again. Do you have time to talk?"

"Sorry, Bill, I don't. I have to march this relief over to the other side of the post and I am a little overdue."

"Well, good luck, old-timer. I hope we see each other back home again before the next year is out."

"Best of luck to you also. The dinner's on me when you get back."

We shook hands and I climbed back into the taxicab. This was the last time I ever saw Lt. McCoffrey. Though neither of us knew it, Jack was to be alive only 17 more days. Months later, when in the Davao prison, a group of American prisoners from Luzon arrived there October 1942. Among those who arrived was 2nd Lt. "Red" Emerson, whom I have mentioned earlier. Jack lived with Emerson and his family back in Logansport, IN, and both had come over on the *President Pierce* with me. Lt. Emerson told me the following story:

"On New Year's Eve we were down in Bataan in a quiet sector. There was a beautiful tropical moon shining that night and several of us were on a hilltop, under a palm tree, drinking a bottle of good whisky (as our celebration of New Year's Eve). I was forgetting the war and we were talking of things back home. One of the boys idly mentioned the name McCoffrey. I pricked up my ears and asked if he knew him. He said Mac had been ambushed and killed on the evening of December 24 while on a motorcycle reconnaissance. Jack had ridden past a road junction that was supposedly in safe territory. As luck would have it, a Nip patrol had penetrated to the road junction and lay in wait for a target. Jack was riddled and they didn't even get his body. This news just laid me low. I had been enjoying myself up to that time, but when I heard that Jack was dead, the evening was spoiled for me. Jack was just like a brother to me."

After leaving Jack McCoffrey, I went on into Manila and back to Sternberg Hospital where I looked up the blonde and got my baggage. From the hospital I took my baggage out to the address Capt. Al Kircher had given me on Sinagoga Street. Finding nobody at home at Al's apartment, I left my baggage with the next apartment neighbor (wife of a British officer in Singapore who had come to Manila on her way back to England and got caught). Then I went down to MacArthur's Headquarters, on No. 1 Calle Victoria, where I found Capt. Kircher.

"Al," I said, "My baggage is now at your neighbor's apartment. I have left the hospital, gotten orders cut at HPD (Headquarters Philippine Department) sending me back to my unit now at Wright, Samar. The boat is the *Don Esteban* and she is being loaded with ammunition and bombs. Some of these bombs are 100 pounds in weight and some are 500-pound affairs. I don't relish a two-day trip on that boat. Have you any alternative suggestion?"

"No, Bill, I don't. Not much is going out now and not much is going to get out. Reports today indicate that the Nips have air superiority now and their Navy is far superior to ours. By this time they must have a pretty good blockade around this island."

"What do you think about my going back to Department Headquarters telling them the situation and asking them for an assignment here on this island?

"If you have orders to go back, you take the ship and start back. It's going to be the same answer in the end. Annihilation! If you get back to Cebu, okay; if you don't, it's too bad. A boat load of bombs means a quick death. There is no telling what you will run into up here. Luzon is going to have her turn in hell before this thing ends out here. The best thing you can do is take the chance and start out on the ship. It is now past 1700. Let's go eat!"

As we left Mac Arthur's headquarters, he asked, "Did you hear or see anything interesting today?"

"I was out to McKinley this afternoon. On the way back I saw a big bomb crater next to the Fort McKinley radio station, which was the result of last night's air raid. The bomb only missed that radio tower by about 20 feet. The crater was about 20 feet in diameter and around eight feet deep. Was there anything of interest at your end?"

"Plenty. The Nips seem to be moving in all directions—Siam, Wake, and several other points. Nobody seems to know when and where they are going to strike next. They just expect the worst very soon. Their bombers hit our airfields again today and our shipping along the coast. It's going to get interesting soon!"

"Yes, too interesting. Where do we eat? I haven't had much to eat in the last two days and now my system is beginning to demand something."

"We'll stop by the Army and Navy Club and then let's go on out to the house. I need some sleep."

"I do, too." I related my experience of the night before concerning the wounded from Clark Field and my holding the flashlights for the nurse while she dressed the wounds of Lt. HuGay.

"You'll see a lot more of that before we are through with this. Here we are at the Club. I'm going to have a steak if possible. We won't be having them much longer."

We dined at the Army and Navy Club, which was blacked out with black curtains over the windows. The lights were few, so that the effect was of dimness inside the Club. The air was hot and stuffy and the sweat streamed off us. We were very nervous as it was, so the dinner was something of an ordeal instead of something to be enjoyed. As soon as we were finished, we went out into the cool of the night where there was a soft breeze blowing.

It was dark outside when we came out of the Club. The city was in almost total blackness right then. Later on, the moon would rise and light up the city again. It took Al and me half an hour walking through the dark streets to get to his apartment on Sinagoga Street. There were mobs of people moving about and we collided with other pedestrians several times. In the streets we could hear (and dimly see) cars creeping along. Several times we heard the noise of collisions followed by angry voices. Sometimes the dialects would be interspersed with English cuss words. I had to laugh at the sound.

On arriving at the apartment, Al and I got my baggage from the British officer's wife, stopping to visit with her and to listen to her radio for news reports. She had a good one and we heard broadcasts from Singapore where her husband was, London, and San Francisco, as well as local reports. None of them were very encouraging. We left her soon, went to Al's apartment and got ready for bed. God only knew when we would have a chance for a full night's rest. I simply unrolled my bedroll in the middle of the living room floor and crawled in. The last thing I remember thinking was, "This is a safe place. It is just another building lost in the mass of the city and it is not near a military installation. I can relax and sleep."

I awoke in the morning to find it broad daylight and Al kicking the end of my bed with his bare foot. I was still flat on my back with one arm thrown over my head. I don't think I had changed positions in something over 10 hours. I was still so exhausted that I could hardly bring myself to get up.

"Better get up and we can get a ride down to the headquarters with another officer who lives here," my host insisted. "You can take your bedroll down to the ship when we go."

"Okay, I'll be right with you." I sat up and stretched. I was very regretful to get up and face reality. That was my trouble—I was afraid of reality! This was Wednesday, December 10, in Manila, December 9 in the U.S. What events reality had in store for us that day!

The day started out quietly enough. Breakfast at the Army and Navy Club, taking my baggage down to the *Don Esteban,* saying good-bye to Al Kircher again and reporting to Maj. Virgil Kerr, the Army officer in charge of the ship. All this was very quiet, taking up to about 1145-2000. About noon I went back to the Cuartel De España, HQ, 31st Infantry to see Capt. J. Truesdale with whom I was leaving my large camphor wood chest with my extra things and equipment. We ate our noon meal at the PX restaurant.

Capt. Truesdale said, "Let's go over to my room and listen to Don Bell, the commentator, at 1245."

"We had better get started then."

On the way to his quarters the air raid siren sounded.

"I'll have to leave you and go to my post. Good-bye and good luck," Capt. Truesdale left at a run.

"Good luck, Captain, take it easy."

I ran to the nearest place where I could climb onto the top of the old fort's stone wall (about 15 feet high and 10 feet wide on top). I wanted to get a look at the raiding planes. I had been afraid of a raid and I didn't intend to stick around that ship loaded with bombs until I had to. In case the harbor was raided and those bombs went off, I was going to be far enough away that I wouldn't be crowding my luck. Here the raid was.

From my point on the wall, I could look out over a small park and get a good view of the sky fairly low down in all directions. At first I saw nothing, so I waited, scanning the sky. Soon from the direction of Manila Bay I heard a few loud explosions. That meant planes somewhere. Looking again at the sky, I found the enemy bombers. When I first saw them, they were in two V-shaped flights of 27 planes, a total of 54. They were so high up that they looked small, much smaller than I expected and they were a silvery white. Being so high and the color they were, they were hard to see until you were familiar with what to look for.

There they were, almost straight over me, yet not quite. Their line of flight would not take them over me, so I stood my ground and watched. Beautiful, majestic, silver birds they seemed to be, floating slowly over the city. I would guess they must have been at an altitude of 25,000 to 30,000 feet up. Suddenly our anti-aircraft opened up and little balls of white smoke appeared in the sky. These little puffs of smoke seemed to reach only half-way up to the planes and they burst behind the formation. Our boys were trying, but they didn't have the equipment equal to the job. We missed those formations so far it was pitiful. As the planes floated over other sections of the city, more of our AA guns opened fire. It was all the same. Beautiful silvery white birds in formation, floating through the skies, unopposed, and spreading terror in the city below. Little balls of smoke appeared in the skies halfway up to the silvery birds and far behind them.

There was a rattle of heavy objects striking the ground near me. I looked down. Ten feet away was a jagged fragment of an AA shell. I ducked down under a thick stone ledge of the wall top not far away. That splinter was sharp and jagged, weighing over a pound, it looked like to me. I didn't want any of that stuff bouncing on my head!

The Nip planes passed on over Manila without dropping their bombs, passed out over part of Manila Bay toward Cavite Navy Yard. From that direction I heard dull explosions. In a few minutes a dark cloud of smoke arose from that area. Plainly there was an oil fire over near Cavite. The show was over from my balcony. I went back to the 31st PX for a drink of chocolate milk.

There were several officers in there like myself. Pretty soon Capt.

O'Donnovan whom I have mentioned before, came in and spoke to us.

In answer to our inquiries, he gave out the information: "I guess they hit the Cavite Naval Yard this time. We don't know how bad, but reports indicate that it was pretty well wrecked."

"First the airfields, now the Navy Yard; what next, our ships in the various ports? At this rate they'll have us paralyzed within a week!"

Soon I left the post, found a taxi and went out to the Santa Monica Courts where I used to live. These courts are on Dewey Boulevard (now Roxas Boulevard), which runs along the bay shoreline, and I could look across an arm of the bay toward the Cavite Naval Yard. Standing on the sea wall, looking over the bay, I could see a tremendous stream of smoke rising seemingly off the surface of the sea. It covered quite a large area from my viewpoint. Some oil supplies had definitely been set on fire. More than that, I could not see or comprehend.

Late in the afternoon before dark and the blackout, I returned to Pier No. 7 and found the *Don Esteban* alongside and still loading. After eating, I walked out onto the pier, up to the gate to the street, through the gate, onto the base of the pier. At that point, I promptly lost my evening meal! It rolled out so suddenly I almost splattered my toes. Why?

There before me was a pile of 10 or 12 corpses stacked every which way. On top was the body of a beautiful little Filipino girl. I say body, but in reality it was only half a body. The head and trunk were intact, but from the waist down, there was only a mass of dark string and ribbons trailing over the pile of corpses, some of them a dozen feet long. The rest of the pile consisted of bodies in a less severed state. I staggered back and leaned against the wall of the pier building where the stench of raw flesh and blood was not so great. As soon as I felt better, I looked around. On the opposite side of the pier from my ship was a Navy ferry or small cargo boat of some type. There were several large holes in her and the glass of every window had been shattered out of their frames by concussion. The masts were bent and her frame looked twisted. There was a list to her. She was afloat, that was all; the boat was useless. Spying a soldier, I walked over to him.

"What's going on around here?" I asked, pointing to the heap of bodies and the wrecked ship.

"They're bringing in the wounded and the bodies of the dead over from the Cavite Navy Yard with the use of a small speed boat, sir. They really caught hell over there this afternoon. The whole Navy Yard is destroyed and a great many are dead. Here comes the Navy ferry now, sir."

I looked at where he pointed. Sure enough, there was a long, steel, gray-looking boat plowing through the bay toward us. I stood by and watched. On reaching the pier edge, the boat drew alongside and some of the crew scrambled ashore. They were a horrible looking lot. Their clothes were half torn off of them. They were covered with blood and one or two had bloody bandages.

A Navy man was on the shore. "Hurry up and get this cargo ashore. Shove it up!"

The crew below shoved up a dark smeared box of some kind. It was filled with bodies. Several bodies were lifted out by hand. The boat had some wounded who were being helped off the other end into a nearby truck or ambulance of some kind. When the unloading was completed, the crew scrambled in again. As it started to pull away, one of the sailors stooped to the floor of the boat, picked up something and threw it toward the soldier standing guard over the area, shouting as he did so, "Here's a present for you." The object fell at the guard's feet. It was a bare white woman's leg; the shoe was still on. I turned away.

"Soldier, how many trips has that boat made?"

"The 'bloodwagon' you mean, sir?"

"Yes, that 'bloodwagon.'"

"I don't know, sir. It was making trips when I came on duty and one of the sailors said last trip they still couldn't see the end of the job."

"I'm going to get out of here. I can't take too much of this."

I walked away. The soldier was right. I did get used to it. I got so used to it that I could stand amid worse; eat and joke while I was standing there. Not only did I become that way, but the men who were alive became that way. It was a matter of "get used to it or go stark raving mad." But that comes a little later.

I got back on the *Don Esteban*. I had seen enough for one night. I felt sick, dizzy, and weak. After lying down for an hour, I got up and went down to the Oriente Motel in the Walled City of Manila where I found my old friend, L. W. Jacobs. I visited with him for an hour before we walked downtown over the Jones Bridge to the Escolta (the main business street in Manila). It seemed strange to see the thriving business center all blacked out. There were scads of people near the entrance of some nightclub. In other parts the streets were almost deserted. We could dimly see the cars and *carromatas*. There were quite a few taxis cruising around without lights. Jacobs and I got one. We went over to the Army and Navy Club for some ice cream and about 2100 we walked home. I went on back to the boat when I left Jacobs. This was December 10 (9 in the States). I did not see my friend again until around January 6 or 7, 1946, when I was visiting in Milwaukee. During prison days I heard twice that he was okay.

On board the ship full of bombs, I got a blanket, went up on deck, spread it out in a cool breeze and tried to sleep. Sleep? Sleep is brought by Morpheus, and Morpheus was hours away. I think he must have gone to Chicago for the late show. When he did come, he was accompanied by a helper, exhaustion. It was the helper who finally did the work!

I awoke at dawn the next morning, went back to my cabin, which was now cool, and slept late. I found Maj. Kerr at breakfast when I entered the dining room. He told me to stick around today because we could leave any time now. I remained on board ship, in the shade of the nearby pier room, until noon. Then I went to the ship's dining room.

The major and I were sitting at the dining table at about 1240 when the air raid siren sounded.

We both jumped up and rushed to the top deck. Maj. Kerr found the ship's captain there.

"Captain, get this ship out in the bay immediately. It's got all its cargo here. Go way out into the bay until you are the farthest ship out in the bay away from all other shipping. Then anchor. I am going ashore for final orders and will come aboard out in the bay. You have perhaps a short five minutes before the Nip planes arrive. *NOW MOVE!*" With that he ran to the pier and disappeared.

The ship's crew was all standing on deck waiting for orders.

The ship's captain ordered, "Cut the shoreline fore and aft. *Sigue* now!!!" He disappeared into the wheelhouse. I immediately heard him shouting in there and ship's bells began to ring far below inside the ship. The ship began to back away from the pier. I have read in books where they cut away the shorelines, but I had never expected to see it done. Standing on the wheelhouse deck, I saw two deckhands spring to the bow shoreline and begin to slash away at the big two-inch rope. Where those ragged devils got those two wicked-looking knives, I don't know, but they had carried them on their bodies somewhere. Before those men had slashed that rope in two, the ship was moving and had the rope taut. It parted with a snap like a rifle shot. I ran around to where I could look at the stern. I saw that rope snap, knocking the knife out of one of the men's hands slashing it. The ship was free in less than a minute and moving in reverse away from the pier as fast as I could walk. About three ship's lengths out in the bay from the pier, there was more ringing of bells, the ship swung in a circle, came to an abrupt stop (for a ship) and immediately started to move ahead. In only three minutes or so, that little liner was racing around the breakwater wall into the open bay at what seemed to me her full speed of at least 15 knots (I am no sailor). I looked at my watch, the five minutes were not quite up, the ship was out in the bay rushing between anchored liners and cargo ships with a great white wave of water rising on either side of her bow. I didn't know a ship could move so fast. It took her sister ship half an hour to perform the same operation in peace time. I still think of that feat in amazement. Of course we had expected air raids at any time after daylight. We had really been sweating them out. Another thing that might have encouraged that ship to move fast, we had a large load of 500-pound bombs aboard. That would make anybody move, in my estimation!

Now that we were free from the pier, I turned my attention to the skies. There was no use in going below with that cargo of hot eggs. One good jolt would send me into eternity. I might as well watch the show.

I saw no formation of Nip planes that day. I saw what I thought were some Jap bombers high in the sky. The sky was sort of hazy and high up in a brassy were some small fluffy bunches of clouds. I definitely saw four of our P-40 planes from Nichols or Nielsen Field climbing hell bent through the skies and searching around the cloud masses for the enemy bombers. I heard later that our boys had been alerted that the Nips were on the way and broke up the formation of the Jap planes. It was a brave thing to see those little P-40s tearing through the skies searching for the enemy. They knew they were hopelessly outnumbered if they ever ran into a group of Nip fighters. Yet, there they were, winging around as if they owned the skies. The memory of them diving through the cloud masses, climbing and diving, still stirs my heart. This day, thanks to them, there was no formation raid over Manila!

The *Don Esteban* continued on out into the bay at high speed all through this air raid. The planes disappeared out of the sky, but the ship continued to speed far out into the bay until it was well beyond all the other ships and the Island of Corregidor loomed in sight. Then the ship slowed down and stopped.

We had to wait several hours until Maj. Kerr finally came out in a speed boat. All this time an American doctor, two sergeants, and I were on deck anxiously scanning the skies for hostile planes. We were now a lone ship way out in the bay. Any hostile planes, which might happen to spot it, would guess that it was something special. It was especially hot, we thought. The four of us anxiously awaited the major at the rail. He came aboard noting our anxious faces.

"Take it easy, boys. We don't move very far today!" Somebody groaned, but nobody asked a direct question. "Later tonight we'll move out to the pier at Mariveles and be prepared to pick up some more cargo tomorrow."

"Any news of the air raid today, Major?"

"I didn't hear of any raids around Manila today. The report is that there was one on the way, but our P-40s broke it up just before it arrived over Manila." With that the major went below.

The fact that we were to stay around that area longer was a great blow to us. Since we were going south, we wanted to get underway. We had been under a terrible nervous strain all afternoon; our clothes were dripping with sweat and the idea of running around on the boat loaded with bombs was enough to make one want to jump overboard.

I went downstairs and stood in my shower for 30 minutes or more trying to cool. Even the cold water was lukewarm, so I didn't get very cooled off. After that I dressed and went up on deck to wait for the evening meal.

Most of us ate the meal in silence, each deep in his own thoughts. As night came on, the weather became somewhat hazy. An hour after dark the ship slowly got under way, moving out toward the Island of Corregidor. We proceeded slowly in the darkness without a single light. I was up on the wheelhouse bridge with the major and the captain of the ship. Suddenly out of the darkness loomed the big hulk of a cruiser (it might have been a destroyer, but it looked too big in the night to be a mere destroyer). The ship's captain moved quickly, spoke into something (speaking tube, I guess) and the ship's bells jingled. The ship came to a sudden stop as the sound of the engines rose high and then began to back up in the water.

Fear gripped us all. We thought we were going to be rammed by the Naval vessel. To us standing on the bridge, we thought the end had come. For those 500-pound bombs to be rammed by that vessel meant "goodbye, dear old Earth." The Naval vessel stopped, we stopped, and the two vessels continued on our course after the Navy turned around.

"That was close! Almost head on. They had been notified to expect us, but I didn't expect to bump noses. We aren't out of the woods yet. That boat is now going to guide us through the minefields to Mariveles," said the major.

I leaned against the rail. "This is enough to drive a man to drink and cigars!"

"If I catch you smoking on this boat, I'll personally throw you overboard!"

I gasped. The major was under far greater strain than I had realized. I said no more.

The next few hours our boat crept through the water bit by bit. Finally I went to bed on deck again where it was somewhat cool. There was nothing I could do and the sensible thing to do was sleep, if I could.

Shortly after dawn the movement of the ship woke me up. On sitting up, I saw a rocky, jungle-covered mountain wall on three sides of me. Getting up, I looked to the back. A few miles away lay the green island of our fortress Corregidor. Turning again to the front, I found our ship was moving toward a long, low pier that extended out into the bay. A quarter of a mile from the pier the ship stopped. I soon found that the sea was too shallow here for the ship to go any closer. The cargo of bombs would have to be brought out by barge and then loaded via winches. The loading got under way fairly early.

After breakfast I got to see several PT boats cruise around the bay while I was standing on deck. One of them approached alongside our ship and hailed us.

"Ahoy!"

"Good morning," said Maj. Kerr.

"Do you have any bread and some butter you can give us? We have been out from our base since Monday morning (this was Friday morning) and are running low on supplies. Most anything would help."

"Come aboard and I'll have the steward fix you up with something."

Standing at the railing I conversed with the PT boat crew and questioned them about their boat. These boats looked like "powerful hornets" to me. When their crew member came back with his load of chow, they took off. They told me their base was on Corregidor, but that they were temporarily stationed in Bataan not far from Mariveles. They were patrolling.

I stayed on the boat and made no attempt to go ashore, that is, until the Nip bombers came. Because we were in the Mariveles Bay we could only see the mountains surrounding the bay and look over to the Island of Corregidor. All of a sudden a plane came swooping low across the front of the bay and went on toward Manila. Farther out, toward Corregidor, were more Nip planes and the AA guns on the island were shooting at them. The little puffs of smoke from the shell bursts were just behind the Nip formation. Suddenly one faltered and dipped toward the sea with a trail of smoke behind it. That was one that wouldn't bother us again.

We heard from around the point of land, just a few hundred yards away, the howl of airplane motors. Immediately I heard a burst of .50 caliber machine gun fire, followed by the roar of the twin engines of a PT boat. The PT boat was in action and this was just over the hill out of sight. What the hell were they waiting for, the Nip plane?

"Captain, order the boats lowered and we will go ashore until the raid is over," said Maj. Kerr.

All of us took to the boats in record time and started for the nearest point of the rocky coast. The plane zoomed over the mouth of the bay and disappeared again. We heard more firing, but who and what, we could not tell. It took us several minutes to cross that open stretch between the boat and the shore. Those minutes seemed like lifetimes. The Nip plane and the PT boat were just over the hill and over Corregidor we again saw AA bursts in the air. When we finally reached the shore, we scuttled like frightened rabbits for the shelter of large boulders on the sandy beach. Once there behind the boulder, I then stuck my head out to see what was going on. As usual when I had reached a grandstand seat, the show was over.

Up to this time, I had failed to remember that there were two other American officers on the boat going to the Southern Islands. One was Capt. Robert V. Nelson (later Major), D.C. He was going down to be the chief dentist for Gen. Sharp's forces. The other was Capt. (later Major) Oliver W. Orson, VC. Nelson was more like myself, just average, but Orson was made of a little sterner stuff. He didn't excite so easily and he liked adventure. What makes me remember him at this time was that he was in no hurry to leave our ship. He wanted to see the show and his boat was the last one to reach the beach.

As things reached a quiet stage, Orson, Nelson, Maj. Kerr and I walked around the shore to the pier. Maj. Kerr stayed at the pier, but the other three of us wandered around the little Filipino town located among the coconut palms not far from the base of the pier. Its name was Mariveles and it consisted of a string of Filipino nipa huts along each side of the shore road that ran around the bay. There wasn't much to see. I took some pictures with a little Kodak I wore on my belt. This took an hour or so. We then wandered back to the pier.

There at the pier we watched the operations. American trucks brought the bombs from their dumps high on the jungle-covered slopes of Mt. Mariveles. From the truck the bombs were loaded by *cargadores* onto the barges. The barges were then towed out alongside the ship where the bombs were unloaded. After talking with some of the truck drivers who had no news, we went back to the ship via a loaded barge. It was mealtime, so we went to the dining room. The crew had returned and our noon meal was waiting.

The loading continued all afternoon and late into the evening. Late in the afternoon the major received a radio message. It told him to stand by to receive a naval pilot who would guide us through the minefield and out into open sea during the night. This announcement brought joy to all our hearts. We had a dangerous, fragile cargo on board and the areas we had been in since the war started were areas of enemy targets. When the loading was finally finished, we had enough TNT in the cargo hold to level a city, let alone blow up our ship. Everybody aboard was anxious to scram.

We ate our evening meal as the Filipino captain and the crew got the ship ready to sail. Afterwards, on deck, we watched a small naval boat approach with the naval officer in it. He drew alongside and climbed the rope ladder that was tossed to him. He went directly to the bridge where he stayed until dark.

I was up on the bridge after darkness watching and waiting for the experience of passing through our minefields. From the way the naval officer talked, I did not doubt that he knew where he was going to guide us.

Suddenly a searchlight on the Island of Corregidor flashed its beam out across the water near us. It didn't flash its beam directly on us, just near us. The pilot spoke to the ship's captain.

"We are ready, Captain. Move ahead slowly."

"Aye, aye, sir."

"Right, left, stop, move ahead, etc."

I am not familiar with naval terms, so I won't describe the language, but word by word and bit by bit, the pilot slowly guided us through the minefields. We passed several buoys anchored in the sea and every time we neared one of those, we turned in some direction. From time to time the searchlight switched its beam as we drew near its edge. At no time were we ever directly in the beam, always we moved in the outer fringes of its reflected light. I lost all track of direction during our twisting and turning. Finally the pilot spoke to the ship's captain who responded by using the speaking tube. The ship's bells jingled and the ship came to a stop. A small naval boat came alongside and waited.

"You are now through the field, Major. I'll go over side now." With that the pilot left the bridge and was soon riding over the waves back toward the searchlight. The light suddenly went out. The darkness was terrible for awhile, but all of us breathed a sigh of relief; we had passed through the minefield. Another event had passed and we were still alive.

Looking back on those days I laugh at my fears. In comparison to events that took place later we were well off, but in those days the war was young and the constant fear of death was new to us. The time came when the day was done and you would hear remarks like, "Who got knocked off today?"

"Nobody I know of."

"Hell! This isn't any ordinary day! Nobody dead, they can't do that to us!"

Maj. Kerr decided that each American officer should take turns standing guard upon deck. I don't remember what turn I drew, but I do remember the night was pitch black and slightly raining at times. We ran into squalls off and on all night. During one of the squalls I was standing on the bridge just under a bit of shelter out of the light drizzle. The sea was choppy and the wind was considerable. The visibility was practically zero. Suddenly in the blackness of the night loomed a blacker shape. Terror struck me. I recognized it as the dark hulk of a ship as large as ours. I thought we were going to crash head on. Then I realized that would have happened before I saw the dark looming hulk. Our lengths overlapped already. There wasn't a single light on that whole dark hulk (neither was there on our ship). Nobody made a sound on it and nobody made a sound on our ship, yet the two passed within 15 feet of each other, with the whole China Sea to navigate in. I saw no watchman on the other ship. There was only the sound of the wind in the riggings and the waves. Surely the watchman on the other ship must have seen ours in the passing. Yet each of us, fearing the other might be the enemy, was willing to let the other pass unchallenged. Perhaps the other ship, like ours, didn't have any guns on board except the pistols worn by the passengers. There we were, two blacked-out ships passing so close to each other—one could almost jump to the other. To this day I don't know if that was a friendly ship. Knowing the Japs as I do, I think it was another unarmed American ship trying to slip into Manila Harbor, hoping for safety. If it had been a Jap ship, I think they would have opened fire.

I remember watching that black hulk disappear, expecting to hear the jingle of its bells and a burst of gunfire. It never came and we continued on our way. I was wringing wet with sweat. With that I decided to go below, undress, and await my turn as guard.

Morning came and we were sailing south with the coast of Luzon low on our left horizon. Soon we lost it. The day was beautiful and bright.

I shall now attempt to make a list of the American soldiers on the boat. There were Maj. Virgil Kerr, officer-in-charge of the ship; a captain, doctor for the ship; Capt. Robert V. Nelson, DC, reporting to Gen. Sharp in the Southern Islands; Capt. Oliver W. Orson, VC, reporting to Gen. Sharp in the Southern Islands; Sgt. George T. Holmes, attached to the ship in QM capacity; Sgt. Paul Snowden and assistant, reporting to Gen. Sharp in the Southern Islands; Sgt. Wilson, assigned to the ship in QM capacity and myself, returning to my unit.

There were several other noncoms attached to the ship in QM capacity. Prior to the war this ship had been transporting ammunition to Australia and other points. The Americans assigned to the ship had been in charge of the cargo. I don't remember their names, or much about them. Some I don't remember at all—the doctor, for example.

While back in Manila, Maj. Kerr had secured two .30 caliber machine guns to mount on the ship for air protection, one on the bow and the other on the stern.

All day Saturday, Holmes, Snowden, and I worked to build platforms in order to mount these guns. It fell to my lot to be in charge of this operation since I was the only line officer on board. Placing the gun on the bow deck was simple because it was flat and level. The stern gun was another matter, though. The only place we could get a clear field of fire back there was from the top of a stack of life rafts. First, we had to lash the rafts more securely. Second, we had to build a level platform on top of the life rafts that was large enough for a man to operate the gun. Third, we had to tie the machine gun down. Before the day was over, we had the job done. After the job was finished, I looked at that setup and felt like the farmer whose farm machinery is held together with bailing wire. It was a good job considering what we had to work with. I'll have to give all the credit to Snowden, Holmes, and Snowden's assistant.

We moved steadily south all that day. Most of the time we were out of sight of land, or it was just a low line on either side of the horizon. Much to our pleasure, the day passed and we saw no Jap planes in the air (we didn't expect to see any of ours; we didn't have any left). Late in the afternoon, I inquired at the wheelhouse about our position and the name of the island that kept looming closer on our left.

"Where are we now?"

"At the end of Negros, sir. That lowland far to the left front is the north end of Cebu Island," said the wheelman.

I had to pass through Cebu City to get to Wright, Samar, but my boat wasn't going that way. This load of bombs had the first priority. We were going directly to Bugo in northern Mindanao. From there the ship would return via Bohol, Cebu City, and back to Manila.

On seeing the Island of Cebu, I remember thinking, "I wish to hell I could get off at Toledo tonight." (Toledo City is a small port on the west side of Cebu Island). I didn't think there was a chance in the world of ever doing that, but as things developed, I almost did. I actually was in Toledo 48 hours later, but I landed that night in San Carlos, Negros Occidental, directly across the straits from Toledo.

I stood on the upper deck after dinner that evening with Orson and Nelson. Maj. Kerr was resting as he expected to be up all night. Together we watched the straits narrow while our boat kept to the middle of them. The sun set, leaving the near shore of Negros dark with the skyline of the island sharply outlined against a rose background. The black island loomed dark against the sky.

On the opposite side was the Island of Cebu. The slanting rays of the sun were fast creeping up the shores and slopes of its mountains. Soon the shore was dark, leaving only the sun-clad mountains etched with shadows. Finally, they, too, lost the last of the sun's rays. Then both of the islands stood dark against the sky. I remember the three of us watched that sun set as if it were to be our last. I don't remember that we talked much.

My turn for the night watch was early, so I didn't retire. I stayed up in the wheelhouse looking out the open window to the south. The strait was clear and the water calm.

"Sir, I have a message I think Maj. Kerr ought to have."

"He is resting. I don't want to disturb him unless it is very important."

"Sir, I intercepted a message from a radio station in southern Negros that five Jap transports and two cruisers are sailing around the southern end of the island toward Cebu."

The radio operator had been instructed to monitor all messages he could pick up.

"All right, I'll get him."

I had no answer for the problem. Our boat was scheduled to pass the southern end of Cebu a little after midnight. If it were true, we would likely run smack into the battle ships. This was a decision for the major. Rapping on the major's door, I called, "Urgent message for you, sir."

"Come in."

I opened his door and walked in.

"Sir, the radio operator has just picked up a message that five Jap transports and two destroyers off the southern end of Negros are heading this way. It looks like we are running directly into them."

"Go back to your post and I'll be up immediately."

I went back to my post and shortly Maj. Kerr passed by and went into the radio room. In a few minutes he came out.

"Call the captain," Maj. Kerr told the sailor on watch.

The helmsman spoke into a phone and the captain shortly appeared hastily stuffing his shirt into his trousers. He, too, looked pretty sleepy.

I think everybody aboard ship had turned in shortly after dark. None of us had gotten much sleep in the Manila and Corregidor areas amidst the air raids. Last night we passed through the minefields and all of us were awake for that. As a result of the events of the week, lack of sleep and rest, mental strain, and fatigue, everybody, including the crew, was dead tired. Tonight, after darkness settled down, a cool breeze sprang up and a light feeling of security settled aboard the ship and everybody had gone to bed. It was now about 2200. This ship was plowing steadily south between the islands of Negros and Cebu and the night was dark, yet clear. The moon would not rise for several hours yet.

The ship's captain conferred with the major a minute and then came back into the pilothouse. What he did, I didn't see, but suddenly the ship's bells rang out quite a number of times, giving us a prearranged alert signal.

When the bells ceased ringing, there seemed to be an eternity of silence in which the only sound was that of the ship plowing through the sea. Then pandemonium broke loose and the sound of subdued voices arose from all parts of the ship. There were cries and curses followed by the sound of human bodies being forced against hard unyielding obstacles. I could not see what was going on; I could only imagine the crew and the various officers and men stumbling and fumbling around in the darkness of rooms, stairways and over decks littered with objects hidden by darkness. Each man carrying a little blanket roll of personal belongings quickly tried to reach his alert post. A feeling of the unknown and fear seemed to pervade the atmosphere.

In the meantime, the ship continued her way steadily southward. As the minutes went on, it seemed to me that we were rushing headlong into the jaws of the enemy. In a way, the alert brought mental relief.

I was no longer the only officer on watch and the responsibility had been taken from my shoulders. Since Maj. Kerr had taken over, I went to my alert post by one of the lifeboats. The major must have had difficulty making up his mind as to what to do. His orders were to deliver his cargo immediately to the Port of Bugo, Mindanao. Only a dire emergency could cause him to change those plans. As the ship continued southward toward the straits where the enemy was supposed to be heading, it became evident that the major could not decide whether to continue on the course or turn aside.

I lay down on the deck next to the lifeboat clutching my little musette bag of personal belongings and a gunnysack of some confidential documents the major had given me to destroy in case of capture by the enemy. With my head on the gunnysack and my arms around it, I fell asleep from exhaustion. I remember the last thought in my mind was that I had better get some rest, as that rest might mean the difference between having and not having the strength to survive the coming ordeal. Sometime later, how long I do not know, but certainly less than an hour, I awoke to a different feel of the ship. Rousing myself and looking up into the night, I sensed that the ship was turning around. A few seconds later somebody coming from the direction of the wheelhouse stumbled over me, and started talking to another person.

"What's up?"

"The major had the captain turn the ship around and they are going back to try to hide behind an island before dawn."

"What a relief! Why didn't he do that in the beginning?"

"Yours not to reason why, yours but to do . . . "

"Blast you. Go to hell!"

That news brought a feeling of relief to all of us. We could hear people beginning to stir around again in the darkness. These were the hours just before the moon rose and the night seemed to get blacker as time went on. It was so dark that it was impossible for us to see the shore, even though we knew it could not be far off. How that Filipino captain sensed his way back up the coast of the Island of Negros, for a couple of hours, through the stygian blackness of the night, to anchor his ship behind a small island a couple hundred yards off shore from San Carlos, Negros, is incomprehensible to me. I remember that we all expressed fervent hope that the old boy knew what he was doing. If he hit the wrong place and ran aground, it would not be hard to guess what the likely result would be.

By and by, the ship almost stopped and we could see land close on our right. Shortly afterwards, the ship seemed to stop and we heard the rumble of the anchor chain. A little later, we heard the major saying, "Well, boys, we'll stop here and go ashore."

"Miner and Snowden, report to number one lifeboat," said Maj. Kerr.

I scrambled through the darkness over some men and made my way to the number one lifeboat.

"Lt. Miner reporting, sir."

"Okay. Where is Snowden? Is he here?

"Coming up, sir." Presently, Sgt. Snowden bumped into me.

"Sergeant, you and Miner, along with some others will go ashore with me to see what we can find out about a place to unload the cargo in the morning if necessary."

We both replied that we understood. A Filipino captain and some of his crew were in the meantime lowering the lifeboat. Maj. Kerr, Snowden, a couple of other Americans (I have forgotten just who they were), and I entered the lifeboat.

While various individuals were groping their way down the rope ladder to the lifeboat, a rifle shot sounded in our midst.

"Quiet, you damn fools. Do you want to alarm everybody on shore? Who is responsible?" asked Maj. Kerr.

There was dead silence. No one answered.

"Who did that?"

"I, sir."

"Who are you?"

"Sgt. Snowden, sir. I bumped my rifle and it went off."

"Don't you know that such mistakes may cost lives? Don't let it happen again. Now, get aboard at once."

With no more mishaps, we got aboard the lifeboat and started toward the shore, which we could now dimly see.

"We had better shout and tell the townspeople who we are, or they may open fire on us. After all this noise and the rifle shot, some of the Filipinos may think we are Japs. Have some of the crew shout 'Americanos' in their dialect."

As the boat approached the shore, all of us shouted as to our identity in all the languages that we knew. Shouts of "Americans," "Americano," "Amigo," and other dialect words meaning friends and Americans rang through the night from our boat. By the time we were 100 feet from the shore, we could hear people running up and down the beach and over boards, although we could not see them. Their excited voices rang sharply through the night. Very cautiously, we nosed our boat in the direction where the voices were loudest.

"If anyone understands English on shore, please answer our hail. We are Americans from an American ship. Do not shoot us. If you have a light, flash it on us so you may see who we are."

There was no answer.

"Stop rowing, men. Don't go any closer as we do not want to be shot."

The major repeated his instructions to the people on the shore. Finally, a flashlight was turned on us and we could hear excited muttering.

"As you can see, some of us are American soldiers. You have no need to be afraid of us. We come from an American ship out next to the island and want to get help from the Americans in the American headquarters in Cebu. We want to come ashore to see about making these arrangements."

Voice from shore: "Okay, American. Come ashore. We will help you."

Our boat pulled up to the pier and all of us scrambled up except the Filipino crew. We were at once surrounded by natives, both men and women, who thrust flashlights in our faces, and peered closely at us. There were excited mutterings running through the crowd.

The men were dressed to a varying degree, from a pair of shorts to a policeman in full uniform. I believe even the mayor was there dressed in a pair of pants and an undershirt. The policeman and the mayor revealed their identity and community offices, offering at the same time to help us in any way they could.

"Will you show us the telegraph office at the Bureau of Posts?"

"I, myself, will take you there. It is not far, sire," said the mayor.

All of us, including the surrounding townspeople started through the town at the mayor's heels. Upon arriving at the building which contained the telegraph office, we found there was no operator at that late hour. The mayor dispatched one of his townspeople to the home of the operator asking him to come at once to the telegraph office. We had to wait half an hour or so for the operator to appear. Then Maj. Kerr sent a telegram to Gen. Sharp in Cebu explaining the situation. While we had been waiting for the telegraph operator, the major learned that there was a large Sugar Central located in San Carlos, Negros Occidental, and that it was managed by a man named Roberts. After sending the telegram to Gen. Sharp, Maj. Kerr told me to go out to the Central and enlist the help of Mr. Roberts. I found a Filipino with a car and started out.

That drive through the night, twisting and turning through the palm trees, among which were Filipino houses, still seems like a dream. The night was murky black and how our Filipino driver found his way to the Sugar Central I do not know. Finally after much twisting and turning, we came out of the palms into an open space. After driving through the clearing, the Filipino drove into the palms again and stopped.

"This is the Sugar Central, sir."

He pointed into the blackness. I looked and could make out the dim black bulk of a house.

"Show me the way to the door. I can't see in the dark."

I didn't want the Filipino to leave before I was ready for him to go.

"Yes, sir," and he led the way.

We moved through the darkness around the house until we came to a broad veranda. Here the Filipino hesitated and I moved on ahead on to the veranda and started pounding on the door. My pounding on the door seemed terribly loud in the stillness of the night. The noise seemed loud enough to wake the devil himself, yet there was dead silence within the house. I banged again. Finally, from out of the silence, came a hard voice saying, "Who is it?"

"I am an American officer off a ship down in the harbor. Some of the Filipinos said that an American named Roberts runs the Sugar Central here and I came to talk to him about disposition of our cargo. If you will come down where you can see me, I can further identify myself."

"Wait where you are and I will be down."

It was a relief to have somebody answer my knocking. In that country, it isn't always wise to go knocking around white men's doors in the dark of night. From the sound of that voice, I felt certain that there was a gun around. Later, I was told that this was true. I waited at the door of the veranda until the figure of a man appeared. There was still no light in the house and I could see that the man was taking no chances in being silhouetted against the light.

(Just inside the door) "What is your name?"

"Lt. Miner and I came off the ship *Don Esteban,* which is anchored off the municipal pier. Are you Mr. Roberts?"

"Yes."

With that a flashlight was turned on me and it scanned me from head to foot. I knew that I was getting a thorough check upon identification by appearance. Roberts then opened the door and I stepped inside. With the aid of the flashlight, we found chairs on the veranda and sat down.

"Maj. Kerr, the officer in charge of the ship, sent me down to contact you about the disposition of some of our cargo for Cebu City while he is contacting Gen. Sharp's headquarters in Cebu. We have some officers and radio equipment which Maj. Kerr wants to unload here before he continues on his voyage. He has directed me to find out what facilities you have for the handling of and storage of this equipment for a short time."

"The Central has its own pier running out into the bay from the bodega. We can't get any men until daylight, but as soon as it is light, I'll send one of my men to get some boys to help. In the meantime, we can have your ship move up to the vicinity of my pier in order that you my unload your equipment at a minimum loss of time at daybreak. I have a motor boat and I'll take you back to the municipal pier where we can find your commanding officer. Wait until I get some clothes on." With that, Mr. Roberts disappeared into the house and I turned to the Filipino man who had driven me out.

"Thank you very much for bringing me out and helping me to find Mr. Roberts. I shall go with him now. You may return to your house and get some sleep."

"Very good, sir, but I shall go back to the pier."

"Okay, I'll see you back at the pier."

After a few moments, Roberts appeared fully clothed and led the way from the house down to the pier where his motor boat was tied up. He started up the boat and we puttered away through the darkness for several minutes. Then we slowed down and Roberts said, "Well, here we are."

The boat bumped something and immediately I made out the vague outlines of the pier. He climbed the pier and the boat while I followed.

"Where will the major be?"

"At the telegraph office is where we agreed to meet."

Roberts turned away without replying. I followed him through the darkness. We passed by the pier and for several minutes went through the streets where few people were moving until we came to the telegraph office.

Here we found a small group talking in low tones. Passing through them into the telegraph office, we found the major still sending his telegrams. A few minutes later he finished and turned to us.

"Maj. Kerr, this is Mr. Roberts, the manager of the Sugar Central. Mr. Roberts has promised to help us in our present difficulty."

"I am glad to know you, Maj. Kerr; I'll do all I can to help. I suggest that you tell me about your difficulty and we'll see what can be done."

"I have an inter-island boat anchored out alongside the island with a small amount of radio equipment and several men whom I want to take off the boat. I want to store the equipment, leaving the men in charge until they receive instructions from Gen. Sharp in Cebu as to its disposal. I wonder if you can provide storage for the equipment and shelter for the men. They have their own bedrolls, but they will need food. The ship's crew can unload the equipment on the pier but we will need several men to carry the equipment once it is ashore."

Roberts said, "I suggest you move the ship over to my pier right away and then as soon as it's light, the crew can unload the equipment onto the pier. You can then move the ship away from the pier at the earliest hour. As soon as it is light, one of my men will get several Filipino boys and move the equipment from the pier into a nearby sugar *bodega*."

"All right, we will get under way at once."

With that, the major arose and the rest of us followed him back through the town and down to the pier.

"I'll take my own boat and guide your ship over to my pier," said Roberts.

"All right, I'll go out to the ship and tell the captain to follow you."

The next hour or so was spent cautiously moving the boats around in the dark, accompanied by much subdued talking. By dawn, the *Don Esteban* was moored close enough to the Sugar Central pier for our cargo to be transferred to it. After an hour or so of labor, this was accomplished and the *Don Esteban* withdrew from the pier and sought shelter on the west side of the small island just east of the town of San Carlos. There the ship remained the rest of the day. True to his word, although it was Sunday, Roberts had a crew of Filipino boys who moved the radio equipment into the shelter of a large sugar *bodega* nearby.

By this time it was the middle of the morning, so Roberts took the Americans up to his house where we met the rest of his family and got something to eat.

The next few hours after breakfast, everybody relaxed and tried to sleep. Then I went back to the *Don Esteban,* got my bedroll, and had it carried into the sugar *bodega*. There I spread it on the floor beside a large pile of filled sugar sacks and went to sleep. The last thing that I remember before falling asleep was wondering how there could be so much sugar in one spot and no ants around it.

By midafternoon, a representative from Gen. Sharp's headquarters in Cebu arrived in the person of Capt. William L. Robinson. He had at his disposal a ferryboat running between the cities of San Carlos, Negros, and Toledo, Cebu, some 20 miles across the strait. Maj. Kerr and Robinson, after a short conference, made their respective arrangements for the transfer of the radio equipment to Capt. Robinson's ferryboat. Robinson then told Capt. Orson and Nelson that they could go back to Cebu with him that afternoon. To me, he gave instructions to see that the radio equipment with its attached personnel were put aboard the ferry and that I was to be in charge of that detail until I delivered it to Gen. Sharp's headquarters in Cebu.

With the help of Roberts' crew and one of his trucks, I transferred the radio equipment to the ferry alongside the municipal pier. By the time this tedious task had been accomplished, Capt. Robinson and the rest were aboard and anxious to sail. The ferry pulled out about 3 P.M. and headed for Toledo. It was good to have respite from duty and relax. As the ferry pulled away from the pier, Capt. Robinson, whom I had known while stationed in Bohol and whom I have previously mentioned in this journal, called me to have a cup of coffee with him. We seated ourselves at a dining room table on the lower deck of the ferry.

"Well, Miner, what do you think of all this?"

"I don't think much of it."

Then I proceeded to relate what I knew of the bombings on the Island of Luzon, mainly those of Clark Field, Nichols Field, Cavite Naval Yard, and the ships in Manila harbor.

"Doesn't sound so good to date. There has been no action in Cebu. There have been some landings, however, by the Japanese in Davao," said Robinson.

"Well, it is only a matter of time until they take a crack at us here. Once on land at Toledo, how do we get this outfit to Cebu City?"

"We have a detachment under Lt. Fossum stationed in Toledo. He will meet us when we arrive at Toledo. You can arrange to stay overnight with him. Borrow one of these trucks tomorrow morning and take the radio and its crew over to Cebu."

"Well, that is a relief. I know where I am going to get the equipment to operate with now."

The rest of the two-hour trip, Capt. Robinson, Capt. Nelson, and I visited and talked about various subjects. Sometime around 5:00 P.M. our ferry pulled into the dock at Toledo. There the three captains departed for Cebu City in Capt. Robinson's transportation.

I was left with the radio, which was charged to Snowden and his crew of technicians at the pier in Toledo.

As Robinson left, an American lieutenant in a truck drove onto the pier, stopping by the ferry. He introduced himself as Lt. Orville Fossum.

"I'm Bill Miner and I'm sure glad to see you. I hope you have a piece of coconut to nibble on and a palm tree that is safe to sleep under."

"I can do better than that. I can give you a boiled egg to eat and a school house floor to sleep on."

"Wonderful! I'm going to think I'm in paradise with all of that."

"Capt. Robinson told me this morning to bring the truck down to meet the ferry and that he had some supplies coming over from Negros. He didn't say what it was. Do you know anything about it?"

"Yes, I do. I have a radio here, which is charged to Sgt. Snowden. He will need some help to load it into the truck."

"My truck driver will get several of the boys [pointing to a crowd of Filipinos on the pier] to help you."

"Okay, let's get some of the boys over there to help with the *cuan* on the ferry."

Fossum's driver sprang out of the truck and started arranging for a group of Filipino men on the pier. In no time at all, half a dozen of them were leaping aboard the ferry.

"Sgt. Snowden, here are some men to help you. The crew of the ferry will also help, so load your radio on the truck as fast as you can and we will go to Lt. Fossum's camp."

The work got underway and, in a short time, the equipment was loaded. Sgt. Snowden, his crew, another lieutenant and his crew, Lt. Fossum, and I all got aboard the truck and set out for the camp. Upon arrival at the camp, which consisted of a company of Filipino soldiers sheltered in a municipal school building in Toledo, we left the equipment aboard the truck under guard. Lt. Fossum, Sgt. Snowden's crew, and I then took our bedrolls from the truck and prepared to spend the night in the schoolhouse.

Lt. Fossum and I became well acquainted that night. He was quite lonesome, having been the only white man stationed in Toledo for several weeks. He practically told me his life history. His home was in Fargo, ND, where his parents had a store, the name of which (I believe) was the Fargo Rubber Stamp Co.

During the course of conversation, I found out he liked to hunt and fish, so we spent most of the evening talking about our respective fishing grounds. Of course, I also gave him all the news I had of the war. We all turned in early as this was the first night in a week that we felt we could go to sleep in safety. I remember that I became dead to the world shortly after nightfall and it was daylight when I awoke. My arms were still flung over my head when I awoke as they had been when I had gone to sleep. I was so deeply exhausted that I doubt that I stirred the entire night.

The next morning, Fossum took me over to the home of one of his lieutenants for breakfast. There I had a complete meal of steamed rice, stewed chicken, and coffee. I remember that I thought the meal very tasteless and found it hard to eat. Yet just a few months away all the American officers on the Island of Cebu and I would have given a small fortune for all we could eat of that same meal. After breakfast was over, Sgt. Snowden, his crew, and I with our equipment climbed aboard the truck with the radio and started over the mountains to Cebu City and Gen. Sharp's headquarters.

I enjoyed the trip across the island. I was much refreshed after a good night's rest and a substantial breakfast. The day was bright and cloudless. Our truck continually passed in and out of coconut palm groves. It seemed good to be alive and driving over beautiful mountains. As we climbed higher, we could look down on the green coastal plains of the island across the straits to the high mountains rising on the Island of Negros. There was a myriad of colors, greens of the vegetation, yellows of the corals and sand, deep blue of the sea, and the distant smoky mountains of the dark Island of Negros. It didn't seem possible that there were such things as a war going on or that 400 miles away to the north on the Island of Luzon events were swiftly culminating in destruction and death for so many of the people and friends I knew there.

As our truck rolled over the mountains and down the east slope of the island, we ran into various troop movements on the highway.

I reported to Gen. Sharp's headquarters shortly after noon and found upon arrival that everyone there was filled with excitement. About half an hour before our arrival, two or three Nip planes had dive-bombed and strafed some oil installations and storage plants on Shell Island in Cebu

Harbor. They had missed their objective and no damage was done. They told me that I had missed the fun. I wasn't the least bit sorry, for I had just had my fill of excitement in Manila and on the way down.

I reported to the adjutant, Capt. William T. Holloway Cook.

"Hello, Miner. Glad to see you again. Where do you come from? I thought you were in Sternberg Hospital."

"I was until 24 hours after the war broke out. By that time, the hospital was so full of seriously wounded that they released the less serious among us. I came down to San Carlos, Negros, on the *Don Esteban*. Across from there to Toledo, with Capt. Robinson yesterday, bringing a radio and its crew of technicians. They are outside on the truck now. Whom do they report to?"

"I'll send a man down to take care of them. I expect you had better wait and see the general."

I sat down in a chair near the general's office and waited. After a short time, out of the office of the general walked a full colonel. On seeing me he stopped.

"Hello, what can I do for you?"

"Capt. Cook told me to wait and see the general, so I am waiting."

"I am Col. Thompson, his chief of staff, and I'll take you in to see the general at once."

"Thank you, sir."

I followed the colonel into Gen. Sharp's office.

"Here is a young man to see you."

"Capt. Cook adjutant, told me he thought the general would like to speak to me."

For the next few minutes, I related to the general and his chief of staff what I knew concerning the events on Luzon. I told them I had gotten this far on the way back to my unit stationed in Wright, Samar. The general and his staff sort of smiled.

"I think we can use you here, Miner. You wait outside the door and Col. Thompson will tell you what to do very shortly."

That was as close as I ever got to my unit. Col. Thompson appeared shortly.

"Miner, you report to Capt. Humber over in San Carlos College. He will tell you what to do."

I saluted and took off. Once outside the general's headquarters, I ran into Capt. Cook again.

"Capt. Cook, I was told to report to Capt. Humber for duty. Can you tell me where my quarters will be and where I will mess?"

"There is an empty room upstairs here and we mess here also. You can put your equipment in that empty room."

"Yes, thank you, sir." Then I moved on.

San Carlos College was only two or three blocks from Gen. Sharp's headquarters in old Fort San Pedro de Cebu. I walked over to San Carlos College and inquired from the guard at the door for Capt. Humber's office.

The guard had an orderly show me the way and, presently, after winding through various stone corridors of the old Spanish college building, I found myself in the presence of a captain who was surrounded by an office staff of Filipino men.

"I am Capt. Humber; who are you?"

"Lt. Miner. Gen. Sharp told me to report to you for duty."

"I am sure glad to see you, Miner. Aren't you the old S-4 man of the 2nd Battalion of the 34th Infantry?"

"That is correct. We worked together on a problem up at Fort Stotsenberg last July."

"They have given me the G-2 office here and I need an assistant badly. I guess you are it."

"I'll do my best and I am glad to work under somebody I already know."

The next few hours were spent in becoming familiar with the duties of the G-2 office. There were large maps hung on the walls which showed all the islands of the Philippines in detail. On them were plotted the positions and composition of the various units of Gen. Sharp's command. In addition, we received reports of Japanese plane flights, which we traced with the use of pins and ribbons on these maps. Any ships reported, we also plotted on the maps. The work became quite interesting. Due to the air-warning system, which had been set up, we could receive reports of hostile planes when they were miles away. After we received several reports on them, we could establish, with reasonable certainty, their course and objective. Once those had been determined, if possible, we radioed or telegraphed a warning to that unit or installation. Late in the afternoon, Lt. Duane Cosper came to the office and asked for me.

"Hello, Duane, glad to see you. Where did you come from?"

"Wright, Samar. I just came from Gen. Sharp and he said to tell you to report to Lt. Bowers in the Bureau of Posts Office of the Customs Building. Lt. Bowers will tell you what your assignment is. The general said that I was to take over your job here."

"Things sure change fast, don't they? Here I am just becoming familiar with the job and they say, move on. I'll introduce you to Capt. Humber."

After introducing Lt. Cosper to Capt. Humber, I got my things and went over to the Bureau of Posts where I found Lt. Bowers. Bowers had charge of the censorship for Gen. Sharp's command. The rest of the day, and part of the night, I spent becoming acquainted with the details of the censorship. The censorship duty there consisted of establishing censorship on all newspapers, radio programs and commercial radio, telegrams, telephone services, and cable services. In the telephone, telegraph, and commercial radio services, government priorities had to be established and maintained. After that, various types of civilian priorities were established. This too proved to be interesting work and had a wider scope than the phase G-2 work that I had experienced under Capt. Humber. The reason that I was relieving Lt. Bower was that he was being transferred to Luzon. Prior to my coming, while on the harbor patrol duty, Bowers had shot a Filipino. For that reason, though just, he was being sent back to a unit in Luzon. His boat was due to leave that night. Bowers got back to Luzon and somewhere during the campaign of Bataan, was killed in action.

I don't remember all the members of Gen. Sharp's staff or his headquarters. I'll mention them and their duties as correctly as I can remember them. The rank mentioned from here on is the rank they attained at the end of the war or as I have known them. At the time of events some individuals might have been a grade or two lower than their final grade.

On Gen. Sharp's staff were the following members: Lt. Col. Floyd F. Forte, often called Sammy Forte. My friendship with Forte was very brief. He did not arrive in Cebu until December 1, 1941. After the war started, he was busy running secret missions for Gen. Sharp in various parts of the Southern Islands. He got over on the Island of Negros on one of these missions and contracted dysentery. This disease caused him to be laid up for several weeks. I saw him in Cebu City on his way to Mindanao from Negros. He asked me at that time how the war was coming in our favor. I remember telling him it was all against us. Sammy was quite a boy and well liked by all who knew him. After he got to Mindanao he saw action against the Nips several times. During those actions, he showed plenty of intestinal fortitude. The details as to his death are not known. He was reported killed in action in Lanao, Mindanao. When he was last seen, he was attacking single-handedly a large number of Japs.

Another at Gen. Sharp's headquarters who met a similar fate was Capt. Charles Bucher. Bucher and I were together in the headquarters on Cebu. I knew him rather well. Bucher sweated out several secret missions from island to island with a narrow escape or two as I heard about him. He then went to Mindanao with Gen. Sharp while I stayed in Cebu. Bucher was killed in action by Japanese artillery somewhere in Mindanao.

Col. John W. Thompson was Gen. Sharp's chief of staff. During the early part of the war, while in Cebu, I got to know Col. Thompson very well. He was an earnest, hardworking man with inadequate facilities at hand for his tremendous job. He went to Mindanao with Gen. Sharp and surrendered with the general in Malaybalay in May 1942. Shortly after the surrender, he was among the group of full colonels and generals sent north to Formosa. After remaining a number of months in Formosa, they were moved to Manchuria and in June 1945 arrived at the Hoten Prison Camp in Mukden, Manchuria, where they remained until the end of the war. When I last saw Col. Thompson, he was in good health.

Col. William E. Braddock was force surgeon for Gen. Sharp. After organizing the hospital facilities and medical troops on the Island of Cebu, Col. Braddock went to Mindanao with Gen. Sharp where he continued to function as force surgeon. Col. Braddock likewise surrendered with Gen. Sharp and ended up in the Hoten Prison Camp at Mukden, Manchuria.

Col. Archibald M. Mison was Gen. Sharp's force communications officer. Col. Mison was among those who went to Mindanao with Gen. Sharp to organize the defense of the island. He was rescued from Hoten Prison Camp in August 1945.

Lt. Col. William T. Halloway Cook was Gen. Sharp's adjutant general. He was a friendly sort of man whenever I was around him. He functioned in Mindanao headquarters until the surrender in May 1942. After a few months imprisonment in Malaybalay, he was moved to the Davao Prison Camp where he, with numerous officers and enlisted men, did coolie labor for the Japanese. In June 1944, he was moved from Mindanao to the Cabanatuan Prison Camp where he stayed a number of months. Finally, he was moved to the Bilibid Prison and was placed on *Oryoku Maru* on December 13, 1944. He survived the bombings by American naval dive-bombers. He was placed in a second ship in Lingayen Gulf and taken to Tokyo Harbor in southern Formosa. He survived a second bombing and performed heroic work in the relief and care of the wounded. When I think of the din and chaos of that wrecked prison ship, I can still hear his voice calling out to give clothes, food and water for the relief of the wounded. The man exhausted himself in their behalf and died later in the ship as a result of exhaustion, malnutrition, exposure, and dehydration. He was a hero who might be alive today had he not been so unselfish.

Lt. Col. Charles I. Humber, commonly called Polly, was the G-2 on the staff. Humber was a big man with a lot of good humor. One of the sidelights of his experiences in the Southern Islands was the securing of some Filipino straw mats of a special design while on one of his trips through the islands. Off the coast of either Samar or Leyte was a small island whose inhabitants wove these special mats. Having the time to make the trip across the water to this small island, Polly secured the services of a native with a banca to paddle him over to the island. On the shore, Polly asked the native, "Joe, how much to paddle me out to that island?"

"Five centavos, sir." (At that time equal to 2 1/2 cents in American money.)

"Okay, Joe. Let's go." He climbed into the boat producing the five centavos. In due time, he landed on the other shore. "Okay, Joe, you wait for me. I come back pretty soon."

Polly secured his mats, came back to the shore and found the native waiting with his banca. Polly tossed his mats in, climbed in and said, "Okay, Joe, let's go back."

Filipino (without lifting his paddle): "You give me five pesos, sir." (Equal to $2.50 in American money.)

Polly exploded for about five minutes, calling the native all the good names this side of heaven. In the end, however, he paid the five pesos in order to get back to the mainland without missing his conference.

Polly, likewise, surrendered in Malaybalay in May 1942 and spent time in Davao, Cabanatuan and Bilibid Prisons. He died on the way to Japan on January 26, 1945. His death was due to exposure, malnutrition, dysentery, and dehydration.

Lt. Col. Robert D. Johnston was the G-4 for the Mindanao force. Col. Johnston, when I first knew him, was my company commander of the Service Company of the 31st Infantry. We went south together in the latter part of August 1941 to assume posts with the Philippine Army. Col. Johnston surrendered in Malaybalay and as a POW worked as coolie laborer in Davao and Cabanatuan. A few weeks later, on January 30, 1945, he was rescued along with the rest of the Cabanatuan prisoners by the rangers.

Lt. Col. William L. Robinson was another member of the headquarters. He was on duty with the Philippine Army September 1, 1941. I found him very likable in the line of duty. He was with Gen. Sharp all the way through until the surrender. Robinson was part of the group that went to the Davao Penal Colony. While aboard the prison ship, which was taking us from northern Mindanao to Davao, he served as one of the executive officers for a group of prisoners. While trying to win some concessions from the Japs in the way of food and water for American POWs, he was violently slapped around the head and eyes by one of the Japanese. He was the first officer of any rank in our group to be beaten by the Japanese. This action by the Jap soldier caused great comment among our ranks. This was worse than some prankster sawing the legs off the college president's chair (almost in two) so that the chair collapsed, spilling the college president on the floor of the chapel stage. However, the POWs made no hostile movements. Later in the Davao prison, he served as farm detail coordinator for a short time. Robinson spent a great deal of his time in the sick barracks or the hospital because of almost total blindness. It was rumored that one of the blows Robinson received from the Nip while on board ship injured an eye nerve causing the blindness. Very little food and a vitamin deficiency failed to improve his eyes. Regardless of the reason, he could hardly see to walk around the camp. He was moved from Davao to Cabanatuan and finally to Bilibid prison. On December 13, 1944, he was among those placed on board the *Oryoku Maru*. He survived the two bombings, but died of malnutrition, exposure, and dehydration about January 25, 1945, on board ship en route to Japan.

Maj. Coleman T. Caruthers was another of Gen. Sharp's staff. He had joined the staff at the beginning of his Philippine Army assignment and remained with him all through the war. His earliest imprisonment was in Malaybalay. He was later in Davao where he, like everyone else, had his share of the work as a coolie laborer. He and Maj. Chrisman used to spend quite a bit of their spare time in prison talking of their families and friends in the Los Angeles area.

Maj. Robert P. Chrisman was in command of Gen. Sharp's message center during the war. As I have previously mentioned, Chrisman had been stationed in Cebu City training Filipino troops prior to the war. He knew all the American soldiers on duty with the Philippine Army on the islands of Cebu and Bohol. He had quite a number of friends among the civilians, Spanish and Filipino families. I had met him socially in Cebu City prior to the war. Picture taking was a great hobby of his. Prior to and during the war, he gathered a great many pictures of interesting people and events on the islands of Cebu and Mindanao. Even after he became a prisoner, he still had some snapshots of pre-war days (although he had no negatives with him). His negatives and private papers he disposed of by burying them or giving them to a Filipino for safekeeping. Chrisman was another that started out on the ill-fated prison ship. He was one of about 105 field officers instantly killed when our Naval dive bombers dropped a bomb into the hold of the ship. The date of his death was December 15, 1944. He was another of the Los Angeles boys in our prison.

Maj. Robert V. Nelson was the force dental officer. I have previously mentioned him as one of my companions aboard the *Don Esteban* on my peerless voyage from Manila to Cebu. Maj. Nelson went to Mindanao and after the surrender, he became the chief dental officer in our prison camp.

Lt. Col. Paul D. Phillips was a 2nd lieutenant when I knew him at the beginning of the war. He was a bright, likable, young fellow and seemed to be right on the ball. He soon became aide to Gen. Sharp, an assignment which he held throughout the war. He went to the Davao prison with the rest of the boys. I'll mention him later while dealing with prison life. He survived the war.

Capt. Duane L. Cosper was one of the assistant G-2s under Col. Humber. He went to Mindanao with Gen. Sharp's headquarters and was one of the boys who did not surrender at the appointed time. Duane took off to the hills near Malaybalay when it came time to surrender. Because of the loose guard at the camp in Malaybalay, there was a little freedom of movement of Americans in and out of the prison area. Somehow or another word got down to the camp as to where Duane was staying and he was contacted. He was found to be very thin and practically without food. He was living in a little one-room house belonging to a Filipino. He had a couple of poor, lean native chickens tied to a bush out in front of the house. The boy was in bad shape with an infected tooth. The whole side of his face was swollen and quite painful. At that particular time, the American prisoners in Malaybalay were living well. They had plenty of food and a fair degree of medical care. One of the colonels who talked to the boy told him that under the circumstances he thought he would be wise to return to prison where he could get food and a fair degree of medical care. At that time, this looked like a wise move, but in view of later events, the colonel told me he was sorry he had ever helped to persuade the boy to come in. As a result of this advice, Cosper did turn himself in. After about three years' imprisonment in Davao, Cabanatuan, and Bilibid prisons, he died on board ship en route to Japan and was buried at sea. The reason for his death was malnutrition, dehydration, and exposure from years in prison.

Capt. Roy B. Gray was another of Gen. Sharp's headquarters staff. He was a six-foot, good-looking young fellow with a quiet temperament. You hardly knew he was around except when he appeared in line of duty. I don't remember what his assignment was, but I do know he was well liked. Capt. Gray will appear later in this story when he served as one of Gen. Sharp's emissaries for surrender of his various units during the fall of the Southern Islands.

Capt. William O'Brien was one of the American officers stationed in Cebu. I think I mentioned him as one of the men I met prior to the war. At that time he was with Headquarters, 8th Military District of the Philippine Army, located in Cebu City. Being Irish, he liked to eat. I remember him coming in for a lot of razzing the night or two that I ate at the 8th Military District HQ officers' mess. He was the mess officer, but he took it very gracefully. He went to Mindanao with Gen. Sharp and I didn't see him again until after the surrender when we were both in Davao. O'Brien and I went on the same work details, so we often planted rice together while there. On February 24, 1944, part of our Davao camp was taken to Lasang by the Japanese to work on an air strip. This detail was composed of 100 men and it was joined by another detail of 650 men. This made a total of

750 men working on the Lasang air strip. On September 6, 1944, the Lasang detail was aboard a prison ship just north of Zamboanga that was torpedoed by an American submarine about 4:00 P.M. As to Capt. O'Brien's
fate, I only know that he went to Lasang February 24, 1944.

Maj. Oliver W. Orson was the force veterinarian. I mentioned him previously as being one of the passengers of the *Don Esteban* when I came
down from Manila during the first few days of the war. Maj. Orson went
to Mindanao and surrendered with the group at Malaybalay. I will refer to
him later when he was camp veterinarian in Davao.

Maj. Jefferson W. Speck, like Maj. Chrisman, came from Los Angeles.
Speck was the man who did a lot of the wire-laying of the telephone and
radio installations in Mindanao. He surrendered with the general and later
went to Davao with the rest of the group. He survived the fearful trip on
board the *Oryoku Maru*.

The final man that I remember as a member of Gen. Sharp's staff was
Maj. Max Weil from Detroit. In civilian life, Maj. Weil had been a postal
inspector. As I recall from several accounts, he found the work interesting;
however, being a reserve officer, he was called to active duty and sent to
the Philippines. His assignment at the beginning of the war was as headquarters commandant for Gen. Sharp. Max was an interesting character and, during the first days of the war, because of common interests, I
got to know him fairly well. Later in the Davao prison, we became very
good friends.

After I took over the censorship office in Cebu City from Lt. Bowers,
things began to grow interesting mighty fast. To begin with, a great deal
of the work had to be done at night. As previously mentioned, the work
concerned all phases of communication with the public radio, telegraph,
RCA, telephone, and newspapers. There were two or three daily newspapers published in Cebu City when the war began. The papers gathered
their news for the morning edition any time up to 11:00 P.M. The censorship demanded that I proofread the entire issue before it went to press.
The same thing occurred around noon for the evening edition. Often the

Filipino editors would fail to send in their proofs and I would have to send a soldier over to the newspaper office with a threat to stop the press unless the proofs were immediately sent to me. It took several weeks and the loss of a lot of sleep to get those editors to send their proofs without fail.

Another day of my censorship, in regard to the radio program in the city of Cebu, was a semi-daily censorship of all news broadcasts and commercial announcements.

Albert Fienstein, commonly called Al Fenton, was in charge of this radio station. Under my supervision, he did most of the actual censorship, but I required a copy of everything that went out over the air. A few commercial announcements prior to the war had been made in Chinese and Spanish. I required that everything be done in English. Shortly after the sinking of the inter-island boat *Corregidor,* we had quite a few requests for commercials offering rewards as to the knowledge of individuals who were believed to have been aboard the *Corregidor.* The originators of these announcements sometimes wanted them in a dialect. People were persuaded to use English. It was the same way with the newspapers. There was one rich Chinese in particular who for days and days after the sinking of the *Corregidor* became known, ran an ad accompanied by a picture offering 1,000 reward for information about the whereabouts of his son who was believed to have been aboard the *Corregidor.*

I mentioned the telegraphic system. Cebu City, being the largest city of the Southern Islands and centrally located in the archipelago, was chosen as the telegraphic central for the Southern Islands. (The telegraphic system in the Philippines was called Bureau of Posts.) The system varies from ours in that it makes use of both wire and radio. On the larger islands, there were telegraph wires strung between the larger towns. These wires were all connected with the main office for that district or island. In this main office was a short-wave radio set operating on a frequency designated by the Bureau of Posts. When a telegram was sent from one island to another, the short-wave radio would send it to the main office of the respective island or district. The radio operator there would receive it, transfer the message to the wire system again, and the message would be delivered to its destination. The Cebu Office of the Bureau of Posts seemed to be the clearinghouse for all the Southern Island stations. Telegrams originating in Tacloban, Leyte, designated for Iloilo, Panay, would be radioed from Tacloban to Cebu City and Cebu City would relay the message to Iloilo. It was the same way with messages from Zamboanga to Manila. The message would be relayed through the Cebu City office of the Bureau of Posts. My duty called for 24-hours-a-day censorship of all messages relayed through Cebu. This duty consisted not only of the censorship of the content of the messages, but it also helped smooth the organization to see that all priorities were duly observed. The wires did not become jammed with nonessentials and speedy, efficient service was maintained every minute of the day and night.

Another phase of the job was the RCA radiograms. For a short time after the war started, we had contact with the Manila office. Prior to the war, the Manila office handled the RCA traffic between the Philippines and the States. When Manila fell, the Cebu RCA office under the Army censorship set about contacting RCA, San Francisco. In a short time, this contact was made and a traffic schedule was established. This traffic schedule was experimented with and developed until a fairly satisfactory contact was maintained, up until a few short hours before the fall of the city of Cebu. The equipment was then destroyed to prevent its falling into the hands of the Japs and being put to use against us. The biggest difficulty that we had with the RCA traffic was not a case of breaking rules or military laws, but the getting of messages accepted was one of them. They would send messages down to Cebu by every possible ship or plane. These messages all had to be sent collect to the soldier's family, if the family were to get the message. A plane would come down from Luzon bringing a whole bundle of radiograms to be sent collect to the families. Then we could not send the radiographs because they were collect. Like them, we didn't have any money to pay for these numerous messages. It was finally ironed out whereby they could be sent collect. This was not until late in the game, however. After the messages were sent, we still had no knowledge that upon being received by RCA, San Francisco, they would be delivered. RCA San Francisco said they were being delivered provided the censor permitted. There again was a ball up. These messages were strictly censored before they went on the air in clear English. There wasn't anything that went over the line from my end that the Japs didn't already know and that the people back home shouldn't know.

We were in touch first hand with the situation while the people in the States didn't comprehend. It seemed a pity when the boys in the battlefield would risk their lives to send a message home, saying they were alive and okay, that the people sitting in safety failed to give immediate action to such morale-building factors for our troops. RCA failed to inform their operators that messages could be sent to the men in the islands from their families. One member of my own family, after receiving several messages from me, finally got one back to me, but it was only after I sent her an RCA message with instructions to reply through RCA. Even in the face of that, the local operator said the message would not go through. Finally, she got him to accept the message on the grounds that if she paid for it he would send it to RCA, San Francisco, and let that office decide what to do with the message. Of course, the message came on through.

A lot of the boys in Bataan would have felt better if they could have had more home contacts. An agency such as the Red Cross could have performed such a service stateside and the public would never have known how the traffic was routed. The last six weeks before the surrender came, a lot of the boys got messages from home which were never delivered to them. By that time, all our ships had been sunk and all our courier planes had been shot out of the skies.

On April 10, RCA Cebu went out of service as the Japs came into the city. It was intended to take the equipment, which had been made semi-mobile, into the hills with us as we fell back into the jungle. The Jap forces, however, were too strong and they advanced too fast for it to be reinstalled after the invasion of Cebu.

The Bureau of Posts was the communication net around which our warning system was set up. Maj. Ernest V. Jordan from Milledgeville, Georgia, was in charge. Because both our duties lay around the traffic of the Bureau of Posts, we decided to have a common office and to arrange or organize our work so that we could relieve each other, thereby giving us time for such necessities as eating, sleeping, and other physical needs. Because there was such a tremendous lack of American personnel in all ranks, many of the men and officers hardly got any sleep for weeks at a time. Through mutual cooperation, Maj. Jordan and I ran our combined offices in shifts. One of the most interesting phases of the duty was tracing flights of Jap planes across the Southern Islands and their inland seas. The air warning system was arranged so that any government or city official, postmaster, Bureau of Posts operator, etc., who received a reliable report of planes flying over his locality would report the number and direction in which they were flying. As the planes passed over various towns and islands, these reports were telegraphed and radioed into our headquarters. This system would forewarn us of an air raid anywhere from 15 to 40 minutes. Any time a group of planes came near any part of this net, the islands of Mindoro, Panay, Negros, Cebu, Bohol, Leyte, Samar, Masbate, and Mindanao, they would immediately be reported and as their flight progressed we would receive a whole flock of telegrams reporting their location and direction of movement. We had a supply of Shell Oil maps, some of which we always kept stored in the desk. As military maps, they were very poor, but they did have all the roads and principal towns on the coast and inland marked on them. By taking the wires that came in concerning a flight of planes and putting pins on the map at the points of origin from the telegrams, we could soon plot the course of the approaching enemy planes. As soon as the course began to take shape, we sent warning messages to any military object over which they might pass. There was never any doubt as to the identity of a large group of planes. The Japanese were the only ones who had any planes in numbers in that area. If we got a report of just a single plane or perhaps two at the most, we would stand by after warning Gen. Sharp's headquarters for the possibility that it was one of our courier planes.

It was rather an exciting game to plot the course of those incoming planes, but the trouble was that the city of Cebu was very often their objective.

The Bureau of Posts in Cebu was located in the Customs Building, which stood right at the waterfront. Directly across a few hundred feet of water lay Shell Island, so named because it had the Shell Oil refinery and storage tanks on it. This was a prime objective of Japanese bombings and strafing during the early days of the war. Other military objectives were ships lying in the harbor and harbor installations. There was no guarantee that raiding Japanese planes could hit Shell Island and miss us. As time went on, we found by experience that the Japs more often missed their target than they hit it. Our office was one of the hot spots of the harbor. Things were always interesting there.

One afternoon a priest named Father Sheridan, who had donned the uniform to become a chaplain, was in the office at about 4:00. A Filipino soldier hurriedly brought a stack of telegrams while we were talking. I received them and started to lay them aside; however, on the top telegram I saw, fleetingly, the words "24 planes." I immediately gave more attention to the telegrams. Twenty-four planes had appeared over the northern end of the island of Negros. The next two telegrams came from points a little farther down the coast, nearer Cebu. The soldier appeared again with another telegram. This time the figure was 18; others had just said many. I knew all I wanted to know by this time: a large group of planes—Japanese, of coursewere headed toward Cebu!

"Father, you mentioned earlier in our conversation—did you not say that you had to hurry to a wedding?"

"No, I . . . "

"I am quite certain you said you were in a hurry to get away from here in the next ten minutes."

"If you are busy, I'll leave."

"Take a look at this telegram." I showed him the telegram that mentioned the large number of planes. Meantime, I picked up the phone connected with Gen. Sharp's G-2 office and Capt. Cosper answered.

"Hello, Duane. Got a surprise for you. A package of 24 pigeons just flew over the north end of Negros headed for the coop on top of your office. From the rate they are flying, you had better spread your umbrella in 10 minutes to catch the droppings. Get me?"

"I get you."

Bang went the receiver and I looked at Father Sheridan.

"Captain, I think you are right. I do have a wedding and I am leaving at once."

With that the chaplain took off and I received another stack of telegrams concerning the approaching planes. The last report we had of those planes, they had left the east coast of Negros just opposite the north end of Cebu and were headed straight east. Those planes never did attack Cebu City. Since it was only about an hour before dark, we believed that they must have headed back to a possible base in the Palau Islands, 600 miles east of Mindanao.

One of the chief troubles we had during these air raids was to keep radio operators at their posts. As soon as one operator got hold of a message saying planes were approaching, it got around to all of the other operators and they would want to leave. The time came when I found it necessary to go stand in the door of the operator's room. Under my supervision, they would remain at their posts.

For assistants on this job, I had two American enlisted men—Cpl. Eckhart and Sgt. Dale E. Dyches. They were both good men and performed excellent work. I put them in charge of the operating room and they divided the 24 hours of duty between themselves. The way those two lads worked together was a grand lesson in cooperation between individuals. One or the other of them was in the operations room all the time. I helped them when I could, which wasn't often (as my day was 18–20 hours in length). It was they who actually read the telegrams, marked them as to priorities, and eliminated the excess ones, preventing jamming of the wires. If there was anything that they were in doubt about, they brought it to me and I made the decision.

During these first days of the war, some of the civilian population were frantic and attempted to send all manner of messages of this and that to relatives all over the islands. Many of the messages were about nonessentials. The message that I remember distinctly had originated in Cebu City. It had gotten as far as the operations room where it was stopped. It was from some local politician concerning the arrival of two fighting cocks from one of the other islands. Somehow or another, through the native operators, the old boy had found out that the message had been stopped, so he came to see me about it. I assured him the message would go through with his priority classification. The truth of the matter was that the wires were so jammed with essentials that the priority rating, under which his message was classified, was never used. These telegrams were filed away and later sent after the rush was over. In order to get rid of him, I took him into the operator's room, found his message and placed it at the top of the priority list, which as I said before was not acted upon until some time later. He then went away happy with my personal assurance that his message would be sent as soon as possible. Of course, before the day was over, it had been buried by other messages of that same priority rating.

As soon as I got rid of this local politician, I immediately traced down the channels through which he had learned that his telegram had been held up. Upon asking the people involved, all of them Filipinos, why they gave out such information to the public, I got the answer. "But, sir, we do not give information to the public. This man is a *politico* and a great friend of the assemblyman in Manila. We do not dare make him angry or we will lose our jobs." I assured them they would lose their jobs faster if they committed that offense again. I went back to my office muttering something about Filipino politics being as foul as American politics.

Another instance I had of information appearing through the grapevine which authorities wanted suppressed, was concerning the sinking of the inter-island line named *Corregidor*. This ship was the second ship loaded in Manila with supplies for the Southern Islands. In addition to the Army personnel, there was a large number of civilians aboard the ship who were trying to get out of Luzon to some safer area.

No one knew just how many souls were aboard. The ship started out from Manila one afternoon and, on reaching the mine field off the island of Corregidor, hit a mine which blew its bottom out, causing it to sink within a period of a very few minutes. There were a few survivors who were able to swim ashore after being in the water for several hours. They told a tale of swift destruction and sudden death in the waters of Manila Bay. Nobody seems to know just who was responsible, but, to say the least, this ship packed to almost standing room sank with almost 100 percent loss of life. Naturally, this was considered terrible tragedy by the entire island. The message was flashed from Manila to Cebu over the Bureau of Posts wires, where it was immediately handed to me. Realizing the commotion this news would cause, in this already chaotic situation, I immediately censored the message except for the proper military authorities and sent the copy to Gen. Sharp's headquarters. In a few minute, I received a call from the G-2 office.

"Miner, what in the hell do you mean by letting news of the *Corregidor* sinking get by you?"

"That message was brought to me as soon as I arrived in this office. It was a personal message from individual to individual and I stopped it at once with instructions to my entire force to say absolutely nothing about it, since there was enough bad news and rumors floating around as it was. I shall immediately look into the matter and warn all personnel that severe punishment will be dealt to any and all who give out restricted information. The only way I can account for this news being abroad so early is the fact it may have been broadcast in a news flash over one of the Manila radio stations, since it is known to the public over there. There is no reason why it couldn't be broadcast in the news."

Wherever that news came from, I don't know. But it must have been a news broadcast, because very shortly thereafter a large number of telegrams came through from various places to relatives in Manila asking if certain individuals were on the *Corregidor* or were safe, etc. We did what we could to keep the situation in hand, but it was several days before we let the newspapers carry the stories.

Previously, I have mentioned two enlisted men in the Bureau of Posts office who helped me as assistant censors—Cpl. Eckhart and Sgt. Dale Dyches. I don't remember much about Cpl. Eckhart other than that he was a handsome young fellow, likable and a good soldier. I may be wrong, but I have the impression that he was assigned to the 31st Infantry of Manila. He went to Mindanao with Gen. Sharp. He surrendered in Malaybalay, worked in the rice fields and the plantations of Davao until February 24, 1944, when he was sent on the Lasang detail. The Lasang detail was aboard a prison ship north of Zamboanga on September 8, 1944, when the ship was torpedoed by one of our subs. There were 83 survivors out of 750 officers and men. I do not know what the fate of Cpl. Eckhart was other than that he was supposed to be aboard this ship at the time of its sinking.

The other, Sgt. Dale D. Dyches, was tall, lean and a Texan. His father was a minister at Goldwaithe, TX. I believe Dale was a career man in the Army, but what his unit was in the Philippines, I do not know. Sgt. Dyches also went to Mindanao with Gen. Sharp and surrendered at Malaybalay. He was with the group in Davao, but instead of going to Lasang, he was one of the enlisted men that remained with the main group of Davao POWs. He was shipped to Luzon with the main group in June 1944. Instead of going to Cabanatuan, he went with the group of enlisted men who were shipped on north to Japan. He survived our air attacks on the Japanese mainland and got back to the Philippines after the war was over. I saw him once at the 29th replacement center near Manila. He was looking fine considering that he was a POW. I later heard from him back in the States and he was then happily married and on leave at Fort Worth, TX.

It didn't take long after I became censor to see that our location on the waterfront was a bad one in every way, whether we looked at it from the standpoint of continued operation or personal safety. It was in the tallest building on the Cebu waterfront and from its appearance, a most likely target for raiding by Japanese planes. Although the Bureau of Posts was on the second floor and there were two and perhaps three floors above it, I did not consider the Bureau of Posts office very well protected. The thing to do then was to move it away from the waterfront into some less conspicuous building back in the city. Maj. Jordan agreed wholeheartedly with me after our first air raid. Accordingly, we both got busy, located a place in one of the downtown theaters and Maj. Jordan arranged with the quartermaster to take over the theater for government use.

Maj. Jordan came into the office one noon and said, "Well, Miner, we sure are lucky. We are going to move from the waterfront pretty damn quick."

"It can't be too quick for me. I can just see those red . . . pigeons dropping eggs around this place. I for one don't want to get splattered with what falls. It isn't healthy."

"Well, we can get under way this afternoon."

"Okay, when you go downstairs, see the man in charge of the B of P and persuade him now is the time to move, not *mañana*."

"Will do. I am on my way."

"Okay, see you after chow."

The next four days were full of feverish haste. We had to prepare the theater in the center of the city to receive the equipment. We had to lay wires, both telephone and telegraph, and have them prepared before we moved the sets from their present seat of operations. We arranged to set up in this manner. The radio and telegraph key receivers and transmitters were placed down on the main floor of the theater. Maj. Jordan and I had our offices on the mezzanine floor. The lobby was used by the public for sending telegrams. When we finally completed the transfer, we had a very comfortable setup in spite of the hardships under which we operated.

Those few days while we were moving were days of anxiety. The enemy planes would appear every once in a while, or by messages we censored and received through the air warning system, we knew that enemy planes were daily at work somewhere in the islands. Sometimes, they dropped their bombs not too far away. I thought we would never get the B of P moved to its new location. The Filipinos in charge were not inclined to be in much of a hurry, for we would ask them to get something accomplished before the end of the day and they would reply, "Oh, tomorrow, tomorrow." This would make the major and me as mad as hornets. They didn't seem to realize that our office was in danger. Their attitude shows the typical philosophy of the tropics—if you don't get something done today, don't worry about it, there is always a tomorrow. He was right. There was a tomorrow, but it was filled with dead men, thousands of his kind, and the reason for their death was procrastination. They were simply too slow to move out of the way of oncoming, clearly perceived attacks.

It was with a sigh of relief that we finally accomplished the task of moving our offices.

About the time that we got our Bureau of Posts moved into the theater, Christmas 1941 arrived, and what a Christmas! I think all of us had the feeling that it would be our last Christmas. It was, for several. In spite of the feeling of foreboding, there was a Christmas dinner under way. Charlotte Martin, wife of Capt. C. J. Martin, both of them old-time residents of Cebu, prepared the turkey dinner for Gen. Sharp and all of his staff. Charlotte had been doing some work in Gen. Sharp's office and she felt so sorry for the boys that she threw a party for us. It really was a grand and glorious party, since we had been out in the jungle and were going back to the jungle. All of us carried on our duties during the day, left our posts of duty in proper care and slipped away to the party for an hour or so. Many of us had arranged to attend in relays exactly the same manner in which we would have done to the ordinary mess hall for our evening meal. This was an old-fashioned American Christmas dinner with turkey and cranberry sauce. It was served by Filipinos and the lights were candles.

There was only one emblem of American womanhood present, Mrs. Martin. I think every man there saw in her a resemblance to his wife or sweetheart back in the States. Not all the evening was devoted to pleasure. Officers would slip in, remain a little while and slip away again. Others would come in and take their places. At this stage of the game, with Jap landings occurring in Luzon, we felt we could expect a landing somewhere in the Southern Islands at any time. In my own case, I had been trying for several days to get some transportation in the form of a truck, so that when invasion came, I could get some of my equipment away for use in the hills. At this time there was, working in the quartermaster pool, an Englishman named Fred Pipe. He had become a good friend of mine and before the dinner was over, I was telling him my troubles.

"You know I'd hate to see that invasion occur tonight. I don't even have a bicycle on which to make a get-away with any of the equipment. There are several good transmitters and receivers among the radio sets. I guess I'd have to evacuate them on my back from the looks of things."

"Do you expect an invasion tonight?"

"No, I don't. There was a new invasion in northern Luzon today, which you already know about. There are no reports of any boats within unloading distance of here tonight. Yet, the general seems to be as jittery as a butterfly on a cake of Jell-O. I am just a lowly captain, so what I expect doesn't count, I guess. I still wish I could get some transportation. Since you work here, why don't you fix me up with something?"

"We do have a truck down at the pool which consists of a cab and a flat bed. There are no sides to it. We have a driver with it and if you think it would do you any good, we will go get it and have it stand by at the theater."

"It would really take a load off my mind to have that truck parked in front of the theater."

"We can go get it at once and be back only slightly late for the next course. The motor pool isn't far from here."

"Let's go."

Arising, I excused us to Mrs. Martin by saying, "Will you please excuse us for about 15 minutes as we have some work to check on. We will be back before the next course is over."

With that, we left the dinner, passed through the double set of blackout curtains and into the night.

"Dong, pssst! Jose, this is Pipe."

"Here, sir."

"Count to 10 out loud, so we can tell where you are. We want to use your car."

"Uno, dos, tres . . . "

By the time the driver had counted to 10, Pipe and I had found the car, a blacker shadow in the black of the night.

"Jose, drive us back to the Motor Pool and go slowly. Don't run over anybody."

"Yes, sir."

For the next five minutes or so, we slowly twisted and turned through the dark streets of Cebu, ending up at the Motor Pool. Pipe located the truck with its driver seated in the cab. He woke the driver up and told him, "You follow us to the theater. If you get separated from us in the dark, you go to the theater . . . *sigue, sigue*. We will meet you there soon. You wait for us. Understand? Wait for us."

"Yes, sir, I understand."

"Okay, you follow."

We again took off through the night in Pipe's car with the truck following us. We soon arrived at the theater and found the truck still with us.

"Driver, you will park your truck here in front of this theater all night. You are to stand by here. You can sleep, you can lie down at the back of the truck, but you stay here all night. Perhaps, very suddenly, Capt. Miner will want to move some boxes to a bodega. You then take Capt. Miner where he wants to go. Understand?"

"Yes, sir. I stand by for Capt. Miner."

"That is good. You understand. You stand by for Capt. Miner. If he doesn't come, you sleep all night. If he does come, he will tell you where to go. Only Capt. Miner will tell you where to go. If anyone wants your truck, you tell them to find Capt. Miner. If you leave before Capt. Miner tells you to, you will go like Moro '*juramentado*.' That would not be good for you. Understand?"

Juramentado is a Spanish word, used in the Philippines, to describe the fanatical insanity Muslims work themselves into when they run 'amok' killing people, anybody in sight until they in turn are killed. The victims are usually non-Muslims. The Muslims believe they will go to the Muslim heaven if they die killing infidels.

With that warning, Pipe and I returned to the Martins' Christmas dinner, having been gone a total of 30 minutes.

During the next hour we finished Christmas dinner, after which Gen. Sharp offered a prayer and there was a sad attempt at singing. The general called the party off very early, much to the disappointment of all concerned. We then returned to our various posts, thankful that we had had an old-fashioned Christmas dinner in the atmosphere of Christmas carols, instead of a prayer on the battlefield as a great many of the boys in Bataan had for their Christmas.

There were several local air raids in Cebu during the first days of the war, most of them having two military objectives: first, the gasoline and oil supplies by the various international oil companies such as the Shell Co. The second objective was the boats in the harbor and their harbor installations. There was also a Proctor and Gamble Copra Factory at Opon, Mactan Island. The Nips never made Cebu a constant objective of raids, but every few days, they would send a photo ship down to take pictures. If there was an inter-island ship in the harbor or quite a bit of small shipping, likely as not, 24 to 48 hours after photo Joe had made his rounds, a bunch of Nip bombers would come over and bomb the port area.

One day, shortly after we had finished moving the Bureau of Posts to its new location in the theater, I viewed a light bombing and strafing attack from the roof of the theater. I had worked the night shift the night before and had just gotten to sleep around 10:00 A.M. That was the signal for the air raid. Shortly after the air raid siren sounded, I heard the sound of planes. I knew that there would be no sleep for me during the raid. Once up, I climbed to the roof of the theater where I could get a view of the city from the mountains to the harbor. At my back, lying at the foot of the mountains, was the Lasang Air Field. To the front, I could see the curve of the harbor with Shell Island on the right and away to my left in front lay Mactan Island and the Proctor and Gamble Copra Factory at Opon. In this particular raid there were three light bombers. After dropping their bombs around Opon and circling the harbor a few times, they headed across the city for Lasang Air Field, strafing the city as they went. Once over the airport, they proceeded to fly low over the field and strafe all installations on and around the field. I could see the planes swoop each in their turn and level off just about even with the roofs of the city. Then they would climb until they reached altitude enough to make another swoop on the airfield. About the time the planes would level off and begin to climb, I would hear the sound of their machine guns. About an hour after the bombing raid was over, I went out to the airfield to have a look at the damage. The hangars, the barracks, and dummy installations were all riddled with machine gun holes. Luckily, the Philippine Air Corps with its two or three little training planes had moved out lock, stock, and barrel and was now located under some tall trees half a mile away. No damage was done to either planes or personnel. This was just a minor raid; nevertheless, it had its effect on morale.

Toward the last of December, Gen. Sharp moved his headquarters from Cebu City to a place designated as Camp X located on the Talisay-Toledo road. The forestry maps had this area designated as Camp T. There in the high valley just under the divide on the western side, the Philippine Forestry had an experimental area. Gen. Sharp moved his headquarters to this area as it had cover from observation from both the air and ground and plenty of water. The place could be reached from either side of the island by this one highway. On the western side the road up the mountain was more or less gradual, though full of hairpin turns. The road on the eastern slope was altogether of a different nature. It was carved out of the side of a very narrow precipitous, winding canyon. Three-fourths of this highway up the canyon was only a one-way road. There was a control station on each end with one in the middle. The traffic was controlled by the use of telephones connecting the three control stations. We generally had to wait at one end of these stations, both going up and coming down. All in all, the place was fairly inaccessible as far as motor transportation was concerned. By foot, it could be reached from all four directions.

Gen. Sharp moved his headquarters up to Camp X leaving Col. Irving C. Scudder in command of the Cebu Provincial Brigade, which was formed for the defense of the island of Cebu. During all this shifting of personnel, I continued as censor of the Island of Cebu.

Since the general had moved out into the mountains, a courier service had to be established between Gen. Sharp's headquarters and Cebu City, still the seat of communication. This courier service was established and operated by 2nd Lt. Paul D. Phillips. Paul had quite a lot of fun, or should we say grief, keeping an efficient messenger service operating over the 24 miles of dangerous, steep canyon road to Gen. Sharp's camp. He evidently did a good job, because he survived the war and was promoted to lieutenant colonel.

The middle of the morning around January 1, 1942, I got a message to report to Gen. Sharp at Camp X. Nothing more was said, no more, no less. I was in a quandary. Should I or should I not take all my baggage? If the general wanted to see me concerning the censorship as he frequently had in the past, I would be back to my post of censorship duty within a matter of a few hours. If he wanted me for something else, God alone knew where I would go. When I reported to Gen. Sharp, I took all my belongings with me. Luckily I did, for within a few minutes I found myself operations officer of a Filipino Corps Message Center located in Camp X. There was a tense air of secrecy about the place. Nobody would say anything, yet anybody bright enough to run a Message Center could see that a move was imminent.

Capt. Chrisman who had been running the Message Center showed me how to operate the encoding and decoding devices.

"Well, Chris, is that all there is to it? Just simply substituting words for letter combinations on this little cylinder?"

"Yep, that's all there is to it. It is all very simple."

"Did you see that loaf of bread on the table at breakfast this morning? It is all very simple to cut and eat a slice of bread, yet a hell of a lot went into the making of that loaf of bread. What is the background of all this Message Center work? I need a background to understand this, Capt. Chrisman."

"The best I can do for you is to leave you this field manual and tell you to read up on cryptography in the front of the Philippine Army code book. The Filipinos here will show you the rest."

"Okay, if that is all there is to it, I'll see what I can do."

The next day at noon, I found myself in full charge of that Message Center. In fact, I was soon to be commanding officer of Camp X.

I learned my cryptography the hard way, by experience only. Because of the nature of the Filipino people and their inadequate use of our language, I had to check everything that came and went out for accuracy.

Gen. Sharp had moved to Mindanao leaving me in charge of his Force Communications Station on the island of Cebu. At that time, the communications station was his only contact with Gen. Mac Arthur.

Capt. Chrisman had gone with Gen. Sharp to run the Message Center at the forward command post designated as Camp Y. These first few days of running that Message Center with Filipino soldiers and not knowing anything about the job gave me merry hell. It took a lot of intensive work and long hours to get used to the ordinary procedure.

Gen. Sharp soon decided that Cebu was far too small an island on which to carry or wage a defensive campaign. Naturally, the most logical place was Mindanao directly to the south. Mindanao is the second largest island in the Philippine group. It is quite monstrous and has quite a variety of vegetation as well as a variety of terrain. He had left Cebu City because it was a military objective that was illogical to defend and he was determined to leave the island of Cebu in secrecy.

With Gen. Sharp's headquarters and most of the troops on Mindanao, the Visayas assumed a secondary importance in the defense of the south. In the event of attack it would be virtually impossible to reinforce any of the islands in that group from Mindanao. Each of the six defended islands—Cebu, Panay, Negros, Leyte, Samar and Bohol—was now dependent upon its own garrison and resources to meet a Japanese invasion. The organization of the Visayas-Mindanao Force established early in January lasted only one month. In early February, in an effort to facilitate the delivery of supplies expected shortly from Australia, USAFFE assumed direct control of the garrisons in Panay and Mindoro, both a part of Gen. Sharp's command. A month later, the remaining Visayas garrisons were separated from Gen. Sharp's command. The five garrisons in the Visayas were then organized into the Visayan Force and placed under Brig. Gen. G. Chynoweth, who had commanded on Panay. Gen. Sharp and Gen. Chynoweth reported directly to higher headquarters in Corregidor.

From time to time, I have mentioned the use of government transportation. This transportation was not regular Army, but consisted of civilian trucks and cars acquired by the quartermaster for military purposes. In Cebu, the Army had taken over whole lines of buses and same on all other islands. In that manner, the Army was able to move supplies and troops from place to place.

Immediately after the beginning of the war, Gen. Sharp started moving all types of supplies back into the interior of the island. He concentrated heavily on food and clothing. He couldn't concentrate on such military supplies as guns and ammunition because these weren't to be had. I have the impression that by January 10, the troops on the island of Cebu had about 10 rounds of ammunition each. A lot of food and clothing was moved into the mountains and was just taken over by the government and held in warehouses so that it would be easily available for shipping to the Southern Islands.

Lt. Col. Marcus Boulware was in charge of the food transportation into the hills. He worked day and night from around December 15 until after Christmas to accomplish this. He ended up going to the hospital due to exhaustion.

The job was too big for just one man. He had to transport the goods with Filipino labor on Filipino time with an American army in back of him saying you will have this accomplished by such and such a date, and that accomplished by such and such a date. An American battalion under American officers could have accomplished the work under American schedule, but one man using Filipino labor was just out of luck. The colonel never fully recovered from the strain of this period of duty. It seemed to have affected his heart and it troubled him all through prison. His bad heart was undoubtedly a contributing factor to his death en route to Japan.

Shortly after Col. Boulware had gotten a lot of the food back into the hills, they had to go get it again, bring it back to Cebu and ship it to Mindanao. He had some fun.

Another American officer who had been connected with supplies was Lt. Col. Rufus H. Rogers. He came into the Finance Office shortly after January 1942 in order to get some pay so he could live. Gen. Sharp was in conference with Lt. Col. Paul S. Beard of the Finance Office. Col. Rogers used to tell this story in prison camp.

"I found Gen. Sharp in there with Col. Beard, the finance officer. They were talking in low tones. They looked up and saw me and went into a closer huddle. Pretty soon the general beckoned to me to come over where they were. I went."

"You are it."

"I am what?"

"The new finance officer."

"You have the wrong man. My branch is the infantry."

"You are the new finance officer now."

"I don't know finance from flour sacks."

"Col. Beard will tell you about finance."

"Yes, sir."

Col. Rogers concluded, "That is the way I became the finance officer of Cebu Island. I just walked into the room and, presto, I became a Buck Rogers finance officer."

Col. Beard taught finance to Col. Rogers the rest of that forenoon and then took off for Camp X with several bags and trunks full of pesos to accompany Gen. Sharp.

On the night that Gen. Sharp left, among the officers left to follow him was Maj. Max Weil. He was headquarters commandant for Gen. Sharp. He was to follow in a day or two with the headquarters troops. The night that Gen. Sharp left, I spent in the company of Maj. Weil. He was very kind in telling me all that he could about the installations of Camp X regarding the caves, tunnels, and supplies since I was to take over when he left. After he finished discussing business, we talked about our future and the immediate war. We both agreed it looked pretty dark. I am afraid I was pretty blue that night, although I had been left behind to run a vital installation. I had the feeling of being deserted and left in one of the hottest spots in the Philippines. It took me some weeks to get used to the idea of "Well, what the hell! You got to go sometime. If I go now, early in the game, I am going to miss a lot of grief and I never did like trouble."

In the days that followed, I was very thankful that my new work of communication officer kept me mentally occupied every minute of the day. When I did sleep, it was because of exhaustion. More than one night I fell asleep at my desk and awoke in the dim hours of the morning slumped in my chair stiff and cold. I have found that physical labor is often the answer to a mind under mental stress. One of the other men Gen. Sharp left behind for a few days was his chief of staff, Col. John W. Thompson. While Gen. Sharp was moving to Mindanao, there were other troop movements to Mindanao from other Southern Islands. Among these movements was the shifting of the 81st Infantry Regiment from Wright, Samar, to Surigao, Mindanao. I believe that Col. Ben Hur Chastine was in command of this operation. The troops had to be loaded on a boat at or near Catbalogan, Samar, where they sailed down the straits between Samar and Leyte to some point on the Surigao Peninsula. Because of a late start, practically all of this troop movement was made in the daylight by a convoy of two boats. All of us, Col. Thompson in particular, were on pins and needles the entire day. About 11:00 A.M., as I remember, we got a report of three Nip planes flying back and forth along the north coast of Leyte and then down the west coast of the same island. They did this for about an hour and then went back north to Luzon. They didn't appear again that day. From the reports of these three planes flying back and forth along the Leyte coast, we knew they were out scouting for something. They had evidently expected troop movements in the Southern Islands. They even guessed the unit and the island involved (or were guessing). But they didn't guess the right route of the troop movement.

Col. Thompson really sweated blood all that day and night. Early the next morning, one of the first radiograms we received was the following: "Two units of transportation safe at Surigao. Signed: Ben Hur Chastine."

Col. Thompson wiped the sweat off his brow as he read that radiogram and said, "Well, this is what I have been waiting for. Yesterday when those planes were flying up and down the coast I was afraid they might find the boats."

On the third day after the departure of Gen. Sharp, I started sending out call signals for his Mindanao radio station. Late in the afternoon we got an answer. After an hour or so of traffic between the two stations for adjustment, the new station 6RC was ready for business. I wasn't satisfied that this was the station I was seeking. Therefore, I determined to make it identify itself in a manner that would satisfy me. To do this, I required from the new station some inconsequential non-military information. There was still at Camp X an American corporal left behind because he was in Cebu drawing his pay when the headquarters left. He was to follow on the next boat. I reasoned that somebody in the headquarters would know who was left behind at Camp X and why. Accordingly, I wired to 6RC the following message: "For purpose of identification, what is the name of the American corporal left in Camp X because he was drawing his pay in Cebu?"

The new station, 6RC, was silent for over an hour. I began to think it was an enemy station. Finally, the radio silence was broken by the following message: "Cpl. Fitzjohn was left in Camp X because he was in Cebu after his pay." The answer established their authenticity with me and I then permitted military traffic to pass over the keys.

The next few days were full and busy ones for me. I was learning a new business. Maj. Max Weil had left with the headquarters troops. Col. Thompson had left to join Gen. Sharp and Col. Scudder, who had been at Camp X for only a day or so until Gen. Sharp left, going back to Cebu City. I now found myself alone, in charge of a Force Communication Station and commander of Camp X installations and supply dump.

I spent most of my time with the radio work, as that was what I was there for. All other things were mere incidentals. For quite some time I did all the coding and encoding work for Col. Scudder in addition to my regular traffic for Gen. Sharp. As the weeks went by, Gen. Sharp would radio for my Filipino Army signal corpsmen. One at a time! I got so low on technical help that I finally complained. The result was that the cryptography work was done in the Cebu headquarters and I was handling only traffic for Gen. Sharp. As he got other contacts with Gen. Mac Arthur on Corregidor, my traffic lessened.

As the military personnel under me were transferred to Gen. Sharp's installations in Mindanao, I had to find civilian personnel to help me operate. To do this I got hold of four men. Three were English and one Scottish. Naturally, with their background, they were all dependable. One by the name of Fred Pipe, a big six-footer, was more American than English. He worked for the Lever Brothers Co. out of their New York office. Pipe had worked for the Motor Pool in Cebu City up to the time that Gen. Sharp left. He was now very willing to help me. The other Englishman, William L. Hocking, was a graduate of Oxford and was working for a commercial company in the islands. The third Englishman was a British first lieutenant, Lawrie-Smith, who, likewise, had been a civilian with a commercial job before the beginning of the war. All three British at the beginning of the war had contacted their country's agency asking to be assigned to duty with the U.S. Army in the Philippines. This, of course, was quite an unusual request to make of the hide-bound British Army. However, the men held the rank in the British reserve and white officers were at a premium in the islands. I don't know whether these assignments became official or not in the British army, but I do know the men performed the services commensurate with their rank.

A little later, I got two Norwegians to come and work for me at the camp. One was a cook and the other, named Jens K. Jensen, had been a ship's carpenter. These two men had been aboard a Norwegian freighter shortly after the war started which was sailing in the Pacific about 200 miles east of the Surigao Peninsula in northern Mindanao. Some Jap planes came over and bombed the ship, sinking it. They did not even know that there was a war on. The ship didn't go down too fast so most of the crew got aboard lifeboats and set sail for Mindanao. In due time, they reached the island and, finally, Cebu City, where the Norwegian consul took care of the sailors. Most of them expressed their desire to help the American war effort against the Japs. They were used in small groups here and there around the island.

Returning to the British subjects, I don't know what happened to the Scotchman after the surrender of the islands. Lt. Lawrie-Smith was killed during the invasion of Cebu on duty with Filipino troops. Lt. Bill Hocking escaped to the island of Leyte during the invasion and later surrendered on Leyte with the American officers. Capt. Fred Pipe remained in my service at Camp X until he was called to Minadanao to work under, I believe, Lt. Col. Robert Johnson whom I have mentioned before. Pipe surrendered with the Americans in Mindanao, but because of some technical standing concerning his commission, he was interned by the Japs as a civilian instead of a prisoner of war. Pipe survived the war. I don't know what happened to my Norwegian cook, but I do know what happened to the ship's carpenter, Jens K. Jensen. He worked for me as civilian in charge of Camp X up to a few days before the invasion of Cebu. At that time Capt.

William English, headquarters commandant, took over the camp and I became communications officer of the Visayan force. Jensen worked for Capt. English until after the invasion. During the invasion, and later, he became engaged in guerrilla activities. Jensen assumed responsibility and was commissioned 1st lieutenant quartermaster in the American Army by Gen. Chynoweth. Lt. Jensen shared my quarters with me at Camp X for weeks before the invasion. During the evenings and at mealtime we got to know each other quite well. He often expressed the desire to become a U.S. citizen, even in those dark days following the American defeat. This Norwegian stoutly maintained that there was only one end to the war, an American victory. He often said that he wanted to be in on the finish. During the course of the war, there were two supply ships from Australia that succeeded in getting into Cebu with supplies. Both were unloaded and got safely out.

Jensen had an opportunity to get to Australia when each of these ships sailed. He refused to go on the grounds that the American Army needed him. From my point of view, he certainly was needed. To this day, I don't know what I would have done without him. He was efficient, reliable and responsible. When the island of Cebu surrendered, he surrendered as a 1st lieutenant in the American Army and took the following years of imprisonment as any other American officer. He survived the war and went to the U.S. on board the same transport with me. He was still a Norwegian citizen and his rank as a 1st lieutenant in the American Army had been authenticated. He was set to go all out to secure his American citizenship once he landed in the States. To this end, I gave him a statement of service and the highest personal recommendations. I can only say that I wish the average American had as much patriotism and stability of character as Lt. Jensen. The U.S. should be proud to have Lt. Jensen for a citizen.

With Gen. Sharp's departure for Mindanao around the first week of January 1942, Col. Irving C. Scudder became commander of the island of Cebu with a provisional brigade of Filipino troops under him. With the exceptions of my Force Communication Station, every military and civilian installation on the island was directly under his command in respect to defense. Col. John D. Cook, IMC, was in command of the port area for operation and I was responsible directly to Gen. Sharp for the operation of my Force Communications Station.

Col. Scudder's staff consisted of Maj. Ernest V. Jorden; Maj. Lyles V. Hardin; Lt. Col. Marcus Boulware; Capt. William English; Capt. Russell H. Cracraft; and assistants to his staff, 2nd Lt. George M. Wightman, British; and 1st Lt. (then sergeant) Doyle R. Armstrong. Maj. Jorden was a reserve officer whose home was in Milledgeville, GA.

Maj. Jorden had worked with me as the air-warning officer in Cebu. When Col. Scudder formed his staff, Maj. Jorden became his brigade plans and training officer and Maj. Hardin took over the censorship duties.

Maj. Hardin came from Rock Hill, SC. He had attended Walford College before coming out to the islands. Maj. Hardin was six feet, rotund and had a wonderful sense of humor. His personality radiated to all that were around him. We never thought of him as Capt. or Maj. Hardin, but he was affectionately known to all as Tiny. His happy-go-lucky smile would cheer the bluest of us. Tiny was a captain during most of the war, but after the invasion, he took over the command of the newly formed MP regiment and did a wonderful job in the guerrilla warfare. That is where he earned his rank of major. Tiny surrendered with Gen. Chynoweth and went to Davao Penal Colony. On February 24, 1944, Maj. Hardin went to Lasang as one of Col. Rogers' barracks leaders. On September 8, 1944, he was killed aboard the prison ship when the boat was torpedoed.

Lt. Col. Marcus Boulware was still in charge of special supplies on the island of Cebu although he was not the brigade officer.

Col. William R. English came from South Carolina. I believe the town was Spartanburg. Bill had been married a short time before he came over and was quite disgusted that the war had come when it did. As I recall Bill was the brigade S-4 and it was through him that I went to get my supplies. He didn't surrender on the island of Cebu when it fell. At that particular time, he was on a special mission for Gen. Chynoweth. When the surrender order came through he surrendered with the American officers on that island. Later he was brought to Cebu as a prisoner, kept in our prison a few hours and shipped on south to Davao. Bill endured the hardships of Davao and in June 1944 was one of the groups moved to Cabanatuan on Luzon. He stayed in Luzon, spending some time in Bilibid prison until December 13, 1944, when, as part of the *Oryoku Maru* detail, he was shipped to Japan. He survived the bombings of December 14, 15, and 16 when our ship went down in Olongapo, Luzon. He was then shipped up to Takao in southern Formosa where he survived a second bombing which killed a great many of us. Finally on board the third prison ship of that trip, January 23, 1945, Bill died from dysentery, dehydration, malnutrition and exposure while still en route to Japan. Bill was an exceptionally good friend of mine. One of the most heart-wrenching things that happened to me was to see him beg for water on that trip. Somewhere along the line, during that trip, Bill had acquired an extra canteen from one of his friends who had died toward the last of the trip when we were getting a half-pint of water per man every other day. He had no use for this extra canteen. But this time he was so weak, such a skeleton of bones and so helpless that he was in the hospital area of the ship's hold. I happened to pass by him on my way to the latrine area and he caught hold of my hand. His tongue was so badly swollen from lack of water that he could hardly talk. He pulled me down to his face and in a thick, halting, hoarse whisper, said, "Bill, will you take this canteen [fumbling with the canteen] and trade it for two spoonfuls of water for me? Just two spoonfuls, Bill." I replied that I would try. I had no water for myself or I would have given it to him. I had no luck in trading his canteen for any amount of water, no matter how small. I can still remember the look in his eyes when I returned his canteen to him saying that nobody had any water to trade. At that late stage in our situation, material things had no value except food and clothing.

Capt. Russell Cracraft worked in the censor's office with Maj. Hardin from the time the latter took over the duties of censor. They were together clear through the invasion of Cebu by the Japs. Somewhere during the battle they were separated and during the guerrilla activities Capt. Cracraft was with me up in the Salambam forest. Cracraft surrendered in Cebu, went to Mindanao, and worked in the Davao Penal Colony until February 24, 1944, when he went on the Lasang detail as assistant barracks leader to Maj. Hardin.

Capt. Cracraft died at the same time as Maj. Hardin due to the torpedoing of their prison ship on September 8, 1944. I don't know much of Capt. Cracraft's life before he came to Cebu, but I have the impression that his home state was West Virginia.

Capt. William English's assistant brigade S-4 was 2nd Lt. George M. Wightman, who was British. He was another of the British who assumed duties and responsibilities of an officer in the American Army. His commission was pending. Wightman had lived in the islands all his life. He knew the native psychology and their ways. He surrendered with the Cebu group on May 17, 1942, and went to Davao with the group in October 1942. He stayed in Davao until February 24, 1944, when he became part of the detail sent to Lasang. On September 8, 1944, his prison ship was sunk off Lily Point just north of Zamboanga, Mindanao. Just what George's fate was during that sinking, I can't say.

Sgt. Doyle R. Armstrong was the chief of Col. Scudder's encoding and decoding center. He had been an enlisted man in the 31st Infantry, if my memory is correct. On September 1, 1941, he went to duty with the Philippine Army in southern Negros. While there, he contracted dysentery and was sent to Cebu City for hospitalization. The war broke out while he was still in the hospital. When he was returned to duty he was assigned to Brigade Headquarters and remained in that capacity until after the invasion when he was commissioned a 1st lieutenant in the Signal Corps. He surrendered with the Cebu group and went with it to the Davao Penal Colony, from where he went to Lasang in February 1944. I don't know what his fate was (other than he was missing) as a result of the sinking of the Lasang detail prison ship.

These men comprised Col. Scudder's Provisional Brigade Staff. There were other American officers with various commands and duties over the island and quite a number of civilians working for the Army who were later commissioned. Those will be mentioned from time to time as I proceed with events.

I won't deal too much with the details of our preparation for the invasion. To say the least, we didn't have much in the way of equipment. There were only a few machine guns on the island and, as I recall, the entire 5,000 Filipino troops had only 81mm mortars (this may be incorrect). To begin with, those who were armed with rifles only had 10 or 12 rounds of ammunition per rifle and the labor battalions were armed only with bolos. There wasn't much of a defense we could put up when invasion came and we knew it, but we were determined to make that initial invasion as costly as possible to the Japs. It was not until Bataan fell that the Japs really turned their attention to the Southern Islands. Prior to that time, they merely captured key points, which would cut off our shipping lanes of supply. They then bypassed us for bigger game in the South Pacific.

From time to time, the Japanese would send large groups of bombers over Cebu City to bomb shipping and supply dumps. I remember two specific instances when the number of bombers was 18 or 20. Another phase was the sending of Japanese cruisers around the island of Cebu to shell and terrorize the people. Finally, on April 10, their task force arrived off shore and landed early on April 11.

FIVE

PERSONNEL IN CEBU

B EFORE I GO INTO THE EVENTS OF THE JAPANESE INVASION OF
CEBU AND THE BATTLE THAT FOLLOWED, I AM GOING TO LIST
all of the civilian and military personnel who were actively engaged in its
defense. The people that I deal with here are those who turned in as
prisoners of war or who were killed in action. From time to time, Navy
men will be mentioned; if the reader wonders why there were Navy
personnel in Cebu, it can be explained in the following manner:

About February 1, 1942, some Navy personnel, newspaper correspondents, and civilians sent to the Southern Islands took a boat to Capiz in
northern Panay, buses from Capiz southward across Panay to Iloilo, and
then a ferry across the straits to Bacolod, Negros Occidental. They continued by bus around the Negros mountain until they reached San Carlos on
the east coast and then took the ferry across to Toledo, Cebu. From Toledo,
buses took them over the mountain ranges to Cebu City. Shortly after their
arrival, a small cargo ship from Australia came into Cebu with supplies.
The civilians and newspaper correspondents went out on this ship while
the Navy personnel remained behind because of orders to report to the
Army for assignment.

As to the personnel in Cebu mentioned earlier, I shall refer to them at their highest rank.

The first on my list is a naval commander, Thomas F. O'Brian, who came from Boston. He was single and made his home with his two sisters. Cmdr. O' Brian was not in very good health due to his war background in Luzon. He worked in the Censor's Office under Maj. Hardin. The commander was a jolly fellow and made friends with everyone.

The second was Lt. Cmdr. A. E. Grove, who worked in the Quartermaster's Office in Cebu City under Col. John D. Cook. Cmdr. Grove surrendered on May 17 with the rest of the Cebu prisoners and went to Davao Penal Colony with the group. He was with the section that went to Luzon and on October 12, 1944, he was put on a Japanese prison ship, which started for Japan. The boat had to dodge submarines all through the China Sea and just outside Takao, Formosa, the boat was torpedoed and there were only five survivors.

The British 1st Lt. Lawrie-Smith also worked in the Censor's Office under Maj. Hardin.

Capt. Orville Fossum has already been mentioned as the American commander of the Toledo Garrison. Capt. Fossum held the command until some time in March, I believe, when he volunteered for the special mission of officer-in-charge of the inter-island ship *Regulas.* This ship was loaded with gasoline and food supplies for Bataan and Corregidor. He got the ship up along the coast of Mindanao some place when it was spotted by some Jap bombers. They bombed and strafed the ship until it caught fire and had to be abandoned. Capt. Fossum was able to get ashore in Mindanao and finally made his way to Corregidor by *banca,* a small native boat. Before going on this journey, Capt. Fossum had talked with Lt. Col. Paul S. Beard, a force finance officer, about getting partial payment of his own salary which was due him. He told the colonel that he needed some money as a security factor on this special mission. The colonel told him that he didn't need money and that the Army furnished him everything. I saw Capt. Fossum a few minutes before he boarded the ship and he told me that Col. Scudder had gotten him about 100 pesos. He said the rest of the boys, like himself, were broke and he couldn't borrow any more. It took most of Capt. Fossum's money to pay for the native bancas that got him up to Corregidor. I saw Capt. Fossum a few days before he died in Davao Prison and he said he couldn't get paid in Corregidor because he didn't belong to the outfit. He told me that after the surrender came, up to the time he ran out of money, he was able to get enough food to keep him going. After his money ran out and he couldn't buy extra rice while in prison, he almost starved to death. He became run down, caught malaria, and contracted dysentery.

When the Japs sent a detail of American prisoners from Luzon to Davao in October 1942, Fossum volunteered for the detail. When he arrived in Davao, I was already there. He was in very bad shape. Most of the Luzon men improved on their arrival in Davao because, at first, there was plenty of rice and work was not too difficult for the ration we received. However, Capt. Fossum was so drained of physical resources that he did not respond to the increased diet and treatment at the Davao Prison Hospital. I talked with him often while he was in the hospital. He repeatedly said that if he could have drawn more of his rightful back pay when he started on this special mission, he could have gotten enough food so that his health would not have broken down from starvation. He said he had several thousand dollars of backpay and it wasn't worth a damn. In January 1943, Capt. Fossum died from malnutrition, dysentery, and beriberi in the Davao Prison Hospital. The last two days he was in a coma and did not suffer much.

Capt. Fossum had quite a number of friends in the Cebu group. His ward in the hospital was often a meeting place for the group after a day's work. Every man present would steal something from the Nips during the day (at the risk of a severe personal beating) and smuggle the tidbit into camp and bring it over to Capt. Fossum. These contributions were never much, but a couple of small bananas, a raw bitter sweet potato, a few pieces of coconut meat, or a piece of ginger root. In spite of the attention of his friends, his body gave out, though the spirit was willing.

Lt. Col. Rufus R. Rogers was left in Cebu as finance officer when Gen. Sharp went to Mindanao. I have already related elsewhere the episode of how Col. Rogers became finance officer. He was a husky, young Texan from Del Rio. He was a farmer's son and a graduate of Texas A&M. He had taught animal husbandry in the Del Rio High School. He had a wonderful sense of humor and common sense stuck out all over him. No situation was so tough that it ever got him down. When things got going the hardest, his big bass voice would suddenly roll out to the strains of "Beautiful Texas." Rogers remained in the Finance Office until the last of March when Gen. Chynoweth assumed command of the Visayan Force and placed Col. Rogers in command of the 33rd Infantry Regiment (located in the mountains northwest of Cebu City). He was one of the American emissaries at the surrender of the American Forces on Cebu in May 1942. Of those experiences and events that concerned him later in the various prisons, I shall relate another time.

Lt. Col. A. B. Carlton, QMC, was one of the men who came down to Cebu from Corregidor after the war started. He worked in the Quartermaster Office of Cebu under Col. John D. Cook. Carlton had been in the last war and later lived in Chicago. He had been on active duty with the Army, as an officer, several years before coming to the Philippines. He worked with Col. Cook's office, along with Lt. Cmdr. Grove and others, until the invasion of Cebu. After the invasion, he still remained on duty under Col. Cook, the quartermaster. He surrendered May 17 with the rest of the Americans on the island of Cebu. He got along during imprisonment fairly well but none too well with his fellowmen. When going got hard, they nicknamed him "Old Lady Carlton." Carlton worked on some of the details in Davao and went north to Luzon in June 1944. He was put on board a ship going to Japan and died en route. He was aboard the ship sailing October 12 or the *Oryoku Maru,* which sailed December 13, 1944. I have the impression he was on the latter; I have no details about his death.

There was a Maj. McClenahan in Cebu who was assistant provost marshal under Lt. Col. Howard Edmunds. Maj. McClenahan had been a school teacher back in Kansas or Nebraska. During the war in Cebu, he was quite a gay bird; after the surrender, I have no information about what happened to him.

I have mentioned 2nd Lt. Al Fienstein who ran the radio station in Cebu. He continued to do this until the Japs took the city of Cebu, when he went and joined Gen. Chynoweth as a combatant. He later joined the guerrillas.

Another of the Navy ensigns, Jimmy Mullins was one of the personnel who came down from Corregidor during the war, in February, I believe. During the war, his duties in Cebu were as an outpost commander along the shore of the island. He would make reconnaissance and keep watch for Jap ships going around the island. With the surrender of the Cebu Forces he became a prisoner of war and proceeded, once we were settled in prison, to become a member of the kitchen force which prepared the prisoners' meals. This was always a choice detail. Mullins then proceeded to get around the Japs enough to learn their language. He became quite fluent in his ability to speak and read it. When we moved to Davao, he became a detail leader there for a while and went north to Luzon with the larger group in June 1944. In December 1944, he was put aboard a prison ship and survived the fearful trip north. From Japan, he was taken to Manchuria where he remained to the end of the war. He made the journey back to the States safely.

Capt. Floyd A. Hawkes, MC, had been in the U.S. Public Health Service before the war began. He had his office in the Customs Building in Cebu and his duty was as port medical inspector for all foreign ships that entered the harbor of Cebu. I believe Capt. Hawkes was a graduate of Indiana University Medical School. His home was Whiting, IN. When the war started, he went into the Medical Service and was stationed in Cebu. He was an excellent surgeon as well as doctor. When the island was invaded by the Japs, Col. Hawkes stood by his wounded patients in the hospital and was captured early in the battle for Cebu. His hospital was located high in the mountains on the east slope of the Talisay-Toledo Road. The Japanese captured the road shortly after they invaded the islands. The hospital staff had warning that the Japs were coming down the road so the American doctors told all the Filipino nurses to run up the mountain and get away before the Japs came. Lt. Col. Dwight M. Deter and Capt. Hawkes stayed by their patients and were captured by the Japs. Col. Deter, being in command, the Japs took him with them and left Capt. Hawkes at the hospital to take care of the patients. This he did for several days until the Japs came and moved him and the patients down to the City Hospital in Cebu.

During the few days after their capture in the field hospital, several Japanese patrols came through. Each patrol looted the food and supplies. Each time the Japs found the clothes left behind by the Filipino army nurses, they beat Capt. Hawkes because he didn't have any of the nurses around and couldn't tell them where they were. When the first patrol came through, Capt. Hawkes had a supply of canned food hidden. He had to hide essential food stuff in the tall cogon grass in the mountains in order to be sure of having food for himself and the patients.

After he was moved to Cebu, he worked in the city hospital, which had been taken over by the Japs for a number of days. After several days of this, he was moved to a cell in the Cebu Provincial Jail and that is where he remained until the American prisoners were brought in to occupy the entire jail. Capt. Hawkes went to Davao and was on duty with the hospital staff there all during the life of the Penal Colony as a POW camp. He was one of the few who was not sent to the field to plant rice. He was with the group that went to Luzon in June 1944. Once we reached the camp in Luzon, he was on the medical staff for awhile for the Davao group in Cabanatuan. On December 13, 1944, he was part of the group of POWs aboard the *Oryoku Maru*. He survived the first bombings and was a wonderful help in the treatment of the wounded on the boat, although he was not a member of the official medical staff which had charge of the sick and the wounded during this trip. I wish to say here that Capt. Hawkes was one of the greatest credits to the medical profession aboard the ship. He gave his services as they were needed wherever he could. He died of exposure and starvation late in January 1945 while still aboard ship en route to Japan.

Lt. Cmdr. Mauricett Spriggs was one of the Naval personnel who came down to Cebu after the war started. The commander's health was not good, although he lived through most of the years of imprisonment. He surrendered in Cebu and went to Davao where he spent most of his days on the old man's hat detail. This was composed of the old, sick, and lame of the Davao Camp who usually sat in the shade weaving hats under the direction of a Jap guard. (A practiced weaver could weave one hat in a day and we figured that the lieutenant colonel, who could weave one hat a day, made a mighty expensive piece of head gear on Uncle Sam's payroll, provided he lived.)

Cmdr. Spriggs was in the group moved to Luzon in June 1944. He was a member of the October 10 detail to Japan whose ship was torpedoed in the China Sea one-half day out of Takao, Formosa. Cmdr. Spriggs was not listed among the five survivors.

Lt. Col. Marcus Boulware, I have already mentioned as connected with the supplies of the Brigade. Since I have mentioned him elsewhere, I shall not go into details of his work on the island of Cebu now.

Lt. Col. Arthur J. Grimes came to Bohol around the middle of October 1941, where he replaced Capt. Paul D. Wood at the Tubigon Cadre School. Capt. Grimes was in charge of the island defenses until around the middle or the first of March 1942 when he and his battalion were moved over to Cebu to augment its defenses.

Lt. Col. Bud Coyle, field artillery, had been sent down to Cebu to the Southern Islands from Gen. MacArthur's headquarters to reorganize an air warning system. Col. Coyle was out to see me several times in regard to this and all his plans were based on receiving equipment from Australia. This equipment never got there.

Capt. Frank E. Merchant was one of the men who went to work for the Army as a civilian and was commissioned on the field of battle during the fighting in Cebu. Merchant was just a young fellow and, I believe, an oil engineer. The Philippine Development Co. employed him as one of a group of engineers who were drilling for oil at the northern and southern ends of the island of Cebu. Indications were that they found what they were looking for because the oil wells and all of their equipment had to be suddenly destroyed along with all the tests they had made.

After the beginning of the war, the oil drilling was naturally stopped. Capt. Merchant then went to work for me in the censor's office where he worked for quite some time before being transferred to the MP Regiment. There his assignment was somewhat indefinite until the invasion. When the Japs came to Cebu, Capt. Merchant's assignment was no longer indefinite. Because of his experience in handling explosives he was one of the men in charge of the demolition crews who blew up the military installations before the Japs captured them. The Japanese tried very hard after they had captured us all to find out the names of the men who had blown up the military installations and indirectly caused the burning of the city of Cebu. Nobody squealed so the Japs never found out about Capt. Merchant. Later in the summer, when the Japanese took all the technicians from our group and sent them to Japan around October 1942, Capt. Merchant was one of that detail. I understand he got safely to Japan, but died of dysentery and malnutrition shortly after he got there.

Lt. Cmdr. Chase G. Lade was one of the Navy men who came from Corregidor to Cebu and was assigned to help the Army. I don't recall what his assignment was, but I have the impression he was associated with the QMC under Col. John D. Cook. Cmdr. Lade surrendered on the island of Cebu and went to Davao with the group. He remained with the large group of POWs and went to Luzon June 1944. He was on the last detail to be sent to Japan, which was aboard the *Oryoku Maru*. He survived the first bombing but when we were bombed in Takao, Formosa, on January 9, 1945, he perished.

Capt. Marion G. Sharp was one of the battalion commanders on Cebu Island. He had come from Bohol with Col. Grimes. I don't know much about Capt. Sharp's home or where he came from. I do know that one time during the war while talking with him, he remarked, "Trouble? You call this war trouble? Brother, you don't know what trouble is. I don't care if I never go home. This is sort of a peaceful place out here."

During the battle of Cebu, Capt. Sharp was killed.

Capt. Frank L. Dixon, Medical Corps Administrative, came down to Cebu from Luzon during the war to set up a medical supply depot. This he did and operated it until the surrender of Cebu. Capt. Dixon spent the usual time in Davao and was moved to Luzon with the Davao detail in the summer of 1944. He was part of the *Oryoku Maru* and survived the trip to Japan. When the remnants of this group were divided into two components, he went with the one that was sent to Korea. Capt. Dixon was rescued in Korea at the end of the war.

C. M. Hunter, USN, CMM, was on the island of Cebu after the later part of March. He was part of the PT boat crews and was wounded during an engagement with some Japanese planes. His arm had been broken, and was useless. A bullet had shattered the bone. The flesh wound had healed, but the bone in the forearm separated; he, therefore, had to carry the arm in a splint to keep it from flopping around. Hunter surrendered with the Cebu group and subsequently went to Davao. On June 28, 1944, he was left at the Bilibid Hospital because of his injured arm while the rest of the detail went on to Japan and Cabanatuan.

2nd Lt. Walter Smith came from the island of Bohol with Col. Grimes about the last of March 1942. I first knew Smith as a Corporal back in the days of the Philippine Army training when he was in Bohol. Smith had come down from the 31st Infantry of Manila to help Capt. William F. Conner, who has been mentioned several times before. Smith surrendered in Cebu, went to Davao and finally to Lasang. His detail was aboard the ship that was torpedoed and sunk September 8, 1944.

2nd Lt. Geo. T. Holmes, QMC, has been mentioned at length before. Lt. Holmes is the same George T. Holmes, then a sergeant, who helped me place the machine guns on the *Don Esteban* when I came down from Manila to Cebu City just after the war started. Lt. Holmes was captured in

Cebu after having been bombed and sunk aboard the *Don Esteban*. They were taking a load of supplies to hard-pressed Bataan and Corregidor when some Nip reconnaissance planes found them off the coast of Mindoro. The planes attacked at once, bombing and strafing with the result that the *Don Esteban* was lost. Holmes was among the crew members, American and Filipinos, who got ashore on the Mindoro coast. From there, by banca, bus, and army vehicle, they got from island to island until they arrived in Cebu City. Holmes was never very well after he got in prison. He went to Davao, Luzon, Bilibid and finally was put on board the *Oryoku Maru*. The trip was too much for him because of malnutrition, exposure and dehydration. He died en route to Japan and was buried at sea.

2nd Lt. Bargvig W. Bardson was another Norwegian who was a survivor of the sunken Norwegian freighter previously mentioned. Bardson was an exceedingly intelligent, fine-looking young Norwegian. He had a chance to get to Australia, but chose to stay and fight with the Americans. He was given a commission on the field of battle (which has been confirmed by the U.S. government), and became a Japanese prisoner of war as an officer in the American army. He, too, was determined, even in her hour of defeat, to become a citizen of the United States. Bardson was sent to Japan as a technician about August 1942. He was rescued in Japan at the end of the war.

Maj. Thomas N. Powell, Jr., CE, was a member of the Cebu headquarters at the time of the surrender. His is quite a story that will be related later.

Percy M. Cotton, lieutenant junior grade, USN, was one of the naval men who was sent to Cebu during the war. Prior to going on duty in the Navy Reserve, Cotton had been in the Merchant Marines. What his assignment with the Army was, I do not know. The Japanese, after the surrender, classified him as a technician and sent him to Japan about August 1942. He was rescued at the end of the war.

Walter A. Shapertine, carpenter USN, was one of the personnel who came down from Luzon about February 1942. He is another whose assignment in the Army I have no knowledge of. The Japanese classified him as a technician and sent him to Japan in August 1942. He was rescued at the end of the war.

Capt. H. D. Weidman was a mining engineer who came from Wisconsin and had been working on the island of Masbate before the war. After the Japs took Masbate, he escaped by banca to join the American Forces in Cebu where he was captured. He was sent to Japan as a technician.

Capt. F. A. Bowen was one of the civilians who went to work for the Army at the beginning of the war. Capt. Bowen was attached to the quartermaster service where he worked all during the war. He surrendered with the Cebu group and was taken to Mindanao. There in the Davao Penal Colony he served on some of the lighter details and went with the group to Luzon in June 1944. On December 13, 1944, Capt. Bowen was left in Bilibid Hospital when the rest of the group were sent to Japan aboard the *Oryoku Maru.*

Joseph A. Allen came down to Cebu from Luzon about the same time the rest of the Naval group arrived. He was attached to Capt. Dixon to work in the Medical Supply Depot in the port area of Cebu City. He surrendered with the Cebu group. He went through the various events concerning the group as far as Bilibid Hospital where he remained when the last of the Davao group was placed aboard the *Oryoku Maru.*

Albert P. Ross was a member of one of Lt. John D. Bulkeley's PT boat crews whom I met in Cebu along with Lt. Bulkeley. His PT boat later sank a Japanese cruiser off the southern end of the coast of Cebu.

Capt. William F. O'Connor has been mentioned before and will be mentioned again. His assignment at this time on Cebu was S-1 for Col. Scudder's Cebu Brigade.

Cpl. Fred R. Shurmm had been a retired corporal at the beginning of the war. When the war broke out he was living in Cebu with his Filipino wife and little girl. He left them to join the Army again and was attached to Col. Edmund's MP unit. He surrendered May 17. When the colonel and his technicians were sent north to Japan, Cpl. Shurmm was sent along as an orderly. When the group reached Manila, he was sidetracked and sent to Cabanatuan. On December 13, 1944, he was left in Cabanatuan Hospital. Shortly thereafter he was rescued by American troops.

2nd Lt. Henry Talmadge had been a civilian at the beginning of the war. He worked for the Army during the war as a well driller for Army installations. At the time of the invasion, he was drilling a well at Camp X and got caught with American Forces between converging Japanese lines. He was given charge of supplies during the fighting and commissioned a 2nd lieutenant in the field. Lt. Talmadge was one of the American officers who carried on guerrilla activities under Gen. Chynoweth. He surrendered with the Cebu group and was subsequently sent to the Davao Penal Colony. On February 24, 1944, he was sent to Lasang to work on the airfield. His detail was sunk September 8, 1944.

Lt. J. G. Otis A. Carmichael was one of the Navy personnel sent to Cebu and attached to the army. What his assignment was on the island of Cebu I don't recall. I believe he was attached to the Quartermaster Corps under Col. Cook. Carmichael surrendered with the Cebu group May 1942 and subsequently went to Davao. For some reason or another, he was never satisfied with prison life. He always wanted to escape. He would sit by the hour and talk about going over the wall in Cebu, then make a dash for the airport, capture a plane, and take off for Australia. While he was sitting around talking about escaping and growling about the chow, he grew a long red beard. Being an Irishman, he liked to talk. The time came when he would sit and mumble in his beard. He talked so much that we all got to figuring that his category was all talk and no action. When we were moved to Davao and we had to get out and work, he sort of snapped out of it and became more normal. He went with the group to Luzon in June 1944 and spent three months in Cabanatuan. A little later he was moved to Bilibid Prison. He was a member of the prison detail placed aboard the *Oryoku Maru,* which sailed out of Manila Harbor late in the afternoon of December 13, 1944. When the ill-fated boat sank December 15, Carmichael was one of those who had to swim for it. He was last seen in a boat with 20 Japs after the bombing. What happened to him after that, I do not know.

Capt. Victor R. Browne has been mentioned before. He was a civilian whom I met socially in Cebu one weekend, when I was visiting the Morrison home (while stationed in Bohol). Because of his extensive knowledge of chemistry and science, Capt. Browne, assisted by Leroy L. Hoyt, USN, began the manufacture of hand grenades in February 1942, when the Army detailed him to this assignment. Before the end of the war, he had perfected a fairly reliable hand grenade, which the Army was beginning to manufacture in large quantities. However, the war ended before they could be put into production.

2nd Lt. Curtis L. Sizemore had come from Bohol as an enlisted man with Col. Grimes. Because of the great need for American officers at the time, he was commissioned as 2nd lieutenant and placed in command of a company of Philippine army troops. Lt. Sizemore has been mentioned before as my corporal at Calape, Bohol. He surrendered with the Cebu group and was a member of the ill-fated Lasang group, which was sunk off Mindanao on September 8, 1944.

Lt. Wilson, QMC, was assigned to the Port Quartermaster after his boat, the *Don Esteban,* was sunk and he made his way ashore to finally reach Cebu. He was the Sgt. Wilson I mentioned as being one of the enlisted men aboard the *Don Esteban* when I made my eventful voyage from Manila to Cebu the first week of the war. Lt. Wilson had been in WWI and been listed as missing in action or killed. After the war was over he returned to the States and was discharged. When he got home, he found his wife married to another man, so he left the situation as it was. He returned to the Army and came out to the Philippines where he remained in the Army. He married a Filipino woman of central Luzon and decided to remain in the Philippines the rest of his life. When the surrender came, Lt. Wilson decided to remain out with the guerrillas. Deciding that the island of Cebu was too small for such activities, he went to Negros. Within a very few hours before I broke camp to join the general in surrendering to the Japs, he came into our camp desiring transportation to the island of Negros. I still had courier contact with Negros, so I sent him on his way on a banca. That is the last I ever heard of him.

Capt. L. Howell was another civilian who was commissioned into the Army. He had been an oil driller prior to the war and was drilling on the island of Cebu at the time the war began. The first I knew of Capt. Howell, he was working in the kitchen as a cook in one of the Army camps after the invasion of Cebu. He surrendered with the Cebu group and in a few months was sent to Japan as a technician. I believe he endured the imprisonment and was rescued at the end of the war.

C. E. Wilson was another of the Navy personnel who came to Cebu in February from Luzon. Shortly after his arrival, he was assigned to me at Camp X as an assistant in communications work. He remained at Camp X on that detail until after the invasion and the headquarters installations were captured, at which time he retreated to the jungle-infested mountains where we carried on our guerrilla activities. He surrendered with the Cebu group in May 1942 and was subsequently sent to Davao. In June 1944 he was taken to Luzon. In August 1944 he was a member of a detail headed for Japan. To my knowledge his detail reached Japan safely.

Capt. Donald C. Gregg, prior to the war, had been a mining engineer working for the Mindanao Lode Gold Mine Co. As soon as the war started, he was one of a group of mining engineers Gen. Sharp sent to work on various defense installations in Cebu. When Sharp went to Mindanao, Gregg was left behind in Cebu and was assigned to me at Camp X where he became my post engineer. While on this assignment, he collaborated with Capt. V. R. Browne in perfecting the hand grenade that I mentioned before. Due to various reassignments by the general, I lost sight of Capt. Gregg during the fighting on the island of Cebu. When we surrendered, Gregg was among the group, and because he was a mining engineer, the Japs classified him as a technician. He was sent north to Japan August 1942 where he remained until rescued at the end of the war.

Capt. Edward L. Short, QMC, was in charge of the Quartermaster Motor Pool for Col. John D. Cook, the port quartermaster. In civilian life, he had for a number of years been the B. F. Goodrich representative in the southern Philippines with his office in Cebu City. As soon as the war started, Capt. Short (along with 1st Lt. David C. Afflick) volunteered his services to the U.S. Army in the field of supply. Capt. Short had married a Spanish girl and between the Spanish contacts and business Filipino contacts, his knowledge of supply sources in the Southern Islands was quite broad. Capt. Short held his post as head of the Port Quartermaster Motor Pool until the invasion of the islands when he and his men did an excellent job of sabotaging their own installations. Capt. Short surrendered with the Cebu group and in August 1942 was sent north to Japan as a technician. I later saw him when we were in prison in Luzon and he told me that he contracted dysentery while on board the prison ship. For that reason, he was left in Bilibid Hospital instead of being sent to Japan. After a number of months in the hospital, he was sent to Cabanatuan where he stayed until the last of October 1942.

By the time Capt. Short reached Cabanatuan, the underground system of communication and supply between the American POWs and friends in Manila had been well established. Over this underground supply line Capt. Short received several thousand pesos, a little food, and some clothing (such as a pair of shoes). He shared the money he received with others in need. Like most men with a good heart, when hard times came for him personally, he found himself without any reserve because he had given all he had to others less fortunate. By the time I arrived, he was broke and had several thousand pesos loaned out. He could have bought food, from various sources, had he had the money. I was in such bad shape that he slipped me a couple of pieces of cornbread one day for ole times' sake. Capt. Short was a member of the *Oryoku Maru* detail and he survived the first bombing. He died of malnutrition and dysentery in January 1945 while still aboard the ship. He was another man who spread sunshine through the prison camp by a cheery word and a generous heart.

1st Lt. David C Afflick had been one of the executives in the Proctor and Gamble offices of Cebu City. Because he was one of the copra buyers in the southern islands, he, like Capt. Short, had a lot of contacts in the southern Philippines, and Dave became one of Col. Cook's assistants. I believe he helped with the administration of general supplies. Dave was one of the more fortunate civilians, in that his wife and child had been sent back to the States along with Capt. Hawk's when the pressure of the war became evident. Hawk lived in Afflick's home up to the invasion of Cebu. Then they stuck to their units during the jungle fighting. Afflick surendered with the Cebu group and went to Mindanao in October 1942 where he worked in the fields with the rest of the POWs. Dave was sent to Lasang as part of the Lasang detail in February 1944. To my knowledge, Dave went down with the Lasang detail prison ship on September 8, 1944.

Lt. Col. Dwight M. Deter, MC, came over from Panay around March (when the Visayan Force was created out of the Visayan and Mindanao Forces). Col. Deter then became the force surgeon. He went to Davao with the Cebu group and was later taken to Luzon. He became part of the October 10 detail of 1,800 POWs whose boat was sunk just outside Takao, Formosa. To my knowledge, there were only five men who survived that torpedoing.

Col. John D. Cook, QMC, PI, was the port quartermaster of Cebu City. He had been in the islands for a long time before the war began. About 10 to 14 days before Pearl Harbor, he arrived in Cebu and took over his assignment, which he held until the surrender. A few weeks after the surrender, he was sent north to Japan with the rest of the colonels and the generals. Years later, Col. Cook was with the group of colonels and generals whom the Japanese brought to Mukden, Manchuria, where I was sent as a prisoner. He was rescued at the end of the war in Mukden.

Col. Irvine C. Scudder arrived in Cebu just before the war started. Shortly after the war began, he was given command of the Cebu Brigade. He fought the war in Cebu until surrender as commanding officer of the Brigade. Col. Scudder was sent north to Japan at the same time that Col. Cook was and he was, likewise, rescued in Mukden at the end of the war.

There were other Army and Navy personnel whom I but vaguely remember who did not surrender with the fall of the Philippines. What happened to them, what adventures they went through, where they were captured, if they escaped, or what their fate was, I do not know and have no way of finding out. For instance, there was a Navy man by the name of Leroy who was a radio technician who worked for me at Camp X. He disappeared the night that our headquarters was captured by the Nips and no trace of him was ever found. I was the last man to see him and he had definite instructions as how to reach our new headquarters back in the jungle. He was still talking to me when the machine guns opened up. As the bullets flew over our heads, he disappeared into the night. There was a Navy ensign by the name of Carson who decided to go to Negros. From all that I could ever find out he is still on his way. There was a young American civilian by the name of Kincaid who worked for the Army in the Quartermaster Camp of Maj. Don Sawtell. There was a rumor that Kincaid and several naval personnel were captured aboard a banca in the Mindanao Sea.

Maj. Don Sawtell had charge of the Quartermaster Supply Depot about four miles down the valley from my camp. This was his detail during most of the war until the surrender. At the time of the surrender, he became separated from the rest of our forces and took to the hills. Several months after the surrender he was picked up by a Nip patrol boat on the southwest coast of Negros. The only reason that the Nips caught him at that time was that someone had betrayed his presence to the Nip patrol. He had the choice of surrendering or being machine-gunned in his nipa hut. He chose to surrender. From there he was taken to Dumaguete in Negros Oriental, where he was kept in the provincial jail for several days. From there he was moved to the American POW camp not far from Bacolod on the central west coast of Negros Occidental. His group of American prisoners was subsequently taken to Davao. Maj. Sawtell was among the Davao group that was taken to Luzon in June 1944. After his arrival in Davao I lost track of him.

There were several other groups of Americans who had tentative plans to escape to Australia. Most of these were Naval men, but some were British. These men seemed to have faded away during the conflict or the invasion of the island of Cebu and how many reached the mainland of Australia I have no way of knowing. If they failed to make Australia, they were evidently lost during the voyage. It is hard to say what is truth and what is fiction in the rumors that flowed up to our headquarters about men attempting to sail to Australia in bancas and small motor boats. There is one tale concerning an ocean-going tugboat called the *Sunmaid* or the *Sunkissed* or *The Sun*. It was fully fueled, supplied, and hidden in a cove of the Surigao Peninsula in northern Mindanao. Reports from native runners said that after the invasion of Cebu, several naval men appeared in a banca and discovered the boat hidden in the cove. They boarded the tugboat, tossed the Filipino caretaker overboard and sailed out into the Pacific.

Before I mention the events of the war in Cebu, perhaps I had better mention what was happening in the rest of the Orient and Southwest Pacific and tell a little of what was known of the Japanese plans.

As I mentioned before, when I arrived in San Francisco, I began to sense things. In Hawaii, the manager of the Alexander Young Hotel personally told me that they would be lucky if Honolulu were not blown off the map. In Manila most of the civilians I talked with expected war before another year was over, and that was what the ordinary businessman in Manila expected.

When I arrived in Manila in June 1941, the Japanese merchants were glad to have customers enter their stores and buy their merchandise. By December their attitude had changed to where they did not care whether customers purchased their goods or not. In June, when a customer entered their stores, they hurried to serve him with politeness. By December, when a customer entered, they would often ignore him and continue to jabber among themselves. If he went up and interrupted them, they would reluctantly wait on him or arrogantly tell him, "We do not have that." They knew what was in the wind and that the time would come when they would be the masters.

Months, in some cases, years, before Pearl Harbor Day, Japan had closed the Mandated Islands of the Pacific to foreign shipping. Why had they closed these island ports unless they were fortifying them? The last Filipino fishing boat I heard of, which was in Palau before the war, came back with its crew saying that there were three of the islands fortified with artillery and that any two or three could fire on the third. Of Truk we know practically nothing except that it was not open to any, but Japanese, ships. Other scraps of information came from here and there. One of our commercial airliners ran into a whole flock of Japanese pursuit ships and bombers lying south of the Mariana Islands toward Truk.

The Japanese established a commercial airline from Japan to Portuguese Timor via Truk and the Marianas. The same crew never made the same trip twice. Although they were in civilian dress, they bore the mark of military personnel. The commercial airline of Timor didn't pay. What then was its justification? There were similar instances of other things; for example, we knew approximately how many ships of various kinds that Japan had from checking on the world ports. By a few weeks before Pearl Harbor Day, I understand there were hardly any Japanese ships in foreign ports. Almost all Japanese shipping had disappeared from the seas into the home waters. What was the reason for this (unless Japan was going to make a hostile move in the Pacific)?

The information we had at our disposal came from all types of sources. Some reliable Filipino or Chinese merchant might go up to Shanghai on business and bring back information that we desired. I know that the British merchants in the Philippines had instructions to send to the British Intelligence Office, by the way of a designated Philippine merchant, anything of military interest they could pick up. There is every reason to think that our commercial agents had the same instructions. Of course, we had the information that came from diplomatic channels through the consuls and vice-consuls, plenipotentiaries, ministers, and ambassadors. Attached to the embassies were the usual military attaches and language students whose primary duty for our government was to gain military and naval information. Often these agents would never get the whole picture. Some agent in Manchuria would report that a large body of troops had moved out of Mukden by rail. Some weeks later some agent in Amoy would report the arrival of a unit of troops. He would observe that some of them were veteran troops and others were recruits. He would estimate the size of the unit and assign it an arbitrary number for identification purposes. For example, he might designate the new unit as 1119th Division, knowing that the Japanese didn't have one-tenth that many divisions. A few days later, down in Shanghai, an agent there would report the arrival of a new unit of troops, some of which were veterans and some of which were recruits. He would make some arbitrary designation of this new unit and send the report into our headquarters. All of these reports reached our headquarters by devious ways and means and our intelligence would sift it, and would come to the following conclusion: the umpty-umph division had left Mukden, Manchuria, on a certain date by train and it had just enough time to arrive at Amoy, picking up recruits on the way where part of it was left, and the remainder proceeding to Shanghai. Then it was logical to assume that the old divisions in Mukden had been divided into two new divisions with recruits being added to bring these divisions up to full strength. These divisions were located in Amoy and Shanghai, respectively. Briefly, that is the way we gained our information.

The Japanese were rapidly expanding their army forces. It was rumored that she expanded her divisions from about 50 to slightly over 100 by the time the war broke out. All her shipping was in her home waters for that purpose, we could only guess. When in December 1941 a large convoy of 100 or so Japanese transports appeared from Japanese waters and headed toward Saigon, it was plain to see that the Japs were on the move. If the Japanese went into Saigon, the British Malay states would be in great danger and naturally the British would have to take counter steps for their defense. It was obvious where the Japs were going to strike when the show began.

With the event at Pearl Harbor, the show was on. The Japs struck at Pearl Harbor, made landings in the Philippines and Hong Kong and set her island forces in Saigon in motion against the British almost simultaneously.

The Japs landed in four places in the Philippines: Aparri, Lingayen, and Legaspi in Luzon, and lastly in Davao on the island of Mindanao. As soon as the Japs saw that they were winning on the mainland and in the Philippines, they sent invasion forces to occupy the Dutch East Indies, New Guinea, and the Solomon Islands. With the fortification of the port of Rabaul on the north end of New Britain, the Japanese were ready to invade Australia. There was only one thorn in their side at this stage of the game. That was the thorn of Bataan and the southern Philippine islands. It was true that there were other locations, which they would have to mop up, but until the American forces in the Philippines had been annihilated, the Japanese could not attack Australia with secure supply lines. That meant that the Philippines must fall before they could move south with safety.

SIX

THE WAR IN CEBU

WHEN GENERAL SHARP MOVED TO MINDANAO HE LEFT COL. IRVINE C. SCUDDER (THE BRIGADE DEFENDER) IN CHARGE OF THE ISLAND OF Cebu. Col. Scudder had two Provisional Regiments under his command plus an MP Battalion, which was later enlarged into an MP Regiment. The whole unit of defense was designated the Cebu Brigade.

The 82nd Infantry, under the command of the Filipino Lt. Col. David, had the defense of the southern half of the island. The defenses of the northern half rested with another Filipino, Lt. Col. Bourbon, commanding the 83rd Infantry. Lt. Col. Howard E. Edmunds, American, was in command of the defenses of the city of Cebu. His MP Battalion was increased to a regiment. Some of these troops were used as labor battalions and were armed only with *bolos*. The Cebu Brigade totaled about 5,500 men just before the invasion. In charge of these troops were 12 to 15 American regular Army and Reserve officers. From time to time civilians were commissioned for definite jobs. At the surrender there were 43 Americans ranking from general to corporal. Hardly more than half to two-thirds of the troops had rifles, which were old obsolete Enfields. The bolts of these old rifles were bad and the ejector mechanism would break. That meant a man had to carry around a ramrod to punch the empty cartridge out each time he fired it.

There was not much time to train the soldiers and when the invasion came, they went into battle without ever having fired their rifles in target practice. There were only 8–10 rounds of ammunition per rifle and we did not dare waste a single round in practice. Shortly before the invasion a couple of supply boats arrived from Australia, but it was too late then to train the men.

The only machine guns on the island were those which belonged to the regimental companies. Our heavy artillery consisted of seven old, semi-obsolete 81mm mortars the U.S. Army had given to the Philippine Army. With all this high-class equipment and highly trained Army we were bound to make a showing when the Japs came in. We knew it! Ha! ha!

In the beginning, the Japs did not pay too much attention to Cebu City. On December 13, the day I arrived in Cebu City from Manila, there was a small air raid on Shell Island and Opon where there were oil and gasoline storage tanks. Not much damage was done at this time because the bombs hit in the water.

Early in January, I awoke one morning about 10:00 to the air raid siren. Since I had gone to bed at 7:00, three hours before, I was dead on my feet from exhaustion. At the sound of that siren I knew I had about 20 minutes before the planes would arrive. (Being censor at the time, I knew all the details about the workings of the air warning system as it functioned off of messages it received over my telegraph wires.) I turned over and went back to sleep. To hell with the Nips and their air raid. I became dead to the world again.

Suddenly I was awakened by a gust of hot air passing over me in three waves. The impact of this hot air was fully equal to the impact of a stream of water from an ordinary hose. I was instantly awake from these three blows and a second or two later, my ears registered three earsplitting explosions. *Wumf! Wumf! Wumf!* The curtains on my windows were flying horizontally from their rods against the ceiling. I knew then what was happening, the Nips were here and had dropped some of their bombs nearby. The waves of concussion had passed through my room from the window to the corridor where my door was standing open. It was a good thing the windows in the Philippine tropics seldom have glass in them. My windows were the shutter-type of shell panels which swung inside the room. They were standing open at the time of the explosions so they were not wrecked nor was I covered with glass. I thought the building was going to fall apart.

I scrambled out of bed and into some clothes. From there I went up to the trap door on the top floor and onto the roof where I could get a good view of the surrounding areas. The Nips were bombing the oil tanks again. There were only three bombers and they were swinging back to try to hit their objective. Two came toward Shell Island, and one swung wide over the harbor. What was the single plane going for? The sergeant was climbing onto the roof near me.

"Sergeant, what is that lone plane after?"

"I don't know, captain, but it just now dropped a bomb. I'll watch the bomb fall."

"We'll soon know then if the bomb is on the way."

Seconds passed, seconds that seemed like an eternity. Suddenly I saw a spout of water and wreckage.

"It hit a ship in the harbor, captain. I heard Maj. Jordan say yesterday the inter-island ship *Basilan* was in the port. I'll bet that's what it was after, yes sir, it was a ship. See that black smoke beginning to rise, that's from the ship," said the sergeant.

Wumf! Wumf! The other two planes had dropped their bombs and one had hit Shell Island.

"Looks like they hit an oil tank on the island. See that flame bursting from the oil tank on the left? Now see the black smoke beginning to rise?"

The sergeant exclaimed, "They really hit that, didn't they!"

We watched the flames steadily mount and the black smoke begin to climb high into the sky.

The three Nip planes seemed to have dumped all their bombs and now turned to strafing the airport, concentrating on the hangars and trees around the edge for any installations they might be concealing. One plane would swoop low while the other two would circle high. The low swooping plane would climb back to the level of the other two. About halfway up to the height it would level off, the sound of its machine guns would reach us. The guns had been fired while the ship was going down but because of the time lag we heard the guns as the plane was climbing. After each bomber had strafed the airport several times, they took off.

I went down to the street when the attack was over and drove down to the waterfront. There I could see plainly the burning oil tank and the damaged ship. The oil tank had not been hit directly. One bomb had burst in the nearby sea and fragments had gone through the seaside of the tank. The white heat of the fragments had ignited the gasoline as pressure forced the gasoline out of the tank. Long streams of fire were pouring out of that leaking tank in several places. James Gushing, who later became a lieutenant colonel in the guerrillas, did some dangerous work helping to get the fire under control.

The ship *Basilan* sank right where she was until her bottom rested on the seabed. This left about a quarter of the ship's body and all the superstructure above the water. That ship lay right there until the Nips floated her after we surrendered. From the air it looked like a good ship in the harbor, and, thereafter, whenever the planes bombed Cebu, they were sure to drop several bombs on the sunken *Basilan*. That got to be quite a joke with us.

Shortly after this attack I moved out to Camp X to take charge of Gen. Sharp's Force Communications Station. In three or four days the Nip planes were back again. This time they concentrated on the airfields. I happened to be on duty near a telephone. I called Gen. Sharp's headquarters in Camp X to report the attack.

The general was not there, but I got Capt. Cosper, the assistant G-2.

"There are three planes down here bombing and strafing. Guess you want to know about it."

"We sure do. The old man wants to know of any attacks so we can lie low up here. I am out on the side of a mountain at an observation post. I'll call you back as soon as I inform the general."

"Okay, I'll hold the phone free for your call."

I hung up and went to the window to watch the low-flying planes, taking the phone with me. In about three minutes, Cosper called back.

"What are they working on now? I just got through telling Gen. Sharp they were over the city. He said to keep him informed!"

"They dropped another bomb near the *Basilan* again but missed it. Right now they are taking turns strafing the airfield. One is diving low over the field right now. In a few seconds, I'll hear the rattle of his guns. There it is!"

"I see them—the three are out over the harbor; it looks like they are coming this way, now they are circling back, one is leaving the formation, now he is diving."

"I see him! He is diving on the airfield from the south paralleling the mountains. He is really coming low this time; it looks like he is almost touching the roofs . . . He has disappeared, now he is climbing again and I hear his gun. He really gave the airfield a long burst. I hope he didn't catch any of our boys out there. If he did, he really played hell with them that time."

"The other two are circling back and they seem to be diving; I can't tell yet what they are going to do," observed Capt. Cosper.

"I see them; they are both coming into the airfield wide apart from the south; both are diving now. It looks like their flight will cross about the time they hit the airfield on the south side; they must have a special target. They are really diving now . . . I hope they hit each other! Up they come, both of them. From the sound they must have used up all their ammunition; that burst must have lasted 30 seconds or more. The lone plane is diving again on the same spot as the other two. Our lads are really catching hell out there."

"I see the two again; they are still climbing. The third is climbing to join them; he is going fast, all three seem to be flying north, and they are leaving from the looks of it. Thanks for all the dope."

"You are quite welcome. I'll phone the boys at the airport and tell them the Nips seem to be leaving. Take it easy."

I called the airport three times before I could get anybody to answer the phone. Finally a scared Filipino voice came shrinkingly over the wire.

"Lahug Airport, Pvt. Gonzales speaking."

"Tell the captain the Nips have left."

"Oh, sir! *(gasp)* That is very good, sir. I will run, sir." Bang went the receiver.

Later I learned that we had partially concealed a dummy plane on the edge of the field and the Nips had strafed it severely.

Many months later, in prison at Davao, I mentioned this raid to Cosper.

"Yes, I remember that very well. The general told me to keep him informed and then he listened in on our whole conversation. The next time he saw me he bawled the hell out of me for gossiping over the telephone! Now what would you do in a case like that?"

"How would I know? I have never been a general."

When I moved to Camp X, I took charge of the Force Communication Station that Gen. Sharp was leaving on the island of Cebu. Gen. Sharp left and Col. Scudder made Cebu City his headquarters. That left me the only A.M. officer in Camp X. There were a few civilians working on some of the installations.

Camp X was a mud home if I ever saw one. A large number of tunnels had been excavated and blasted out of the sides of the mountain wall in the valley where the camp was located. The work was still going on and every wheelbarrow of mud and rocks wheeled out of the tunnels was dumped so as to shelter some of the buildings. Rain in these high peaks made the mud worse. Since it was being dumped around the installations, the mud was naturally tracked all over everything and got quite deep in some places. The buildings and installations were housed in shacks, which were blacked out for the use of lights at night. Everything had been hastily "sandbagged" by filling sugar sacks with the mud and rocks out of the tunnels. Because of the dampness the sugar sacks soon rotted and the bags had to be replaced. The staff worked and lived in the tunnels while Camp X was there.

When I found myself left with this mess on my hands, I immediately set about organizing a place to fit my needs and to cleaning up the mess in general. After I had been out there a month, Col. Scudder stopped by one day as he was inspecting other installations. He was very complimentary when he saw how shipshape the camp had become. That month had been a nightmare though.

"Hell, Miner, just dropped by to say hello on my way over to Toledo."

"Glad to see you, sir. Won't you have the noon meal with me? It gets lonesome up here."

"I'll stop long enough for a cup of coffee. I am out looking over this Talisay-Toledo road. The more I think about it, the more certain I am that this camp will be my field headquarters and last defense area when the Nips come in. If I send supplies up here, would you help me see they are properly stored away?" (I was still one of the assistants on Gen. Sharp's staff and was outside his command.)

"I will, sir."

The colonel left soon afterward.

Before going any further, I should explain the location of Camp X. The island of Cebu is around 100 miles long and only about 30 miles wide at its broadest point. There are two roads across the island from east to west. One, the Talisay-Toledo Road, cuts the island right in half at its broadest part. The Carcar Road divides the southern half of the island into almost equal fourths. In this broad part that the Talisay-Toledo Road passed were the highest and most rugged mountains, some of which were heavily forested. Camp X was up in the top of these mountains set down in a valley between two high mountain ridges running lengthwise on the island. There was a hogback that ran from one mountain to the other forming a right angle with each. This hogback was the watershed divide between the east-side canyon and the west-side canyon. Any camp located in the forest on the hogback would be protected by high mountains on the east and west sides with deep canyon approaches from the north and the south. By using the road from either side of the island, the forces from either side could fall back to these more easily defended areas. The plan looked good, but the hitch was that we had no equipment to defend the canyons with. Rifles alone would not do it and we knew it, yet the old bolt-action Enfield rifle in the hands of a half-trained native who had never fired a rifle was to be our only weapon of defense.

The defense of the island of Cebu was planned around Camp X. The few supplies we had were stored out in the regimental defense areas. About the middle of February and the first of March, two cargo ships slipped through the Japanese blockade. The *Anhuai* and *Doña Nati* brought in a lot of food from Australia and quite a bit of ammunition. From that time on, we were not short of rifles and machine gun ammunition. There were also some artillery shells, but we had no guns to use them in, and by that time, it was impossible to get a ship up to Bataan or Corregidor. Those shells were unloaded and stored. When the Nips came in, they were set off. All the supplies off these ships were stored in the mountains. No sooner were they stored than Gen. Sharp ordered a lot of it sent down to Mindanao. It had to be trucked down to the piers and sent in small boats to Mindanao. Such a mess!

In general, the defenses of Cebu Island were nil.

Camp X was made the hub around which the island defenses were built. Cebu City was used as a temporary headquarters prior to the invasion when Camp X would be the center of things.

In any war, communications are one of the most vital needs. Here, too, we had to improvise. The telephone lines running out of Camp X were too few for what we needed and built of anything. Imagine how efficient a telephone line made of bailing wire and Coke bottles would be for ordinary commercial use in your home. This was war, our lines had to run through steep mountains and endure tropical storms. Some were built of bailing wire hung on Coke bottles which were, in turn, wired to bamboo poles stuck in the rocky earth (on a mountain so steep you could hardly walk). Some farmer's carabao would find the pole while grazing and knock it down while rubbing its back on it. Then we would have to send a repair crew out to trace the wire and repair it. This crew had to carry with it the extra poles and wire for the repair.

How those Filipinos ever climbed up and down those slopes with those heavy loads I'll never know. I could barely climb over them with absolutely no load.

Other lines were covered electrical wire that was laid on the ground. All the farmers would burn the cogon grass off the slopes before they plowed them. Wire that happened to be laid in these areas had the covering burned off so it had to be replaced. There was unceasing repair to be done day and night.

One of the hardest things to do was to get materials to repair with. All the standard radio tubes had been sent to Gen. Sharp in Mindanao. If we burned out a tube, my technician had to tear the radio down, take out the tube socket, and solder a special socket into the radio in order that an off-brand, odd-sized tube could replace the burned-out tube.

Towards the last, we were running out of these old tubes for replacement. Then the set was no good. That was our communication equipment to fight a war with—old tubes, bailing wire, and coke bottles!

For the equipment to be used, we had to have operators. There weren't any! Gen. Sharp had taken all the good ones to Mindanao. We had to train new ones from young Filipino students. They made mistakes galore, often because they hardly understood the English language. Because of their lack of knowledge of English, they would often fall back to using their native dialects. The messages then were so undeveloped that they could be used for generalities only but not for specific details. This caused more confusion. The frustrations were enough to drive an insane man to saneness.

Small units stationed on outpost duty had only one radio, which was their only contact with their headquarters. Because of the rough handling the sets received, they often would not work. For hours at a time, we had no contact with these units.

Supplies for these units often had to be carried to their base by *cargadores*. The work was slow and straining.

While the fortification of the island was going on, we were subject to various types of raids from the Nips. For several days following the bombing and strafing of the airport, things were quiet. Then one beautiful sunny morning, I went down to Cebu City and got caught in another air raid. Eighteen heavy bombers came floating over the city of Cebu from the direction of Pelas Island. Their first flight over, they designated their targets by dropping bombs on the ships in the harbor and the oil tanks and installations. The poor, sunken *Basilan* was again bombed. The oil storage tanks on Shell Island and Opon had some very close calls. I had been in the Brigade headquarters when the bombing started, so I left the offices and went to the top of the building, which was quite tall and overlooked most of the city and harbor. Capt. English went with me, while Maj. Jordan stayed down below. We got on the roof in time to see the first bombs land.

"Look at those babies splash. *Ouch.*" Capt. English was interrupted by the sound of the explosions: *Wumf, wu-wu-wumf,* followed by blasts of concussion. "Where the hell is my cap? It's blown off my head!"

I looked around. English stood upright, bareheaded and holding his ears. Three feet behind him on the roof lay his overseas cap.

"Horsefeathers, that concussion blast was not that strong. You just knocked it off your head when you tried to cover your ears. You ole. . . ." *Wumf*—an invisible blow struck me in the face followed by others, all of which were strong enough to shake me, but not strong enough to blow my hat off my head!

"Bill, did you count those explosions? There were 32 in that series. See where the water is still churning around from them falling in the harbor? I'll bet the Filipinos have fish for supper tonight!"

"The group is splitting up into two bunches and are turning. I wonder . . . one group is turning toward Opon and the other is going south."

"They are doing a damned poor job. They must have dropped 50 bombs and haven't really hit anything yet. Most of them fell in the sea and the half dozen that hit on land didn't hit anything to speak of. That second group is turning now. It's headed toward Shell Island."

"The first group is coming lower over Opon. They can't be over a mile high now; they must have been 8,000 or 9,000 feet the first time they came over. They dropped some bombs; I saw them leave the bays. It won't be long now."

"This second group is also way lower. I hope they don't keep coming this way much longer; they are on direct bombing line with us now . . . at least they are turning toward the sea again. I'm sure glad to see that."

"Me, too," said Capt. English.

A series of explosions again shook the air over the city. Most of these bombs again landed in the water along the shore of Opon. The oil tanks were lined up in a row along the water for convenience of the tankers when they docked. They presented a very narrow target to the planes. Shortly thereafter, the second series of explosions took place by bombs falling to the sea around Shell Island. Neither of us could see that much damage had been done there.

"Those babies are certainly coming down low this time. They can't be over 2,000 to 3,000 feet high."

We watched the two groups slowly float over the harbor again. This time they dropped only a few bombs.

"That must be their last load of bombs and they certainly are rotten shots. They haven't really hurt anything," I said.

"I hope so."

After the raid by the 18 heavy bombers, things were quiet for awhile. Then came the day we got news of a large Japanese Task Force coming south through the China Sea. The report was that it was passing Luzon and headed toward the Southern Islands. We really sweated out that event. The task force went right on past the Philippines to the Dutch East Indies. It was headed toward Java. This task force got as far as the Straits of

Macassar where it was struck by our combined sea and air forces. The report on that action was that the task force was destroyed. The Macassar Straits lie between Borneo and the Celebes Islands. Our forces caught the convoy in these narrow confines where it could not maneuver and get away. I don't know the particulars of the action, but there were rumors and radio broadcasts that reached us which said the Japanese lost at least 100,000 men due to the sinking of their ships. One airman told us, after we were prisoners, that he took part in the action. A member of his crew counted over 100 Japanese ships either sunk or on fire (and there were beached Japanese craft on both sides of the straits in the area that he flew over). The way he talked, the Japs took a hell of a beating in that battle. But the facts of this battle, true or false, had a great morale effect on our troops in Cebu at the time it happened and on us in prison camps, when our fellow prisoner told us his account of this action he had taken part in.

A few days after the first raid by 18 bombers, a single small Nip plane started flying daily over the island of Cebu about 10 or 11:00 in the morning. It always came from the direction of the city of Iloilo on the island of Panay, flying over Bacolod, the provincial capital of Negros Occidental, and over Cebu City. At Cebu City it would circle around the harbor a couple of times, fly over the airfield and after awhile it got to flying out over the valley where my camp was supposed to be hidden. One of the boys got a pair of field glasses and told us it looked like he was taking pictures. Since he always came at the same time of the day we would arrange our schedules for a siesta or quiet period when "Photo Joe" was due. This was just a single, slow, antiquated Jap plane and we used to get so mad that we didn't have a gun with which we could fire at him. He came absolutely whenever he pleased, and did what he wanted! We had not one plane or one gun with which to chase him out of the sky.

The second raid by 18 bombers also caught me in Cebu City, but this time I was on the way back to Camp X. It came without warning while I was still in the main port of the city. I wasn't surprised because we always expected the Nips at any time. The first flight over, I took shelter in the gutter of the street I was traveling. My Filipino chauffeur, Federico Cortes, did likewise. There were no bombs that fell near us, although the explosions were quite loud. The Nips were again bombing the oil and harbor installations and I was a good half mile away from the nearest of these. However, when you are looking at planes 8,000 or 9,000 feet up in the sky it is pretty hard to judge just where the bombs will fall, especially when there is a heavy breeze blowing from them to you. As the planes passed over us and receded in the distance to circle around and come back, my chauffeur and I got in the car and raced toward the outskirts of the city. As the planes again approached our location, we pulled up under a couple of coconut trees in the street and stopped again. Again my chauffeur and I "hit the dirt" of the street just in case. We were far enough away from the car to be out of range of breaking glass unless the car was directly hit. This time we saw the bombs drop out of the planes and knew that we were not in the line of the falling missiles. When the planes had passed far enough over us that we would not be in any danger, we ran to the car and again took off down the street. By the time the planes had swung around for their flight across our installation, we were near a coconut grove on the edge of the city. I directed my chauffeur to drive the car into it. With our car hidden under a coconut tree, the chauffeur and I got out and walked back to the edge of the grove where we watched the big Japanese bombers float back and forth unmolested over the city of Cebu. They had complete air superiority. When the planes had dropped the last of their bombs, they went back toward the east. Then my chauffeur and I got the car out of the coconut grove and headed back toward the city to see the damages inflicted by the raid.

After the second raid by 18 bombers, we had an uneventful time for a few days. Then excitement again! This time it wasn't an air raid but a Jap cruiser sailing through the straits around Cebu. It would shell a nipa village on the shore with a salvo or two and then take off and repeat the process in some other location. At the north end of the island of Cebu, near the town of Medellin, we had established an observation post under the command of one of the Naval officers sent down to Cebu from Corregidor. This commander was on the shore when the cruiser approached. I believe it was the first salvo (it might have been the second) the cruiser fired, in which one of the shells struck the commander and severed his head from his body. As I recall, the report said the shell hit him in the neck and caused his decapitation. The cruiser didn't make a landing there, although it may have sent a small boat ashore to see if it could capture a native or two. The rest of our outpost retreated from the shore as soon as the commander was killed.

The cruiser left the north end of the island and steamed south down the east coast creating panic among the Filipinos along the shore. When it arrived at Mactan Island, which shelters the harbor of Cebu City, it slowed down and finally stopped at the south end of the harbor. From there it started shelling the city of Cebu, but it didn't venture inside the harbor. Two or three shells struck my old quarters, Fort San Pedro de Cebu, and left holes in its massive, thick stone walls. Other shells landed out in the city. One landed in a garage, managed by a man named Burbinggame, where considerable repair work for the Army was done. Another landed in the palatial home of one of the Spanish families. After half or three quarters of an hour the cruiser ceased and sailed on south past the sound end of the island of Cebu.

Time was growing shorter for the Americans. The Japanese were growing bolder day by day. We couldn't stop them. All we could do was await their pleasure.

As I previously mentioned, about the first of March a U.S. cargo ship from Australia arrived with ammunition and food supplies. The first one that arrived in mid-February had hardly been unloaded and put to sea before a second one arrived. Both the *Doña Nati* and the *Anhuai* came in the space of about two weeks. I don't remember which came first. Under Col. John D. Cook, the port quartermaster, facilities worked night and day to unload these ships so that they would not be caught in the harbor by an air raid or by a cruiser roaming around the waters surrounding the island.

One of the boats took 16 days to come about 1,500 miles. It had to make so many changes in its course that it could barely make more than 100 miles a day. One morning at dawn, after a night's sailing, it found itself almost within sight of one of the Japanese-mandated islands. The captain knew he could not sail by the island unobserved in the daylight. He turned around and sailed back away from the island for 50 miles or so and then "lay low" until nightfall hoping that none of the Nip patrol planes would discover the ship. No planes came and with the fall of night, the ship sailed past the island undetected by the Japs.

There were several civilians and newspaper correspondents who had been sent from Corregidor to Cebu City to see if they could be sent on to Australia. Among the last was *Life* magazine's photographer Jacobi and his wife. I talked with them briefly at the service club one day. These people went out on the first boat when it sailed and they arrived safely in Australia. Later we heard that Jacobi had been killed in an airplane crash in Australia.

The first boat had hardly left before the second one came. The second one didn't have navigation charts of Philippine waters, I guess, because it ran aground on a sandbar between Cebu and Bohol about an hour out of the Cebu harbor. The ship lay out there in plain sight for several days until its load was lightened by barges and it could be towed off the bar. It also had food and ammunition on it. In addition there were several P-40 planes in a dismantled state. Finally the ship was towed off the bar and came into the harbor to finish unloading. It, too, set out for Australia as soon as it could. The waters of Cebu were much too warm to be healthy for any Allied ship.

The food and supplies that were to remain on Cebu from these two ships were taken back into the hills and mountains just as rapidly as it was possible. We knew that the more we got back the more we would have to live on when the going got tough. Invasion was imminent and we all knew it.

First word of the approach of the Japanese reached us in the afternoon of April 9. It was reported that three Japanese cruisers and eleven transports were steaming for Cebu from the south. That night further news was received that the Japanese force had split in two, one sailing along the west coast, the other along the east. By daylight, the enemy vessels were near the island, with the larger of the convoys reported to be close to the island's capital, Cebu City, midway up the east coast. Shortly after dawn the Japanese in this convoy landed at Cebu City; at about the same time the men in the other convoy came ashore in the vicinity of Toledo.

On April 11, the Nips attacked in great strength before dawn. They made quick work of us and our position on the Talisay-Toledo Road was untenable, so we were forced to pull back. Being the force communications officer, I refused to abandon my post. With the Japs less than 50 yards away, and under constant fire, I remained to destroy the communications installation at Camp X and deny hostile use of the vital equipment.

With the enemy in possession of the cross-island highway, the fight for Cebu was over in a matter of hours. Nothing more could be accomplished in central Cebu. Gen. Chynoweth, with about 200 men, started north to his retreat in the mountains. From there he hoped to organize the few units still remaining on the island into an efficient guerrilla force. The Japanese did not claim the complete subjugation of the island until April 19, but Gen. Wainwright had already acknowledged the loss of Cebu three days earlier when he ordered Gen. Sharp to re-establish the Visayan-Mindanao Force and take command of the remaining garrisons in the Visayas.

NOTE:

During the guerrilla campaign between mid-April 1942 and the surrender in mid-May 1942, there is strong evidence that my father was with a group known as the "Blackburn Raiders." They were considered up-close shooters. I do remember my father saying that he used a Winchester-Pump rifle during this time. He also told me a story that when he was sitting on a ridge one day looking for Japs, he saw a silvery flash coming towards him. He ducked as this "silvery flash" passed close to his head and hit a bamboo tree behind him. He was asked later, "Miner, are you trying to telling us that you dodge bullets?" This leads me to believe that he was a "close-up shooter." *(Lewis Miner)*

SEVEN

THE SURRENDER

THE SILENCE RESTED UNEASILY ON SUDLON FOREST AS I DESCENDED THE JUNGLE-COVERED TRAIL ON THE SIDE OF BALANBAN MOUNTAIN EARLY in May 1942. It lay heavy and oppressive, broken now and then by the subdued chatter of a monkey or a forest bird. As I moved cautiously down the trail, I reviewed the events of the last few weeks. Bataan had fallen, Corregidor was about to surrender. The few American forces on Cebu had been decimated by the troops of General Masaharu Homma, the "Beast of Bataan," and our guerrilla action had been limited on the island, due to the lack of effective weapons with which to fight. I was now on my way to Gen. Chynoweth's headquarters.

Upon arrival, I was received by Lt. Col. Marcus Boulware who informed me that Corregidor had surrendered and that Gen. Wainwright had broadcast a surrender order to all American forces in the Philippine Islands. He also stated that Gen. Chynoweth wished to continue to fight by moving our command to the Island of Leyte where we would operate as guerrillas on the larger, less populated island. However, there was some question about his having authority to refuse to surrender.

Late in the afternoon, I was instructed to go back to my outpost and return with my men the next day. Darkness caught me toiling and stumbling through inky blackness up in the steep canyon on the side of Balanban Mountain. Fortunately, I knew the trail well and still had a flashlight. Otherwise, I would have had to spend the night on the canyon side.

The next morning Lt. Henry Talmadge, Capt. Russell Cracraft, Maj. Ernest Jordan, and I, accompanied by some Filipinos, made our way back down the mountainside and, after hours of travel through the oppressive heat of the jungle, arrived at the general's headquarters.

After reporting to Lt. Col. Boulware and learning that we were to surrender, we sought out Gen. Chynoweth.

We found him sitting on a log looking at the jungle-covered wall. He looked around as we approached and saluted. "Well, boys," he said, "the news is bad."

"General, do we have to surrender?" I asked.

"The orders from headquarters specifically state that all troops will surrender and anyone who fails to surrender will be charged with refusal to obey orders. Officially, I have tried my best to be authorized to continue the fight in Leyte."

We were struck by the sadness and bitterness in his voice. Here was a young man who had spent all his life preparing to defend his country. Now he was forbidden to do so and was ordered to surrender.

I finally broke the silence.

"General," I said, "Maj. Jordan, Capt. Cracraft, Lt. Talmadge, and I have already laid plans against the time when we could not operate here. We have acquired a sea-going banca [outrigger canoe], stocked it with canned goods and coconuts, and we have secured a Filipino navigator. Will you give us a mission to Leyte or some other island that will permit us to set sail for Australia?"

Gen. Chynoweth looked at us sharply. "Have you had any experience in navigation, and do you have a compass?"

I shook my head and replied, "We do not have a compass, but our navigator assures us he can sail by the stars."

The general looked thoughtful and after a long study said, "I'm sorry, boys, but I cannot consent to it. You will have to go on your own."

Cracraft, Talmadge, Jordan, and I looked at each other. I finally said, "General, if you are going to surrender, I will stay with you." The others did the same and we left.

It was a heavy blow to face the idea of imprisonment when we could escape. I left the encampment and walked alone along the stream. The afternoon became hotter and more oppressive and when I came to a large pool of water below a small waterfall, I stripped and went swimming. The cool water seemed to soothe my tormented mind and body. I perched on a ledge in the water at the floor of the falls and rested. Suddenly, I became aware of a Filipino officer standing on the edge of the pool beside my pile of clothes on which my rifle lay. My first thought was what an ignoble way to meet my end. Then I recognized him. It was 1st Lt. Gavino Lapura, one of my officers from camp.

"Lapura," I exclaimed, "I thought you were gone," and plunged for the shore to dress.

"No, Captain," he replied, "I have come through the Japanese lines to join you. I want you to come with me and I will take you through the Japanese lines to the south end of the island of Cebu. From there we will take a banca to my home island of Bohol where I will hide you until the Americans return. You must not surrender to the Japanese."

This was one of my hardest personal decisions and I thought along time before I finally said, "No, Lapura, I think I had better surrender. However, this is my suggestion to you. Take my rifle and go back to Bohol until the Americans return." (He became a captain in the Bohol guerrillas and aided the returning American forces.)

The next morning our little band of hungry, weary Americans left our camp in the valley and traveled all day in a southerly direction over mountains and valleys. As darkness fell, we made torches by binding grass and wood together. Late that night we arrived at the edge of the forest where we camped on a high ridge above a large grass-covered valley.

The next morning Col. Irvine C. Scudder, Gen. Chynoweth's chief of staff, directed Cracraft and me to lead an advance party to Camp X and prepare it for the arrival of our few forces. Our party of 10 descended 1,000 feet into the valley and climbed the near vertical opposite side, always traveling in a southerly direction. Late in the afternoon, we descended a long ridge and as we approached the highway in the vicinity of Camp X, we affixed a white flag of truce to a bamboo pole; this precaution proved unnecessary as the area was deserted.

At last we entered the forested area of our old headquarters. There, under the trees of the valley floor, scenes of shambles and destruction met our eyes. Cracraft and I were stunned by how little was left of what had once been an orderly camp. Finally, we sat down and viewed the scene with heavy hearts. This was the end of our efforts. It was the end of the American forces in the Philippines. We were the lost men of a lost cause and we could see only imprisonment and an unknown fate before us.

Later, as we crossed the road, a car came swiftly around a nearby curve and skidded to a halt when its driver saw us. Out stepped a Filipino mestizo.

"What are you doing here?" he inquired.

"We have come ahead of our forces to plan for the camping of the American Forces which will surrender here day after tomorrow," Cracraft replied.

"Good," he replied. "I will report this to the Japanese commander at Toledo." With that he stepped back into his car and sped down the road.

The next morning we heard a motor and a shout from the road. Cracraft and I decided we had better investigate and when we reached the road it was the Filipino mestizo, accompanied by an armed Japanese soldier.

"You are to come at once to Toledo where the Japanese commander will question you," said the mestizo. There was little else we could do. We entered an American car and were taken to the Japanese headquarters at Toledo, which was located in a schoolhouse. Cracraft and I grew very uneasy as we stood in the schoolyard surrounded by vicious-looking armed guards. Finally, we were led into the building where we entered a large room with four Japanese officers seated in a semi-circle. There were four guards with rifles in the room, one in each corner. The rifles were cocked and the bayonets were fixed. In front of the seated officers were two tables littered with maps.

Our guide, who could speak English, shoved us into the open part of the circle facing the four officers. He then walked around to stand behind one of the officers who proved to be the senior. Finally, after a period of at least two minutes of searching scrutiny, the senior officer let out a shout. Cracraft and I must have batted our eyes because the youngest officer smiled an instant and then recovered his gravity. The English-speaking Japanese soldier behind the senior officer then spoke to us.

"What are your names and rank?" I answered and gave my rank. Cracraft did the same.

"What were you doing on the highway in the mountains?"

"We are the advance party of Gen. Chynoweth's forces on their way to surrender to the Japanese at Camp X," I replied bitterly.

"When do you plan to surrender?" was the next question.

"Tomorrow," Cracraft answered.

"What units of your forces are coming to Camp X and how many men are in the units?" was the next question.

Cracraft and I shifted uneasily and looked at one another. Out of the 5,500 troops on the island of Cebu, we expected only a few dozen to surrender. We realized we were in a tight spot and the air became charged, as we remained silent.

The Japanese officer spoke again sharply and the interpreter said, "Answer the question."

"To be honest with you," I said, "we do not know exactly how many to expect."

The interpreter spoke in Japanese. The Japanese officer roared in anger at my answer and after a full minute of verbosity, he ceased and the interpreter spoke. "It is very foolish for an American officer who is on a general's staff to lie and say he does not know how many men his general has. The major says he is tempted to strike off your head with his ancestral sword. For your own safety you must answer him."

I made my decision, deciding to tell the truth and resort to flattery. "The Filipinos reported that there was a Japanese general with a large Army here in Toledo and another in Cebu City. All our communications have been disrupted and I do not know how many troops we have. There has never been anything in the history of the U.S. Army like the astounding defeats, which your forces have inflicted upon us in these last few days. So complete has been the annihilation of our forces that I would guess the only Americans left alive are at our headquarters. I am sorry if my answer does not please the Japanese commander, but if he doubts my word he has no idea how effective his troops have been."

The interpreter relayed my message and after much conversation, the interpreter turned and asked, "Will 15 large trucks be enough to transport your headquarters to prison?"

"His estimate is very sound," I replied in relief, realizing that he had accepted my statement.

"We are going to continue to treat you as official emissaries for the American forces and we will return you to camp. Tomorrow morning at 11 A.M. our forces will enter that area and formally receive your surrender."

The Japanese then treated us to a cup of hot tea and after a few minutes of informal conversation, sent us back to camp.

The next morning, May 17, a few minutes before 11:00, 43 Americans and approximately 100 Filipinos gathered in the little open area along the side of the road running through our camp. We were a compact, silent group as Japanese trucks filled with troops rolled into the area. A Japanese officer ordered his troops out of the trucks and motioned for them to surround us. He then requested Gen. Chynoweth, our chief of staff, Col. Scudder, and the two emissaries (Cracraft and myself) to come forward.

"Do you have all your men ready to surrender?" he asked.

"Yes," replied Gen. Chynoweth.

"Show my men where your arms are," the Japanese officer instructed.

"Scudder, you and Cracraft show them," the general said.

I remained near the general and slightly behind him as the other two moved off, accompanied by several Japanese soldiers. I watched the general square his shoulders and look at the sky. His look was one of bitter disillusionment and I realized that he was taking the surrender with far more feeling than he had shown. This was a personal defeat for him as well as a most disgraceful way to end a career in the defense of his country. We stood in the sun waiting, surrounded by Japanese. The green forest near us beckoned longingly.

Col. Scudder and Cracraft, sweating profusely, returned with a Japanese soldier who talked excitedly to the Japanese officer who, in turn, angrily demanded of us, "Where are your swords? Are there no swords with your arms? Have you destroyed or hidden them? We must have them!"

"American officers do not wear swords," he was informed. "They carry pistols."

"This is preposterous!" he replied. "All officers have swords. Even sergeants have swords," he said, pointing to a Japanese soldier. After much conversation, the officer accepted the fact that there were no American swords to be captured.

The interpreter turned to us and told the general to prepare to surrender his troops. Gen. Chynoweth relayed the information to our troop commander and our little group came to attention. The Japanese officer barked an order, spoke a minute or so in Japanese, and then turned on his heel. His detail commanders, in turn, barked orders and the Japanese soldiers surrounded us. I was shoved into the ranks. Shortly, the Japanese soldiers were among us searching each man. They took our few remaining personal belongings such as pocket knives, watches, pens and pencils, family pictures, rings, billfolds, anything that caught their fancy. Lt. Byron Lee Johnson stooped and started to pick up his empty billfold after a Jap soldier tossed it at his feet. The Jap instantly kneed him in the groin and he fell in a heap. There were other incidents of similar violence.

After the plundering of our personal items, we were ordered to climb into the waiting trucks. With dragging footsteps our little band approached the vehicles and climbed the best we could into the truck beds amid the sound of rifle butts striking human flesh.

The American forces on the island of Cebu had surrendered to the Japanese.

As the trucks started down the canyon road, we were on our way, to march as Roman captives in a triumphant Japanese parade through the City of Cebu, to 39 months of torture, shipwreck, and death before our release in faraway Mukden, Manchuria.

EIGHT

PRISONERS OF WAR

A FTER THE SURRENDER ON MAY 17, 1942, I WAS CONFINED IN THE CEBU CIVIL JAIL. I REMAINED THERE FIVE MONTHS UNTIL OCTOBER 17, 1942. At that time I was moved to the Philippine POW Camp #2, Davao, Mindanao. It was at that time Lt. Junsaburo Toshino and Mr. Shusuke Wada, a civilian interpreter, first appeared. Mr. Wada was the first to appear and he arrived in camp sometime around December 1942 or January 1943. His designation at camp was the official Japanese interpreter who spoke English for that camp. His job was to act as liaison officer between the Japanese army officials in charge of the camp and the American prisoners of war. From the very beginning, Mr. Wada was inclined to look upon the Americans as criminals to be punished, beaten about, and made to suffer. He held the attitude that, instead of being honorable soldiers overcome by superior forces, we had committed an unpardonable crime because we had dared to oppose the imperial forces of the Japanese Emperor. At every opportunity, Mr. Wada would do his utmost to discredit the American POWs with the Japanese camp officials. Under the policy of the Japanese camp commander, Maj. Maeda, all the personnel in the camp were required to work regardless of age and rank. There were exceptions in respect to internal officers of the camp and some of the really sick. Mr. Wada, once or twice a week, would go through the sick barracks of the camp with the American camp commander examining the sick people. He would point to some man, who perhaps had malaria within 24 or 48 hours and who was just beginning a short course of quinine and ask, "Why is this man not out at work? He is not sick, he does not even look sick. The Japanese soldiers are always on duty even though they pretend to be sick." All explanation given in respect to such cases would only infuriate Mr. Wada and he would leave camp very angry. During such occasions the American camp commander would be as diplomatic as possible and do his best to give the sick man a chance to recuperate. Very often, after such occasions, the camp would be shorted a sack or two of rice. When our camp commander asked Mr. Wada why we were shorted in our ration (which consisted mostly of rice and wheat soup and was far inferior to what the Japanese soldiers were eating), Mr. Wada answered, "But you do not need food because you have so many sick. The sick do not work and we cannot feed people who do not work." The result of all this was that our rations would be shorted for a day or two.

Mr. Wada often came out to the fields where the men were working. One incident occurred in the sweet potato field. Mr. Wada personally walked out among the potato planters and found Capt. Milton Whaley, who had gotten a little too much dirt covering some of his sweet potato slips. Without any warning, Mr. Wada proceeded to use his stick that he was carrying to beat Capt. Whaley. As a result, Capt. Whaley was put in the sick barracks for two days. Capt. Whaley was doing a decent job and his sweet potato plants were as efficiently planted as any of the others. By Mr. Wada's manner, it was easy to see that he was looking for something to make an issue of. After beating Capt. Whaley, Mr. Wada lectured the whole detail of about 150 to 200 men on doing a very bad job of planting sweet potatoes. As a result, the whole detail had to stay out on the job for an extra hour with no rest periods during the later three-quarters of the day. Also, after Mr. Wada talked to the guards, they became very vicious and before the day was over two or three other Americans were beaten or clubbed.

Often our little hospital would run out of medical supplies and we would have to ask a Japanese doctor for new supplies. Officially this had to be done through Mr. Wada. At such time Mr. Wada would say he would see to it and our camp commander would hear nothing more about the medical supplies. Finally the Japanese doctor would make an inspection and inquire as to why there were so many more people in the hospital, and Lt. Col. Dwight M. Deter, the American hospital commander, would immediately tell the Japanese doctor that we had run out of quinine, anesthetics, bandages, etc. He would also very pointedly tell the Japanese doctor that we had asked for supplies and that they had been promised to us, but they had never arrived. Often, very shortly after that, a portion of the quantity of supplies asked for would be brought into camp by a guard. Mr. Wada, after such occasions, would be extremely harsh and revengeful in his contact with all Americans. During such periods he usually beat Americans and would go out on inspection details and by ingenious ways make the detail almost unbearable. For example, in cutting weed greens and bringing them into camp, the American detail would carry these greens in big baskets swung on a pole and borne by two men. He would force us to load our own baskets far beyond the weight that we could ably carry. This overtaxed our strength to the point that some of the men would grow so weak that they would fall under the weight of their load. On such occasions the guards would beat them for failure to do the work. The only thing we could do was to leave a basket on the way and double up with the weakened detail members. As a result, the camp was again shorted of food.

On the logging detail, several times Mr. Wada would come and complain that the men were carrying just sticks instead of good firewood logs out of the jungle. We were beaten until we carried out logs of a size that he desired and we would be kept overtime until dark when they were afraid that we would escape. As a specific example, I was one of two men who had to carry a 10-foot log, which we estimated to weigh 200 pounds, through the edge of the jungle for about half a mile. This task would have been a large one for healthy men on good rations. We were barefoot and naked to the waist. As a result of this, we were badly bruised, both in the feet and the shoulders, and so exhausted that we could hardly move when we reached the railroad car that we were loading. There were many other details who performed feats that were equal to, or similar to this. I give this just as an example.

In respect to the need of our camp and specifically when our camp commander would protest the beatings of Americans by the Japanese, Mr. Wada was the official go-between the American camp commander and the Japanese officials. On all such occasions, Mr. Wada (in translating what our camp officials were saying to the Japanese camp officials) would take three or four times as long to translate to the Japanese officials what our camp officials said. For a specific example in regard to food, Lt. Col. Kenneth S. Olsen asked Maj. Maeda for more food. The conversation went something like this:

Lt. Col. Olsen speaking: "Major, we need more food; all our men are losing weight and we cannot work and maintain our health on the rations that you are giving us." Mr. Wada took the greater part of seven or eight minutes, in my estimation, to translate these two or three simple statements. As he talked, Mr. Wada would become increasingly vehement. After he was finished, Maj. Maeda spoke a few words and Mr. Wada again talked angrily for several minutes. At this point, Lt. Col. Olsen made a simple statement: "We need more food." Mr. Wada then turned back to Maj. Maeda and talked for at least five minutes. The end of the conversation was a statement from Wada to this effect: "Maj. Maeda will see if he can get you more food, but all Americans must work harder; they have been lagging on their details."

It was very plain to see that Mr. Wada was coloring the situation with his personal animosity far beyond the statements made by our camp commander.

This was the background and attitude of Mr. Wada at the Davao Penal

Colony. This camp lasted for 21 months and was broken up in June 1944 by which time there were 1,200 men left at the Davao Penal Colony with a detail at Lasang under Lt. Col. Rufus H. Rogers, which was working on an airstrip. The approximate number of American prisoners in the Lasang detail was 750.

When they moved out 1,200 from Davao to the prison ship at Lasang, we were taken in trucks from camp. Each truck, which was a 1 1/2 ton, contained 40 men in the truck bed. We were placed standing five abreast with our hands tied behind us and ropes tied around the waist of each of us running from one person to another and the men at one end or the other of the rows were tied to the row behind. The result was that every man in the truck had his hands tied behind him and was tied at the waist to his neighbor. Sitting on top of the cab was a Japanese guard with a long pole in his hand. Our instructions were to keep our head bowed and look at the floor of the truck during the entire trip. The guards used the pole on anybody who happened to look up. This trip lasted about six hours and it became extremely torturous to all the American POWs. Some of the men almost went mad from the pain and it was nothing to hear them moan or cry out. Wada was interpreter during this trip and he frequently made the ropes unduly harsh as we were tied.

When we were placed on the ship, there was insufficient room for us to lie down. Lt. Col. Olsen protested to Mr. Wada concerning our crowded conditions and Mr. Wada was able to do nothing for us, so he said, because the captain of the ship had no more room. The 1,200 American soldiers were placed in one hold (on one deck) towards the bow of the ship. There was not enough room for the men to lie side by side with their bodies touching. The best we could do was have four men sit with their knees drawn up against their chest in the space that one man's body would normally take. This trip lasted 21 days as I recall. During this time Mr. Wada was asked to get us disposal cans for our bodily waste; he got us a few, but not near enough what we asked for.

During our time in Cabanatuan or Philippine POW Camp No. 1, Mr.

Wada had very little association with us. We did not see him again, with the exception of one or two times, until December 13, 1944, when he and Lt. Toshino were placed in charge of the group of 1,619 American prisoners placed on board the *Oryoku Maru*. Lt. Toshino was the Japanese officer in charge of our group of POWs with Mr. Wada as his assistant and interpreter. Lt. Toshino was also in Davao during the last few months of existence of the Davao Camp. As one of the Japanese officers in the Davao Camp command, he proved himself very unfriendly to the American prisoners. His conduct was the same harassing style as that of Mr. Wada.

I desire to make it plain at this point that Mr. Wada was undoubtedly following out the policy laid down or at least condoned by the Japanese prison commander. Lt. Toshino, likewise, followed this policy and used every chance he had to make the Americans uncomfortable. In Davao, Lt. Toshino had used all the ingenious Japanese devices, which have been mentioned as part of Mr. Wada's technique. Lt. Toshino, being an officer, can be held as more responsible than Mr. Wada for the roughness of the policy pursued by the Japanese officials and guards toward the American POWs.

On October 12, 1944, we were moved again to Bilibid Camp, Manila, where we remained until December 13, 1944.

The afternoon of December 13, 1944, 1,619 American prisoners were placed in the hold of the *Oryoku Maru* in such a manner that they did not have even standing room.

The prisoners were marched into the hold at the point of a bayonet. The hold became so filled by men sitting down that it was impossible for any more men to enter. At this point, the Japanese guards, under Mr. Wada's direction, made about half of the prisoners stand up. With the prisoners standing up, it was possible to force more Americans down into the hold. There were three Japanese guards who directed the placing of the prisoners. Two of these men had bamboo poles about six feet long. The third had a shovel or spade. With these poles and spade they beat Americans, both standing and sitting, until they were squashed into huddles of solid flesh and bones. Then more Americans would be forced into the hold. With the men that were standing the Japanese held their poles horizontal and shoved against the chests of the men as they stood in mass against the side of the hold. While the two guards with the poles were shoving with all their might against the solid mass of prisoners, the third guard with the spade went up and down the line beating them to make them shrink closer against the wall.

In the course of a few minutes a large group of the prisoners were standing in an oblique position of perhaps a 45° angle. This was due to the fact that the feet were broader than the thickness of their chests. The time came when the mass of perhaps 200 prisoners against this wall was actually lying against each other in an upright position. When the Japanese finished loading Americans into the hold, I estimate that there must have been at least 500 American POWs in the lying-standing position. During this loading operation, Mr. Wada and Lt. Toshino were up on the deck forcing the Americans into the hold. The fact that there was no sitting room in the hold and that the POWs were standing in great numbers made no difference to them. Both Toshino and Wada would glance into the hold and then at the remainder of the group of prisoners yet to be loaded and would order more into the hold. After each decision by Toshino, Mr. Wada would lean over the edge of the hatch and cry out, "More men, more men down here." When the Americans would protest that there was no more room, Mr. Wada would answer, "It does not make any difference, more men must go down." There was no argument that was effective. As near as I can remember, a general estimate in my section of the hold, the number of prisoners forced into that hold was around 800. This included what little baggage each one was carrying. Since this was December we knew that it would be cold in Japan and we tried to take with us what few clothes we had. When the Japanese finished loading us into the hold, it was practically impossible to move. We were wedged in so tightly against each other that we could not move if we tried. In a period of about six hours, we were able to shift ourselves a little and make more room for the standing. As a result, most of the American POWs who had been lying against their fellows in an upright position were able to stand upright. As soon as our hold was loaded, Toshino ordered the hatch closed and we were left in darkness. There was no attempt made to give us ventilation. Even in December the weather in the Philippines is exceedingly tropical. As soon as the prisoners could arrange themselves so that they could move, they started taking off their clothes in order that they would not perspire so much and to keep them being overcome by heat. Within a few hours practically everybody was stripped to a pair of shorts or "G" string.

The ship pulled out into Manila Bay as soon as the American prisoners were loaded. The POWs were not the only passengers on this ship. For a period of about four hours we waited at the dock while Japanese civilians, a small number of troops, and a large number of Japanese women and children were loaded onto the ship. These passengers were placed in the passenger quarters and on the various decks.

The ship appeared to get underway as soon as they had fastened the hatch covers. Within an hour, the American POWs were beginning to faint from lack of air and from the heat. There was no water available except what each individual had in his canteen or any type of receptacle in which he could carry water. Within about eight hours, fully half of the 800 POWs had used up their small water supply. Within four hours after the hatches had been closed people were beginning to go out of their minds, thrash and struggle around and to scream. That first night was so nearly a reality of hell that I cannot begin to describe the situation as it really was. Men went stark raving mad, screamed, cursed, and beat each other up as if they were mad animals. Several times during the night somebody would scream out, "He is killing me, he is killing me; get him off of me!" All during this time the hold was pitch dark and it was impossible to tell what was going on or who was going mad or who was killing whom. In the morning a little light penetrated through the canvas that covered the hatch and we could dimly see the men lying upon one another. There were several men dead, perhaps 15 or 20 this first night. It was impossible to make an accurate count. Some of those dead showed marks of violence with gashes on their throats and wrists. There is no doubt in my mind that some people had gone entirely crazy and reverted to an animal status. Teeth marks would indicate that there had been attempts to suck blood from these victims.

Shortly after sunup, Cmdr. Bridgett, who was the American in charge of our hold, quieted talk in the hold with the following information: "The time is at hand to show ourselves true Americans and not to lose our heads; our convoy is under air attack." I won't go into detail concerning the air attacks. Mr. Wada and Lt. Toshino appeared once during the day, looked into the hold and went away. That day we got one meal that consisted of a handful of rice per man—the volume of this rice in my ration was equal to perhaps a teacup. We received no water and there were some who received no food. All during this time no provision had been made for our bodily waste. Quite a number of the men were sick with dysentery and with weak kidneys. Our hold was fast becoming wet and filthy from these bodily wastes. Wada and Toshino were told of this the one time that they looked into the hold.

As the air attack continued during the day, the hatch covers were taken off of the holds in order that the Japanese guards could see what the prisoners were doing. The men who were directly below the open hatch could see our planes in air attack. We estimated that our ship was under actual dive bombing 12 or 15 times that day. It was hit several times and partially wrecked. Some of the Navy men said that the ship's rudder had been destroyed from the way she handled. During this first day's bombing, the ship was very near the old location of our Naval Base at Olongapo. During the night the ship limped up to shore and discharged the Japanese soldiers, civilians, women, and children. In the morning she moved offshore slightly and anchored just offshore from the tennis court at Olongapo. The American prisoners and some of the Japanese guards remained on board the ship. Mr. Wada and Lt. Toshino were nowhere about. The second night was far worse than the first night in respect to American POWs going stark raving mad. In the morning our dive-bombers were back attacking the remainder of the convoy. By 10:00 A.M. we had undergone a series of dive bomb attacks. At approximately 10 A.M. we underwent a dive bomb attack during which a bomb lit in the hold where I was and blew the side out of the ship. The bomb fell between 20–30 feet away from me among a group of about 115 field officers. There were only eight or nine survivors of this group of approximately 115 men. One of the survivors was Lt. Col. John Curtis. The result of this bomb landing in the hold of the ship was chaos. There was wreckage of all types from the ship and pieces of bodies all over the place. There were wounded men unable to move; others, pinned down by wreckage, who were unable to get free. When the wreckage quit falling, the American POWs began to stir around, and some started toward the stairway to the deck, which was still standing. Immediately the Japanese guards, who were uninjured and still at their positions, up on deck, tossed hand grenades down into the hold, started firing their rifles, and some used their pistols on the American prisoners who were attempting to climb out of the wreckage. A man about two feet away from me sat up out of the wreckage, got to his knees and placed both hands on the stairway to the deck. He was immediately shot in the chest, very near the heart. He took two full breaths, flopped back into the wreckage and died. While I was watching him die, there were other shots from the deck through the hold. I heard some prisoners say that Lt. Toshino was present and fired his pistol into the hold. I saw a Japanese, who might have been Toshino, but due to the confusion I did not pay particular attention to him and I could not swear that Toshino was the man with the pistol. After a few minutes of this type of treatment, the Japanese guards left their posts and the American prisoners started climbing out of the hold onto the deck of the wrecked ship. Some jumped into the seagoing through a hole in the side of the ship. I went up the ladder and onto the deck where I saw several dead Americans who had been shot and a few dead Japanese. Finding a life preserver among the dead, I put it on and jumped overboard. Once in the sea I started swimming to the nearest point of the shore. During this time there were still Japanese guards on the boat and they were firing at American soldiers who were swimming in the water. Several men were killed by those shots. Those of us who went as direct as possible from the ship to the shore were not very often fired at. Those Americans who attempted to swim to more distant points of the shore were often shot as they swam. There were a few who undoubtedly got to shore. After the majority of the survivors of the boat had been recaptured, Japanese details went along the shore searching for escaped prisoners. For several hours after I reached the shore I heard firing in the region of the wrecked ship. The Japanese were undoubtedly mopping up any Americans whom they found alive and attempting to escape.

When we left the ship, it was burning and although the American POWs themselves attempted to remove wreckage from the wounded and the helpless, we were so weakened that we were unable to save many. The Japanese made no attempt to rescue any of the wounded. These poor devils were left to burn with the ship. Due to suffocation the first two nights, we estimated that between 50 and 75 Americans died in the hold and it is estimated that 230-some men were killed in the actual bombing or left on the burning ship.

When the Japanese recaptured the majority of the survivors we were herded into a tennis court. Once in the tennis court and settled, we found that there was just room enough to lie down by lying alternately. By this I mean that every second individual had his feet lying near the head of the individual on each side of him. There was no food given us on this day, December 15.

NINE

DIARY EXCERPTS

THIS IS THE MEAGER DIARY OF THE MOST FANTASTIC AND HORRIBLE SHIP TRIP I EVER TOOK, AND ONE OF THE MOST HORRIBLE VOYAGES OF WWII.

TUESDAY, DECEMBER 12, 1944. The camp commander of Bilibid Prison was informed late in the afternoon that 1,619 American POWs were to leave in the morning.

WEDNESDAY, DECEMBER 13. We were placed on board the *Oryoku Maru.*

THURSDAY, DECEMBER 14. We were bombed all day and received one meal.

FRIDAY, DECEMBER 15. We underwent several bombing attacks and around 10:00 A.M. a bomb exploded inside the hold of the ship blowing the side out and setting it on fire. No food.

SATURDAY, DECEMBER 16. The American prisoners who were able to get ashore, approximately 1,333 of 1,619, were confined to the tennis court with water, but no food; torrid sun. I was wounded slightly on both hands and right cheek by flying bomb fuse during raid by our bombers.

SUNDAY, DECEMBER 17. The group of POWs were still on the tennis court. There were four deaths and we received our first food since

December 14. This food ration consisted of 2½ mess kit spoonfuls of dry uncooked rice. There was no way to cook this rice, consequently it did us very little good. To boil it down, we had one sack of rice for 1,333 men.

MONDAY, DECEMBER 18. This day is a repeat of the 17th and our food ration was three mess kit spoons of raw dry rice.

TUESDAY, DECEMBER 19. Men can hardly walk, heat stroke by day and freezing by night. Four mess kit spoons of dry rice.

WEDNESDAY, DECEMBER 20. Four and one-half days on the tennis court with 13½ mess kit spoons of raw dry rice for our total ration. By this time, Mr. Wada and Lt. Toshino had made arrangements to take us out of the tennis court. Just as they moved us they brought in some wornout salvaged tropical Japanese uniforms which were nothing but rags. I received two pairs of shorts. By wearing both pairs at the same time I was still unable to cover myself up. During these days on the tennis court we had plenty of water, no food except a few spoonfuls of raw rice. No sanitation, except a trench just outside the gate of the court and absolutely no medical attention. Many of the men were wounded. In one case a man had his leg amputated on the floor of the tennis court under the tropical sun. Naturally he died after, but it was the best that could be done. Between the damp cold of the night and the fierce rays of the sun by day, the men were failing rapidly and beginning to die.

THURSDAY AND FRIDAY, DECEMBER 21–22. The group was moved from Olongapo to San Fernando, Pampanga, where we were lodged in the provincial jail and a cockpit. During the days that we were there the flies were terrible. They crawled all over us as though we had been covered with honey. One reason for this attraction was the fact that the Japanese had given us no opportunity for bathing and we were unspeakably filthy with our own filth.

SATURDAY, DECEMBER 23. We received an estimated 300 grains of cooked rice. One death occurred this day.

SUNDAY, DECEMBER 24. Moved to San Fernando, La Union, by the way of small box cars on the Luzon railroad. The Japanese placed 180 Americans standing in the particular car that I was in. There were also sick American POWs placed on the top of the prison cars. We were in these cars from about 10 A.M. until 3 A.M. the next morning. During this time we received no food, no water. The hardship of the journey packed in these cars, which were exposed to the tropical sun, caused many men to faint.

MONDAY, CHRISTMAS DAY, 1944. The group was in a school yard, received two meals and a little water. The amount of rice is estimated as one canteen cup and the water ration is estimated as half a canteen cup. This is the lowest Christmas I ever had; we are without hope, almost.

TUESDAY, DECEMBER 26. The group was moved to some sand dunes not far from the San Fernando pier waiting to be placed on board another ship. The day was terribly hot sitting and lying on the sand exposed to the direct rays of the sun. Our ration was five mess kit spoons of water and a half cup of rice.

I want to make it very plain that on both of these days there were wells very near our location and plenty of water could have been given us had Lt. Toshino and Mr. Wada so directed. No amount of pleading with them would do any good. They refused us water. By this time it was very apparent that the more inhumane they could be, the better they liked it.

WEDNESDAY, DECEMBER 27. We were placed on board a large empty freighter, *Enoura Maru,* at dawn and got underway. One meal of a third cup of rice and half-pint of tea; one soldier, an officer I believe named D. C. Brown, was shot when he attempted to jump overboard and escape.

THURSDAY, DECEMBER 28. Half-cup of rice, a little piece of fish, and third cup of water for our day's food and water ration. As the ship went north, the atmosphere became cool and the men did not suffer so much from the heat. The ship that we were placed on was a large freighter that had just brought a cavalry unit down to Luzon. No attempts had been made to clean the place. As a result we were forced to sit and lie in horse manure and urine. We just had enough room to sit down if we curled up. This hold was filled with flies, millions of them, which persisted in swarming over us making us more miserable than we were. Again, there was no sanitation.

FRIDAY, DECEMBER 29. One meal of half-cup of rice and no water.

SATURDAY, DECEMBER 30. Half-cup of rice, five mess kit spoons of soup, and half-pint of water.

SUNDAY, DECEMBER 31. One and half meals today, arrived in the Port of Takao on Formosa.

MONDAY, JANUARY 1, 1945. Ship lying in the harbor of Formosa; men were dying. Received two meals and no water.

TUESDAY, JANUARY 2. Still on board the ship; more dead; usual ration of rice which was half canteen cup, also received one cup of soup to be divided among six men. We received half a cup of water.

WEDNESDAY, JANUARY 3. We received three spoons of dry rice, half-cup of cooked rice, quarter cup of soup and one pint of water.

THURSDAY, JANUARY 4. One meal plus a little soup, received one water ration of half-pint. Thirty-four dead since leaving Olongapo; no medicine or dressings of any type. Dysentery is bad. Since boarding the ship, Mr. Wada had appeared almost daily; asked him for more food and water. Lt. Toshino appeared once or twice; all of our requests were either refused or ignored.

FRIDAY, JANUARY 5. One meal; no soup and one water ration received. Six men died, making a total of 40 since leaving Olongapo. The estimate, 1,293 survivors to date, out of 1,619 that started on the *Oryoku Maru* on December 13, 1944.

SATURDAY, JANUARY 6. Japanese were all day loading supplies on board the ship. Part of our detail which had been on board another ship was brought on board. We received two meals with soup each time and a short ration of water, which means less than half-pint. Four more dead.

SUNDAY, JANUARY 7. Recheck on number: 1,619 left Bilibid, 279 lost on the *Oryoku Maru* or 1,340 arrived on the tennis court. Fifteen of the most seriously wounded were sent back to Bilibid; 1,309 got on board the boat at Lingayen Gulf. 1,262 alive this morning. Two meals and water today. Fifty have died since arriving on tennis court.

MONDAY, JANUARY 8. Still in Takao Harbor clearing up the ship's mess; we received one meal and one water ration, group was divided into two holds, sitting room only, sitting much worse than before.

TUESDAY, JANUARY 9. It is about noon and we have just been hit by five bombs in an air raid by our planes. We are still in the harbor of Takao. Ten days now, many are dead. Japanese not doing anything for us.

WEDNESDAY, JANUARY 10. Many dead in the other hold, estimate about 236, about 40 dead in this hold, many are wounded, myself included.

THURSDAY, JANUARY 11. Japanese cleaned the dead out of the holds, one case of diphtheria today. One meal with soup; very cold at night.

FRIDAY, JANUARY 12. Night very cold, sleep in shorts, meals the same, nine more dead from wounds. Dr. Whaley killed by bomb. Repairing boat by placing wooden plugs in the small holes; two meals.

SATURDAY, JANUARY 13. Moved to another ship, *Brazil Maru*. One meal and no water. Wounded are dying for lack of medicine and moving. In reference to the bombing, these figures are as near accurate as I could get at the time. There were many who were seriously wounded that we had to move to another ship, about a dozen and a half died while they were being moved. We were bombed on the 9th and it was not until the 11th or 12th that the Japanese made any attempt to give us any medical care. I believe it was on the 11th when the Japanese took the carcasses off the ship that they gave us this farcical medical treatment. The treatment consisted of everybody who was able to walk, who had a wound, forming in a line and having a Japanese first-aid man paint his wound with some red disinfectant and perhaps receiving a bandage. The most beneficial effects of this visit was the fact that some of the wounded received some bandages. We had no bandages with us and what little care we ourselves gave the wounded was done by donation of clothes from our own backs. The Japanese made no effort to give us bandages, disinfectant, or any kind of care. The attention they did give us did not come until the odor pile of dead directly under the hatch became so strong that it must have been unpleasant on the deck. It was terrible down where we were.

SUNDAY, JANUARY 14. Moved out to sea at dawn in convoy; one meal of quarter cup of rice and no water.

MONDAY, JANUARY 15. Ship sailed north all day; we had two meals and no water.

TUESDAY, JANUARY 16. Ship still sailing north; men dying; very cold and we have no clothes.

WEDNESDAY, JANUARY 17. 32 men died last night from exposure and disease; boat stopped and anchored overnight.

THURSDAY, JANUARY 18. The boat anchored at night and sailed north all day; two light meals and quarter canteen cup of water; weather very cold.

FRIDAY, JANUARY 19. We had two light meals and two rations of water. The ship anchored all night and sailed all day.

SATURDAY, JANUARY 20. Ship stopped at night; had two meals and one water ration. It is very cold and the men continue to die at the rate of about 30 a day. The boat sailed all day.

SUNDAY, JANUARY 21. Two meals and one water ration. Ship sailing north. The usual number of men are dying. At this point I want to make clear that the ship was sailing north every day and each day the weather got colder. We were still naked at this stage of the trip as we had been when we started out from Lingayen Gulf. As the men died, which they did at the rate of 30 to 50 a day, the Japanese continued to decrease our ration accordingly so that in spite of the vast numbers dying, those remaining alive received no additional food. Mr. Wada and Lt. Toshino would come around and demand to know exactly how many had died each day. They decreased the food that they were giving us accordingly. A time or two there was a discrepancy between the figures that we gave and the count of the Japanese. On each occasion Mr. Wada would refuse to give us food until they could agree on the figures.

All during this time the Japanese had straw mats and life preservers aboard the ship which they could have given us to cover ourselves as protection against the cold. This they refused to do. I am absolutely certain that these mats were available because I was one of the first in this hold and saw them lying on the floor. The hold had been used for the transportation of Japanese troops and there were dozens and dozens of mats and life preservers left scattered around by the Japanese troops. We started gathering up these mats and life preservers for our use, but the Japanese ordered us to put them in a designated place in which they were stored. Afterwards, I traded a fountain pen for one of these mats. There is no doubt in my mind that receiving this mat through trading with a Japanese guard was what saved my life. Not only did it save my own life, but it also saved the lives of Lt. Col. Robert Lawlor and Maj. F. L. Berry. The three of us huddled together covered by this mat. All during this trip there was an open hatch in the center of the deck above our hold. The Japanese refused to entirely cover this and there was always an open hatchway in the deck above. Through these openings rain, snow, and sleet often fell. The wind always blew down through the openings over our exposed bodies. Most of us had to lie upon the bare steel floor of the hold or upon the bare boards of the upper tier. No amount of pleading with the Japanese would get them to give us more food and water, give us the unused mats they had taken from us, stop the openings on the deck above, and close a ventilator which blew from another part of the ship throughout the hold. Under these circumstances, men were physically numb most of the time. We never knew from one hour to the next who would be alive and who would be dead. After we started this last leg of the journey on the 14th, we had between 30 and 50 deaths daily. Every day the cadaver detail, composed of the strongest POWs in the group, would go through the bays and pull out the dead which were piled up in the little open space in the center of the hold. Sometime during the day the Japanese guards would have our detail drag the bodies up on deck and leave them there. Then the Japanese ran every American POW down below and closed the hatch for half an hour. During this half hour the American guard, who happened to be stationed at the bottom of the stairway to the upper deck, often peeped out through a crack and reported that the Japanese were knocking the gold and silver filings out of the teeth of the cadavers before throwing them overboard.

All during this time the sanitation in the hold of this ship was unspeakable. We only had 8–10 buckets as catch-all for the bodily waste of this large body of men which numbered around 1,000 when we started out on this ship. The Japanese took no special pains to see that we had an opportunity to empty these buckets. There were times when we could go out to a latrine, but only during daylight hours. Most of the men were sick with dysentery and diarrhea by this time and, of course, they had to attend to bodily needs during the hours of darkness. The Japanese refused to let us go on deck. As a result, these 8–10 wooden buckets were very far from adequate for our sanitary needs. As a result, with so many men sick, the buckets ran over nearly every day. In the area of the hold where these buckets were, the human filth was at least two inches deep in some places. It ran out into the bays where men were lying and lived, slept, ate, and died in it. No amount of requesting the Japanese for adequate facilities brought relief.

MONDAY, JANUARY 22. Very cold, two meals, and one water ration. Some of the men were going down into a lower hold and getting sugar to eat. The Japanese had forbidden our stealing sugar under the pain of death.

TUESDAY, JANUARY 23. Snowed all day and the snow blew down over our exposed bodies.

WEDNESDAY, JANUARY 24. Snowed all day and seemed unusually cold. We got two meals and one water ration this day.

THURSDAY, JANUARY 25. We received two meals and one water ration. About 30 were dead. As the ship drew nearer to the mainland of Japan, it would anchor for hours at a time. On many days we would hardly sail for four hours of the 24.

FRIDAY, JANUARY 26. Anchored four hours at night. Sailing between large islands. Pine trees on shore. Two meals and no water.

SATURDAY, JANUARY 27. We received one meal and one water ration; men continue to die at the rate of 30–50 a day.

SUNDAY, JANUARY 28. Received two meals. The ship sailed a little while during daylight hours; men continued to die.

MONDAY, JANUARY 29. The ship underwent another submarine attack in the dark hours just before dawn. Submarine attacks have not been mentioned previously because they were merely minor incidents on the trip. From information I could secure, I estimate that we underwent from 10 to 12 separate submarine attacks. At one point the ship following us was damaged by a submarine and our ship was towing it. This was one of the reasons for the slowness of the trip. We reached our destination about four or five hours after this last submarine attack.

The ship pulled into the harbor of Moji shortly after daylight. During the morning the boat was inspected by some high-ranking Japanese officers. Mr. Wada and Lt. Toshino were not in evidence that I saw; however, some of the men said that Lt. Toshino was standing in the background as the Japanese inspection party stood at the top of the hatch and looked down upon us. Shortly after this inspection party boarded the ship, the Japanese demanded a roll call of all survivors of the trip—this was done. Later, one of the doctors told me that the Japanese had forced him to sign a statement that all the men lost on the trip had been due to American forces bombing Japanese prison ships. Of the 1,619 Americans that started out on board this ship there were less than 500 who got off the boat alive. The survivors of this trip continued to die in the camps that we were taken to for almost a month after we were taken off the ship. The last estimate that Col. Ovid O. Wilson and I made indicated that there were 303 survivors left out of the 1,619.

TUESDAY, JANUARY 30. The Japanese took us off the boat, marched us a mile through the town of Moji, put us on trains, and sent us to various camps on the island. I went to Fukuoka Camp No. 3. Once inside this camp, where there were numerous Dutch, American and Chinese POWs, we had a chance to survive. I desire to say at this time that the major in charge of Camp Fukuoka No. 3 personally was a liberal and as good to us as any individual Japanese that I saw. I think possibly he would have been kinder to us had the policy of the Japanese army permitted it.

WEDNESDAY, JANUARY 31. I am alive 31 days longer than I ever expected to be. I think we will make the grade through the war now. Everybody grand to us. 80 lbs.

THURSDAY, FEBRUARY 1. Have the dysentery. Had beef soup and 1/4 fresh fish tonight. Am very cold here.

FRIDAY, FEBRUARY 2. Sleep when I can; not too cold. Runs bad. Soup and rice chill before we can eat it.

SATURDAY, FEBRUARY 3. Coldest day here. Enlisted men moved out last night so we have whole barracks.

SUNDAY, FEBRUARY 4. Diarrhea better; appetite no good; so cold I can't get warm in bed.

MONDAY, FEBRUARY 5. Cold as heck. 25° in hospital. Three meals a day!

TUESDAY, FEBRUARY 6. Js won't let us lend each other our money. We now have to share Red Cross with camp.

WEDNESDAY, FEBRUARY 7. Received half chocolate bar from Red Cross. Very cold; many men going to hospital with runs and exhaustion.

THURSDAY, FEBRUARY 8. One man died so suddenly nobody in the barracks knew he was dead. Snowy and very cold. Js very wrought up.

FRIDAY, FEBRUARY 9. Very cold. Got put on intravenous beriberi shots today. More men dying.

SATURDAY, FEBRUARY 10. Snow, cold. Runs still continue. Very miserable.

SUNDAY, FEBRUARY 11. Pudding issued again. Corned beef in rice and four tangerines. Warmer.

MONDAY, FEBRUARY 12. Usual day, sunny. Butter issued today; a little salmon in night's soup.

TUESDAY, FEBRUARY 13. Fish at night. A little warmer today.

WEDNESDAY, FEBRUARY 14. Another died today. Our 100 is now reduced to 90. My diarrhea grows better gradually. Coffee with cream in it tonight.

THURSDAY, FEBRUARY 15. Cheese and jam issued today. Weather is warmer.

FRIDAY, FEBRUARY 16. Wrote a 40-word radiogram to folks. "Safe in Japan. Plan our homecoming to take place immediately after my return. Answer this radiogram in all letters. Bob and Marion say hello to E.P. Lawlor, Columbus, OH and Mrs. Adda Bates, Louisville, KY. Love, Bill."

SATURDAY, FEBRUARY 17. More Red Cross. Three squares of chocolate and one tangerine bloated me like a balloon last night. Rumors that one of our task forces bombed Tokyo with carrier planes.

SUNDAY, FEBRUARY 18. Nothing new; no news. Fish on the side for supper tonight.

MONDAY, FEBRUARY 19. Another day; issue of coffee and sugar (four men to a coffee can). Nothing new.

TUESDAY, FEBRUARY 20. Feel better. Runs receding so I feel better.

FEBRUARY 21–28. More Red Cross items issued. Small countries climbing on bandwagon.

WEDNESDAY, MARCH 1. Am just beginning to feel better, like I am gaining in strength. I think we lived on our reserve for two weeks after we arrived. February 27 we were officially made members of this camp. Eighteen of us have died since our arrival; most of them seem to relax and give up, some pneumonia, etc.

SATURDAY, MARCH 31. Since the night of March 1, four more have died, 22 now. I feel a lot better, am doing light garden work 8:00 to 11:30 and 1:30 to 4:30. We have had a dozen air raids the last of the month, mostly at night. The boys are active all around. Tinko is at 5:00 A.M., 7:00 A.M., 12:00, and 8:00 P.M. Have had more numerous inspections, etc. Chow is the same. Red Cross food is now eight men to a box. Bob Lawlor and I still are together sleeping in the same bed.

SUNDAY, APRIL 1, EASTER. Big shakedown by the Js this morning. All officers are in disgrace because two men stole some potatoes slated for the kitchen.

WEDNESDAY, APRIL 25. Transferred from Fukuoka Camp #3 to Hoten Prison Camp, Mukden, Manchuria.

TEN

RESCUE FROM THE JAPANESE IN MUKDEN, MANCHURIA

MONDAY, AUGUST 13, 1945. The factory men of T.K.K. and M.K.K. were left in camp. The day before there were many rumors from Chinese and Koreans that the war had about ended. We hardly believed the rumors yet the good sources claimed them reliable.

TUESDAY, AUGUST 14. Half M.K.K. men went to work, total 198 remained in camp and 202 went to work; all T.K.K. went to work (36 men). There were many rumors that the war was over. Many of the men thought they would not go to work. Rumors reported Russians had taken Harbin through the junction of three Russian columns. Russia's border reported penetrated in several other places. Three main columns approached from east, north, and west and all reported advancing down railroads. Rumor also said seven landings on mainland of Japan.

WEDNESDAY, AUGUST 15. About 9:30 A.M. the air alert signal blew. Men from M.K.K. and T.K.K. came rushing in at noon and the Nips were very downcast. The branch camps were beginning to come in. Hot rumors that the war was over and Russians were advancing fast in north Manchuria. No air raid materialized. From the Japanese attitude we knew something was up in the way of bad news for them.

THURSDAY, AUGUST 16. Men did not go to work. About 10:30 or 11:00 A.M. six men dropped, via parachute, out of a strange (not Nip) large plane. The chutes were varicolored: red, green, white, etc. About 4:30 P.M. six strange men were brought over to Nip headquarters. They were reported variously as American, Chinese, and Russian. The Nips smiled and shook hands with them (it was rumored). The Americans gave our workers the okay "high sign." Excitement ran high that night in camp as we recognized by their colored parachutes, these men as the six who had dropped out of that strange plane. Rumor was hot that the war was over and many bets were made. Many officers stayed up all night playing poker, reading, and talking. The Nip guards failed to fix their bayonets in some cases; they did not order us to bed as they usually did and they did not beat us for smoking after hours and out-of-reach of ashtrays.

FRIDAY, AUGUST 17. About 8:00 A.M. Gen. Parker, Air Vice Marshall Maltby (British), and the Dutch general were called to Nip headquarters for a conference. Shortly afterward these leaders came back and told us an armistice had been called between the U.S., Great Britain allies, and Japan. We were instructed to remain quietly in camp. Later Maj. Hennesy, leader of the six men, came into camp and visited with us. He brought with him, via chute, a radio and medical supplies. American planes were supposed to precede him here dropping leaflets. These two planes failed to arrive, so the major and his five men soon found themselves surrounded by a Nip battalion of bayonets. The American-born Japanese interpreter had to talk pretty fast to save their lives as the Nip troops did not know the war was officially over. Finally they persuaded the Nips of the reality of the armistice and they were brought to this camp where all the Nip colonel promised to do was not to shoot them. By the morning of the 18th, the Nip colonel had the news as to what was what and he didn't refuse Maj. Hennesy anything he wanted. It seems the American headquarters in Chungking under Gen. Weidmeyer jumped the gun at the knowledge in order to forestall anything happening to the American POWs at Camp Hoten.

The Nip guards failed to patrol through camp after this announcement.

We were given an issue of Nip cigarettes and some of the remainder of the Red Cross food stored in the canteen was issued. Again people stayed up most of the night as Hennesy's party had told us a little news of the States and the outside world. Coffee jags also had a lot to do with the general sleeplessness of the camp.

SATURDAY, AUGUST 18. Maj. Hennesy had the Nips bring the 14 airmen into camp from the annex 300 yards away. These men had been shot down in raids last December. The British, Dutch, and American units began to organize their men in their various organizations. These 14 men under Capt. Campbell had a lot of news about war conditions in the States which was all new to us. Americans assumed interior camp guard. Weight down to 60 lbs. If the war had not ended when it did, I would have perished in a few weeks.

SUNDAY, AUGUST 19. I was asked by Gen. Frank to help distribute the remainder of the Red Cross supplies. I am now working in the canteen with Lt. William Don Thompson. The portable radio of Maj. Hennesy brings us world news several times a day now. We sent out via radio for food, medicine, clothing, guitar strings, etc. As soon as diplomatic arrangements can be made with the Russians, these supplies will be flown in.

MONDAY, AUGUST 20. Put out the remainder of Red Cross supplies by early P.M. Men are still exclaiming in delight about being free men. The camp organized a jam session for 7:00 P.M. Around 4:30 P.M. a large American plane flew over camp dipping its wings. The men of the camp cheered wildly. With the exception of the 14 flyers, none of us had ever seen such a large plane. Personally, I knew the war was over because I saw an American plane and it didn't bomb or shoot at me.

At 7:00 P.M. the men gathered for the jam session and started singing. The session was interrupted by a call for the senior officers of the three nations in camp to meet the Russian representative at the headquarters. The Russian was a captain, 31 years of age, who had been in Vienna, Austria, Prague, Berlin capitulation, and had had contact with the American 9th Army fighting in Germany. The POWs gathered around him where he stood on the hospital steps where he made the following dramatic speech:

"Liberty, on the very day when our units have occupied the City of Mukden, we visited the Mukden camp for American and British war prisoners. Small, bowing, commander of the camp Col. Vsiaki came to meet us.

"In the inner yard of the camp the war prisoners had formed. When we came into the yard their ranks were immediately broken, and the men rushed toward us shouting their greetings in various tongues. 'My God! At last you have come! We knew soon you would come!'

"With tears in his eyes, Michailov, a Russian-American from the state of Washington, came forward and offered to be our interpreter."

The representative of the Soviet Military Government ascended an improvised speaker's stand and began to speak:

"This morning our units have occupied the City of Mukden. I am empowered to inform you that from this hour all American, British, and other Allied war prisoners in this camp are free!"

It is hard to describe the emotions of the liberated men. Up went their military hats, handkerchiefs; the men kissed each other and shed tears of happiness. The word "liberty" was repeated over and over again. Hundreds of the British and the Americans inhumanely (uproariously?) shouted it in the Russian language: "Liberty, Liberty, Liberty!"

"In the name of the Soviet Military Government," continued the officer of the Red army, "I congratulate you on the victory of the Allied troops over the Japanese imperialism!" And again the storm of applause swept the assemblage.

"Oh, Russian youth!" the voices shouted, "the Russians are so strong! We are your friends."

The meeting went on. Up the porch ran Alexander Biby, speaking half in English. "The Russian troops have brought us liberty. Three and a half years we have suffered in the Japanese prison. Thousands of us have died of hunger and thirst. In that time only four were able to escape from this camp and were recaptured by the Japanese and done to death. Words cannot describe the cruel deeds of the Japanese to the war prisoners. My

Russian buddies, it is to you that I address myself, with words of burning thankfulness and love. Not one of us will ever forget this day. For life you're our faithful friends and this friendship we will bequest to our kin."

We saw the faces of the people who heard Alexander Biby and we realized that he spoke for the multitude.

The Soviet officer announced that the Japanese camp guard would, at once, be disarmed and those guilty of cruel and inhumane treatment of the war prisoners would be arrested. Temporarily, before the arrival of the Soviet troops, the administration of the camp would be conducted by the American and British generals.

This announcement was met with the unanimous approval of the liberated war prisoners. We became acquainted with the generals. We were introduced to Gen. Parker, who was the ranking and oldest general in the Mukden Camp. He was tall, lean, very pale. He had the face of a man of knowledge, a face of parchment with narrow bluish streaks. He asked interpreter Michailov to tell us that he was overjoyed to see the Russians and that he was amazed at the miraculously rapid advance of the Red army. Gen. Parker was asked to take temporary command of the camp.

Gen. Parker thanked our officers for their trust in him and assumed the command. At once it was seen that he was a man who had commanded troops all his life and was able to accomplish everything brilliantly.

Also introduced were Vice Air-Marshall Maltby of Great Britain. Then came Generals Jones, Sharp, Chynoweth, all commanding Corps; generals Brougher, Pierce, Funk, Drake, Stevens, Lough, Beebe, division commanders.

We got acquainted with the widely known Dutch journalist Joel, who became prisoner three years before. He declared, "I will write about you Russians, the senders of light into our darkness."

Within 30 minutes of our arrival all the Japanese formed in front of the war prisoners and lay down their arms. Here, with exceptionally fine organization, the Americans and the British took up the Japanese arms and posted their own sentinels.

Gen. Parker occupied the office of the Japanese camp commander. There, for a conference, went all the other generals.

"The men would not let us leave. Each man wanted to shake our hands and to receive our autographs. They asked us about the Red army, of her battles with the Japanese, and in unison said, "Russians can fight! We are surprised at them! We will mention them at home!" Somebody from the Russian-speaking war prisoners said aloud: "Now we will go home soon! Home to our families and children!" and this feeling spread all through the camp. The people's faces changed and no words could describe their feelings. Now these men were free, and peace and quiet were not far away!

"And so, that day, liberty had come to our camp. It was brought to us by the Red army fighting and marching over the trackless swamps and desert and the Great Hinken." *(Translated from a Russian newspaper by Sgt. Hurley, 31st Infantry)*

After the representative of the Soviet Military Government, the young Russian captain's speech, the men carried him on their shoulders around in a circle. The jam session continued until we were told to get inside the barracks while the Nips' camp guard were disarmed on the compound parade ground. Not many people went inside, just lined up in front of the barracks. The Nips—officers and men—marched out into the field, formed up and laid their arms in a pile, and formed again. The Russian officer then called for some American prisoners to form a guard, take up the surrendered arms and form a guard around the dejected Nips. The Russian officer then had our guard march the captured Nips around in front of us and away to the guardhouse. The Nip officers were allowed to keep their swords. There was a mighty cheer from the spectators as we saw the Nips who had kicked, beaten, starved, and humiliated us, march away under our guards. This was a new experience for them.

After this, the Russian officer answered some questions about his trip here, 1000 kilometers in 10 days. When he left we all went back to our groups or barracks, had more coffee, and spent another sleepless night!

TUESDAY, AUGUST 21. Today the Americans had the pleasure of seeing the Nips go out to the fields, dig potatoes, lug dirty wet sacks of vegetables, and step to the tune of a bayonet. Last night some of the men got into the Nip storerooms and rifled them for food, writing materials, etc. Things were quiet around camp except the repatriated units were trying to organize themselves and they overlapped in claiming men. It was an awful mess trying to portion out cigarettes, etc.

WEDNESDAY, AUGUST 22. Another plane came in today. Col. Hillsman's son, a captain in the airborne infantry, says we will likely fly all the way over the Pacific to San Francisco. (Dramatic meeting between Col. Hillsman and his son.)

THURSDAY, AUGUST 23. Worked around the QM most of the day. About 4 P.M. went with Capt. Grow on a truck out to a Nip food dump the Russkis had taken over. The dump had an area of about 20 square kilometers which contained every conceivable type of food essentials, tobacco, and small equipment facilities. On the way back the Russkis gave Grow and me some Nip arms. Personally, I got a Nip non-combat saber, an American .45 pistol, and a German Mauser pistol. I hope to take the first and latter home. Among some other things the Russkis told us we could have were some Japanese kimonos of which I took three, one each for my mother and two sisters. I also got a carved lacquer table that I hope to take home.

Mukden was very deserted-looking. The only vehicles moving were American-made Russian equipment and a lot of captured Nip motors in the hands of the Chinese, Russkis and interns. The Russians were bringing Nip prisoners into town in large numbers. What they were doing with them I didn't know and I didn't care.

The Nip prisoners were scared stiff three ways: scared of the Americans they had as prisoners, scared of the Russians, and scared of the Chinese they had lorded over for 12 or 13 years. Most of the Nip prisoners I heard quoted doubted if they would ever get back to Japan. Well they might have doubted, such had been their actions in the past!

The Nips never have been able to understand American psychology; they never could break our spirit. As one Nip interpreter here in camp said, when the guardhouse sentence of some men was over and the men were released, as he overheard the Americans' uncomplimentary remarks about their treatment, "I can't understand your attitude. I can't understand why you are not humble and downcast. We punish you by giving you little food so you are very hungry, we make you stand at attention all day until you faint from exhaustion, you have no blankets or mosquito bars so your nights are cold and miserable, we strip you of all your clothes in the sub-arctic cold winter and pour cold water on you, and when we let you out of the guardhouse you do not say 'Thank you.' All you say as you walk away is a contemptuous " . . . 'em!" They killed many Americans, trying to break their spirit, but they had no luck in general. We knew that America was going to win, kill us though they might. Today, the vanquished Nip has no future even if he does live; the American always had a future if he lived."

This morning Maj. Jacobs of Chicago left on the first plane carrying sick prisoner patients out of camp. With him he took a radiogram to the folks as listed below:

- one to folks
- one to Bob Inman
- one to H. G. Ingersoll
- one to Herb Heller

These letters would likely be home before I ever get out of here.

SATURDAY, AUGUST 25. Worked around QM today. More milk and canned meat were brought in. Am dead on my feet; have been working too hard.

SUNDAY, AUGUST 26. Nothing new except a lot of supplies came in from off a couple of planes.

MONDAY, AUGUST 27. Gen. Wainwright was in camp a few minutes this morning. Giving the major general 30 minutes notice, he flew out with them and his aides. I believe he is to go to the Tokyo show. I am still dead on my feet.

TUESDAY, AUGUST 28. Work around camp, etc. Nothing much new or doing.

WEDNESDAY, AUGUST 29. I went to town in one of the official cars. All I did was to ride around as a passenger wherever it happened to go. Met a Col. Leath of Los Angeles who is one of the six men who parachuted in to get us out.

On return to camp I found the "processing detail" of 19 men had arrived on the plane in the P.M. Among them is a Bud Pearson of Toulon (about 30 miles out of Galesburg, IL). This was like meeting an old neighbor. Needless to say, we had quite a visit.

Just at 6:00 P.M. three B-29s came over and dropped food, candy, and clothes via parachute. Many of the chutes didn't open so the food cans were smashed. The falling cases knocked out our power lines, fell in the swamp and foxholes, and were stolen by swift appearing crowds of Chinese.

THURSDAY, AUGUST 30. Yet more B-29s dropped more supplies. Supply rooms are a mess of broken crates, mud, and smashed supplies.

We now have up-to-date newspapers in camp, magazines, radio, and movies. Several men, after seeing the movie, remarked they couldn't get enthused about seeing an American girl again; they would rather have seen a steak and chop dinner; the show was *To Have and Have Not*, with Humphrey Bogart and a girl called Slim.

FRIDAY, AUGUST 31. Another delay was the day. It's been over two weeks since we were first contacted, a plane a minute goes in and out of Chungking; we are still here, Uncle Sam isn't the "fast on the ball" man I thought he was.

I understand the censorship of the U.S. is full of bunk like the Nips. All I can freely say is, "Dear Mama and Papa, I am well. How are you? Love, etc."

Seven more planes dropped food. Met a processing man from Macomb. Movie again (Duane Coshill).

SEPTEMBER 1–6, 1945 (INCLUSIVE). Have been working in the QM all this time. Made several trips outside the gates on missions. Brought a group of Belgian Fathers (Priests) out to get clothes and shoes. A Russian enlisted man, a sentry at an old schoolhouse, gave me an officer's sword (Japanese). I was scheduled to fly out the 7th, but the plane went on another mission so I wait to go until day after or the 8th, if I go by plane. I hope I do.

I have met some pilots who are ferrying food in and men out: Maj. R. B. Young, Mitchell, SD, Phone 2087; Capt. W. A. Thompson, 1301 North Oregon, El Paso, TX or Rancho Patrillo, Palma, NM. Maj. Young took a letter out to send air mail to folks telling them I am on the way home. I feel like flying and I hope to be able to do some at home.

SEPTEMBER 7. Stood by all day for the plane out. Rested some.

SEPTEMBER 8. Flew from Mukden, Manchuria, to Hsian, China, about 950 miles. Tomorrow we fly on to Kumming just north of the Himalayan Mountains. Hope to go out to India from there. Today we flew over the Gulf of Korea and then up the Yellow River of China. It sure looked yellow, brown, and red from the plane. Our altitude was 7,000–7,500 all the way. Passed over several mountain ranges, saw the Great Wall of China where it began at the sea and ran inland.

The erosion of China is tremendous—great gullies hundreds of feet through nice farm land. There are no forests or trees on the mountains. None of the mountains I saw today were over 7,500 feet high.

SEPTEMBER 9. Hsian to Kumming, China. The most used airport in the world here, a plane in or out each minute of the 24 hours. There are always four to seven planes in the air. Once at Kumming, we were taken to the base hospital and fed. Everybody treated us grand, brought us ice cream, Red Cross had a little bag of toilet articles on our bed. We were given part of a complete physical examination. For the first time since May 1942 I saw an American woman. The Army nurses are quite a jolly crowd. They are dressed in fine striped (white and tan) smocks for a uniform, slacks, GI trousers, and leather jackets, leather boots, field shoes, women's shoes, anything that's adaptable to comfort and activity. They sure looked good. Every American I have met has acquired a broadness of adaptability and tolerance foreign to our race. Everything new and foreign they take in their stride. I am proud to be an American.

MONDAY, SEPTEMBER 10. Finished the physical examination. Am okay for travel! Left the hospital and moved downtown to a hostel (converted hotel). Sightseeing around Kumming.

TUESDAY, SEPTEMBER 11. Slept late. Looked around the town of Kumming. Went through town Club of Red Cross, saw its setup, saw a show, etc. At 10:30 left for airport to catch plane for Manila. Took a C-54, left Kumming 11:30 and arrived Manila around 7:00 A.M.

WEDNESDAY, SEPTEMBER 12. Arrived Nichols Field, Manila around 7:00 or 7:30 A.M. Immediately sent me to 29th Replacement Depot.

Rec. Per. Sec.

(688 Co. Tent D-3)

APO 501

c/o Postmaster

San Francisco

Found many of the people here who left Mukden prior to me. Nobody knows when we leave. Sent Red Cross message to home folks.

THURSDAY, SEPTEMBER 13. Rested, got my physical examination this P.M. Registered for mail with Red Cross. Sent message home to folks in A.M. Meeting more friends. Got uniforms, etc., yesterday and today. Wrote letter to President Osmeña and Dr. Francisco Benitez in Manila.

FRIDAY, SEPTEMBER 14. Got my first radio from folks. Everybody okay. It gave me a great feeling of relief to know they were okay. Was processed this P.M. and got my records up to date. My major's promotion "will likely be retroactive and I will end up a lieutenant colonel." Meeting more friends.

SATURDAY, SEPTEMBER 15. Checked up on more copies of my promotion order to be made. Rested around camp.

SUNDAY, SEPTEMBER 16. Chester Richards took me into Manila to see a Spanish girl named Pilar Deren who was the fiancée of Capt. Harold Bishop. I had the unpleasant job of telling her of Bishop's death.

Also met Betty and Miriam Wright, Mrs. Wright, Mrs. Deren, and Don Danon, brother of Mrs. Wright. It is a miracle any of them are alive because in the siege of Manila the Nips raped and pillaged. The Nips sent out personnel destruction squads who shot down anybody and everybody.

SEPTEMBER 17–23. Have been hanging around for an entire week now. Tomorrow the third boat since I have been here goes out and I am not on it. My papers got mixed up and General Headquarters didn't know I existed. I tracked this down three days ago. Ever since, I have gone in every day to check on things. Maj. Earl Short, Charlie Underwood, and Bill Nealson, all left today. I stay in town at Wrights' and last night because it was so rainy and . . .

SEPTEMBER 24. Stayed around camp this P.M. after going into Manila and getting my orders finally. Went to bed early. No word from home; I should have included all addresses in my messages, I guess.

TUESDAY, SEPTEMBER 25. Am to finally get on a boat for home. Cleared myself at camp and came into Manila before noon. Left my baggage at Capt. Paul Coker's office in the P. Samanillo Bldg., had dinner with him. After eating we went and picked up Betty Wright with whom he had a date and went and had a second meal!! (at Rizal Stadium). Rode around the city, ate ice cream, visited Pelie Terren at her job and found her scraping the paint off her fingernails. She couldn't go for a swim in Cavite with us so Paul and Betty took me down to the pier (15) to check on the sailing of my ship, the *Stormking*. Supposed to be on by 8:00 P.M.

After this we went back and got Pelie (Pilar Teren Goiri), went for something to drink at the Bacombo Nite Club (this was 4:30 P.M. so the club wasn't open but we knew the manager and got fixed up). After this we returned to the girls' home for dinner.

Paul had promised to have a jeep pick me up in front of Santa Mesa Church at 7:15 P.M. It never came. So I hitchhiked down to the motor pool without saying good-bye to my friends. Got a staff car and took my baggage to the ship. After checking in, I found I could stay out until 11:00 P.M. I took off for the Wrights to pick up my musette bag and say good-bye. Arrived about 9:00 P.M.

Pelie was waiting for me and all were guessing I had hitchhiked to the boat and left my bag. Said farewell to the older folks, took Pelie, Capt. Fred Garrett, and Miriam Wright and went to a new nightclub, the El Cairo, for an hour. Said farewell to Mrs. Wright and Betty there and the four of us left for Pier 15 at 10:40 P.M. On arriving at the pier the ship was still loading troops so the girls and Fred waited with me in the car until almost midnight when the operation was through. The girls had to work the next day so I said good-bye to the three of them, started them home in the staff car, and boarded the ship. Once on board I met some men who came over on the *President Pierce* in June 1941. Most of us are gone.

This is another trip I am not expecting to enjoy even though it is the road home. I have lost every close friend I had out here. I have been through filth, destruction, near death many times, and lived under conditions that warp men's souls. I haven't come through unscathed in the latter. Now that I return, I dread the coming days of inactivity; with good food and rest my mind is beginning to become active again. I go home to a land of memories and hope, leaving behind me a land of memories—memories of love, hate, fear, heroism, sacrifice, atrocities, destruction, torture, death, and of living friends. There is only one answer to this state of mind: work and physical activity.

Looking back on these last 53 months, in which I have lived more than half a dozen people ordinarily do in their entire lives put together, I wonder of what avail are all these events. When I boil it all down all I want out of life is "quiet happiness." All the glory, riches, power, pomp, and splendor I have ever had or even seen I would throw away for happiness and a healthy physical body. Such is life. It's a pretty empty affair at times.

All through the boat there is no hilarity among the POWs, mostly a feeling of sadness, weariness, and boredom!

SEPTEMBER 26, 1945. Terribly hot on the boat. I am in a room about water level with 30 other officers from the rank of major on down. Spent the day sleeping and sweating. I slept through the fun last night. Our ship, about midnight, near the west end of San Bernardino Straits struck a 60-foot Filipino fishing boat, cutting it in half. The ship stopped and the searchlights picked up swimming Filipinos and wreckage. A life boat rescued more than half a dozen from a floating half just as it went down. Out of 17 Filipinos one was lost. They brought the Filipinos on board. Later they sighted another Filipino craft and put the survivors on it.

THURSDAY, SEPTEMBER 27. We passed out of the San Bernardino Straits before noon. Saw the last of Samar about 11:00, more land for two weeks now. This morning I got up about 6:00 A.M. and watched Mayon Volcano in the distance as we passed by. It has the reputation of being the world's most perfect volcanic cone. A grayish white smoke was drifting in a stream for miles across the sky from its cone. It was quite an impressive sight.

FRIDAY, SEPTEMBER 28. Another day. I slept some, read some, wrote a letter to James A. Wright telling him of my trip after I left him. Now, about 1,100 miles out of Manila. Running into a storm tonight, sea very rough.

SATURDAY, SEPTEMBER 29. Another day on the road home. Spent the day getting my citation and promotions ready to send to MacArthur. Wrote letters to Dr. Francisco Benitez, c/o Bureau of Education, Malacanang Palace, Manila; Mr. and Mrs. K. L. Morrison of Loh Cebu City; Bob Irrmann and Helen DeVault, c/o LU. At 9:00 P.M. we passed the island of Ulithi of the Mariana group. It is about 150 miles northeast of Yap.

SUNDAY, SEPTEMBER 30–OCTOBER 7. One monotonous day follows another. I sleep as much I can. Today, the 6th, at 7:35 we crossed the International Dateline back into the western hemisphere. I am back in the Occident after 52 months in the Orient. We have two Saturdays or two October 6s.

MONDAY, OCTOBER 8. Arrived in Honolulu at 3:00 P.M. Got shore leave, hitchhiked with Lt. Meis down to telephone control and called folks back home. Cost $56 for 15 minutes. Camp Ellis has taken the farm and the folks now live in Vermont. Ruth gave me the address of a Wave, Marjorie Fulton, at Kaneohe Naval Air Base to look up. Took two hours to call her.

WEDNESDAY, OCTOBER 10. Got up at 6:00 A.M., left ship at 7:00 A.M. for Kaneohe, arrived around 9:00 A.M. Visited Marjorie for about 50 minutes and got back to ship by noon. About 1:00 P.M. a big liner anchored just ahead of us; it looked familiar. Bands came to serenade it. Tommy

Harrison and I sneaked down the gangplank and over long side. Sure enough, some of the men who left Manila two days before us were on it: Charlie Underwood, Earl Short, and Bill Nealson.

OCTOBER 11–14, 1945. More monotonous days. Read and wrote letters. Practice debarkation runs.

MONDAY, OCTOBER 15. Debarked about 2:00 P.M. and taken to Letterman General Hospital and quartered in Ward 15. Got about 19 or 20 letters at the pier. One from Florence Smith said Mary Pickering was in San Francisco. Called her up about 8:00 P.M. and she told me to come on out. We talked until almost midnight at the Drake-Wilkshire Hotel. Took her back to her room at the Federal Hotel in the 10 hundred block on Market Street, Room 705, phone Underwood 4946. Mary works for TWA, 441 Post Street, Phone Export 3701.

TUESDAY, OCTOBER 16. Bought clothes and chased around all day. Met Mary at TWA and went to the sky room at Hotel Mark Hopkins about 20 (?) stories up. Went across the street to another large hotel, had dinner in the Birch Room (hotel?) and danced in the Circle Room.

WEDNESDAY, OCTOBER 17. More Army red tape. Brought Mary out to hospital for dinner; showed her my pictures and we went to the nightclub Bal Tabarin where there was a floor show, but didn't dance. Back early.

THURSDAY, OCTOBER 18. Cleared from Letterman today; got authority to take my own transportation. Mary is fixing things up so I can fly to Chicago via Los Angeles so I can visit K. L. and Buster Morrison. San Francisco to Chicago via Los Angeles on TWA costs $98.27. Went to a show with Mary called *Orders from Tokyo,* showing authentic technicolor pictures of the destruction of Manila; home early.

FRIDAY, OCTOBER 19. Went in to TWA at 11:00 A.M. to speculate on a trip to Los Angeles and took out for the airport at 11:30 A.M. All thanks to Mary. Arrived at K. L. Morrison's around 9:00 P.M.

SATURDAY, OCTOBER 20, 1945. Visited around Whittier with Morrisons. They are well.

End of Diary

THIS ENTIRE ACCOUNT HAS BEEN RECONSTRUCTED FROM MEMORY WITH THE HELP OF A FEW NOTES I MADE ON A FEW SCRAPS OF paper, mostly Japanese toilet paper that I happened to have in my pocket. Many of the few notes are not readable at this time or the account would be more specific and definite. All of these notes were processed by the 19-man processing crew who came into our prison camp a day or two after the Japanese surrender. This processing crew was sent from Gen. Wedemier's headquarters in Chungking, China. The camp they went to was the Hoten Prison Camp at Mukden, Manchuria, which was the camp I was in when I was liberated.

Lt. Col. Ovid O. Wilson, assisted by Lt. Col. Thomas Trapley, and various other senior officers of our surviving group, wrote up a complete history of this boat trip, which I have just described. This history was written at the direction and under the supervision of this 19-man processing group who processed everybody before they left the camp. All of the information I have placed in this account should be found in a more detailed account in Col. Wilson's history of the trip.

Later I saw a newspaper clipping stating that Mr. Wada and Lt. Toshino were on trial in connection with this trip. There is no doubt that their inhumane treatment was a cold deliberate policy of murder in respect to the American prisoners they had charge of. They could have gotten clothes for us and given us enough food to live on had they desired. There was absolutely no reason that the sanitation on the ship could not have been adequate for that occasion.

To the best of my belief and knowledge there is no material in this account which has not been included in previous reports made at Mukden, Manchuria. These facts were common knowledge to all the survivors.

Note: Junsaburo Toshino, former Lieutenant and Guard Commandant aboard the "Hell Ship," was found guilty of murdering and supervising the murder of at least 16 men and sentenced to death as Class B war criminal at Yokohama. Shusuke Wada, whose charges paralleled those of Toshino, was the official interpreter for the guard group. (Both Toshino and Wada had supervised the San Fernando murders). Wada was found guilty of causing the deaths of numerous American and Allied Prisoners of War by neglecting to transmit to his superiors requests for adequate quarters, food, drinking water, and medical attention. Wada was sentenced to life imprisonment at hard labor.

EPILOGUE

BY CHARLES, GEORGIA, AND LEWIS MINER

D URING DAD'S TOUR OF DUTY IN THE PACIFIC, HE WAS INVOLVED IN BATTLES AND CAMPAIGNS FOR THE LIBERATION OF CHINA, bombardment of Japan, Philippine Defense Campaign, Philippine Liberation, Mindanao, Cebu and Luzon. He also received the following decorations and citations: Silver Star, Purple Heart, Asiatic Pacific Ribbon w/ 4 Bronze Stars, American Defense Ribbon w/ Bronze Battle Star, Philippine Liberation Ribbon w/ Bronze Star, Presidential Unit Citation w/ 2 OLCs, Philippine Defense Ribbon w/ Bronze Battle Star, Victory Medal, seven Overseas Bars, Atlantic-Pacific Campaign Medal, and POW medal.

After Dad's return to the States from the Pacific in 1945, he married Clara Charles in 1946. He continued his interrupted (due to the war) education at Indiana University where he received his master's and doctorate degrees. In 1950 he accepted a position at Eastern Illinois State College (now Eastern Illinois University) in Charleston, IL. He and his wife Clara adopted three children: Charles, Georgia Ann, and Lewis. Dad was a faculty member at the University until he retired in 1980 and continued to live in the Charleston area until his passing away in 1998 at the age of 83.

Of our father . . .

Despite all the inhumane treatment that Dad suffered as a prisoner of war, he was one of the most "human" of people we have ever met. He did not let his POW experience overrun his life. Instead he lifted himself up and proceeded on, utilizing the experiences to his benefit. Once we asked him why so many continued to suffer after the war and why he seemed to take it in stride. He replied, "When I saw all of those returning POWs and the various conditions that they were in I decided right then, that there was nothing wrong with me and that I had a future." Dad was a man of strength, discipline, and courage. He was also a man of deep emotions and concern. We never saw him quit or get openly discouraged. He was the type of person who did what he said and followed through on things.

Dad talked about his experiences as a POW and he could hold you spellbound with his stories. Despite our best efforts to really understand the pain and suffering that he and others endured at the hands of the Japanese, it was difficult to fully comprehend such atrocities: people being treated worse than the lowest form of creature. That might be one reason Dad did not go into a lot of detail of the brutality. "It was unbelievable." At the time of liberation, "I weighed approximately 60 pounds and on the verge of death. If you did not have the desire to eat what was given to you each day, you would die. If the war had not ended when it did, I would have died." There is no question in our minds that the starvation, sickness, disease, dozens of beatings, physical torture (and witnessing physical torture of others), psychological torture, and long-term stress he suffered during the 39 months of captivity, took its toll on him every year. He suffered from nightmares for many years and did seem to wake up in a daze at times, not knowing where he was. Dad did not have any vices and took care of himself physically and kept himself mentally sharp. He did suffer from back and vision problems as well as an irregular heartbeat and edema. At the age of 65 he developed diabetes. He might have had other conditions, but Dad was not one to openly discuss these things with us. He was an individual with great common sense and vision. He truly understood the meaning of sacrifice, duty, honor, and country. We never met anyone who did not admire and respect our father.

One of the main themes that Dad had was that if you are not willing or able to maintain a strong national defense, which involves the commitment of its leaders and citizens, then someone will come and take away your freedoms . . .

Dad passed away peacefully on May 8, 1998. Chaplain Robert E. Holmes expressed the following: "The march of our comrade is over and he lieth down in the house appointed for all the living. . . . Our comrade is in the hands of our heavenly Father and God giveth His beloved sleep."

He will be laid to rest, but let us cherish his virtues and learn to imitate them.

POSTWAR TESTIMONY

FOR THE WAR CRIMES OFFICE
JUDGE ADVOCATES GENERAL'S DEPARTMENT
WAR DEPARTMENT
UNITED STATES OF AMERICA

****

In the matter of atrocities committed
by Japanese personnel, Lieutenant
Junsaburo Toshino and Shusuke Wada,
involving American Prisoners of War

Perpetuation of the testimony
of William D. Miner, formerly
Lt. Col., ASN 0-343468,
United States Army

****

Taken at :	Military Office, Indiana University
Date :	28 March 1947
In the presence of :	Lee R. Ballard, Special Agent, CIC.
Questions by :	Lee R. Ballard, Special Agent, CIC.

Q. State your full name, permanent home address, former Army rank, and serial number.

A. William D. Miner, 1407 East 10th Street, Bloomington, Indiana, Lt. Col., ASN 0-343468

Q. State the date and place of your birth.

A. I was born on 26 June 1914 in Table Grove, Illinois.

Q. What is your marital status?

A. I am married but I have no children.

Q. What education have you had?

A. I am a college graduate.

Q. When did you return to the United States from overseas?

A. I returned to the United States from overseas on 15 October 1945.

Q. Were you a prisoner of war?

A. Yes, I was a prisoner of the Japanese.

Q. Of what military organization were you a member prior to your imprisonment as prisoner of war?

A. I was a member of Headquarters VISAYAN Force.

Q. State the approximate dates and places of your confinement as a prisoner of war.

A. I was captured by the Japanese on 17 May 1942 on the Island of Cebu and was confined in the Cebu civil jail. I remained here for five months until 17 October 1942 at which time I was moved to the Philippine P.O.W. Camp #2. We arrived here on approximately 27 October 1942 and remained here until 28 July 1944, at which time we made a 21-day trip to Cabanatuan P.O.W. Camp on Luzon. On 12 October 1944 we were moved again to the Bilibid Camp, Manila, Philippines, where we remained until 13 December 1944 at which time we were sent aboard the prison ship *ORYOKU MARU*. On 30 January 1945 we landed at Moji, Japan and were confined at Fukuoka #3 until 25 April 1945. We were then taken to the Hoten P.O.W. Camp, Mukden, Manchuria, where we remained until our liberation on 18 August 1945.

Q. At any time during your confinement as prisoner of war were you under the supervision of these Japanese personnel, Lieutenant JUNSABURO TOSHINO or SHUSUKE WADA, a Japanese interpreter?

A. Yes, I first was under TOSHINO and WADA at the Philippine Prisoner of War Camp #2, Davao, Mindanao. TOSHINO first appeared in the camp some time during the twenty-one months of my confinement there but as to the actual date I am not able to say. Whereas WADA appeared on or about January 1943, as a civilian interpreter. I remained under their supervision until approximately 30 January 1945.

Q. Were you a witness to any atrocities committed by either of these men toward American Prisoners of War? If so, state the full details as to the causes of such treatment.

A. Yes, I was a witness to a great many atrocities committed by these men. When I first came to the P.O.W. Camp at Davao, Mindanao, they immediately began punishing the men for minor reasons, nothing ever serious to the best of my knowledge. They looked upon the Americans as criminals to be punished, beaten about and to be made to suffer. At every opportunity they would do their utmost to discredit the Americans before the Japanese officials. WADA would make an inspection of the sick barracks in the company of the American camp commander at least once or twice a week with the purpose of examining the sick. During this inspection he would ask why the men were not working because he felt that they were not sick enough to remain in quarters regardless of what their illness might have been. There was never enough food and if we asked these Japanese why, they would always answer "but you do not need food because you have so many sick, the sick do not work and we cannot feed people who do not work." As a result of such an inquiry our rations would be still shorter for one or two days. WADA, who was the "right-hand man" of TOSHINO, would often come to the fields where the men were working. One incident that occurred in the sweet potato fields was when WADA found that one Captain Milton Whaley had gotten a little too much soil over some of his sweet potato slips. Without warning WADA proceeded to beat Captain Whaley with a club that he always carried. As a direct result from this beating, the Captain was confined to the sick barracks for about two days. After beating Captain Whaley, WADA lectured the entire detail of about 200 men on the consequences of doing such a poor job of setting sweet potato plants. After the lecture all of the men were forced to work an extra hour without a rest period. During this last hour the guards became very angry and at least two or three Americans were beaten or clubbed before the day was over. Like the case of Captain Whaley, there was no reason for this atrocity except for the delight in beating Americans.

Oftentimes, our small hospital would run out of medical supplies and when we asked the Japanese for new and more supplies, they, either WADA or TOSHINO, would make promises to look into the situation but we never heard another thing about it. During the inspection by the Japanese doctor, our American camp commander would tell him exactly what was needed and the supplies asked for would be delivered. After such contacts with the doctors, WADA, no doubt upon the orders of TOSHINO, would beat the Americans for no reason whatsoever. For a lengthy period after that all work details were actually used as a method of punishment. They were made unbearable by some ingenious method. One such occasion, resulting in cutting weeds and greens, the men were forced to bring them into camp in a large basket swung on a pole and carried by two men. They werer forced to load the basket far beyond the weight they were capable of carrying and this extra weight caused some of the men to fall because of their inability to carry it. On such occasion the guards would beat the fallen men for their failure to do the work and then force them to leave their load and double with the weakened members of the detail thus causing another shortage of rations for the camp.

On the logging detail WADA would come out and complain that the men were carrying just sticks instead of good firewood logs out of the jungle. We were beaten until we carried logs that met with his satisfaction. We were often kept overtime until dark when they were afraid that we might escape. At one time I was one of the two men who were forced to carry a log about 10 feet in length and weighing about 200 pounds. We carried this log about one-half mile through the jungle. We were bare to the waist and as a result of this we were badly bruised, both in the feet and shoulders; we were hardly able to move by the time we reached the loading point. We remained at this camp for approximately twenty-one months and it seemed that each day brought about more severe punishment by the Japanese in command of the compound.

Q. At the end of this twenty-one months of confinement in Davao were you associated with TOSHINO or WADA?

A. Yes, I was associated with them after this period. In June of 1944, men were left at Davao under Lt. Col. Rufus H. Rogers who was supervising the work done on an airstrip. This was the Lasang detail in which about 750 Americans took part. When we left Davao en route to the prison ship at Lasang, we were taken in trucks of about one-and-one-half-ton capacity. Each vehicle contained about forty men standing abreast with their hands tied behind their backs. The Japanese put ropes around the waist of each man, running from one man to another until all men aboard the truck were tied together. We were made to ride for about six hours, standing and facing the door of the truck. If at any time a man raised his head to look around, the guard who was seated on top of the truck would strike him on the head with a long pole. Some of the men came very close to insanity during this trip but were given no assistance by the Japanese. When we arrived at Lasang we were placed aboard the prison ship which afforded no standing room for us. Complaints were made to WADA who stated that there was no more room aboard and we would have to make the best of it.

Both TOSHINO and WADA were in charge of the 1,619 American soldiers aboard the *ORYOKU MARU*. TOSHINO did everything he possibly could to make our confinement one of torture. It is my opinion that he can be held responsible for the actions of WADA inasmuch as he was continually telling the Japanese interpreter how we should be treated. On the afternoon of 13 December 1944 we were placed in the hold of the prison ship.

The Japanese guards, under the supervision of TOSHINO, carried long poles or long-handled shovels with which they would beat the Americans until they stood in the hold of the ship instead of resting which was more than needed by all of these men. If the men were slow about moving they were beaten across the head until the Japanese were satisfied with the condition as a whole. Conditions on the ship were deplorable inasmuch as we had men aboard who had become infected with dysentery, malaria, etc. There were no latrine facilities and the men were forced by circumstances to use the floor of the ship upon which to dispose of all human wastes. After we were loaded, TOSHINO ordered the hatches closed and locked, leaving no means of light or ventilation for the prisoners. There were approximately 800 men in one hold and only about one-half pint of water per man was derived from the supply carried by each man in his canteen. After a short period of time the men became as wild animals, screaming and fighting among themselves. The Americans were passing out one after another due to the lack of air and water.

Shortly after sunup of the following day we were told that there was an air raid in progress and that we should act as American soldiers and, if at all possible, we should not show our fear. For that entire day, our rations consisted of one handful of rice and no water. Every now and then TOSHINO would stick his head into the hold but saying nothing he would turn and walk away. The following morning we were sitting just offshore Olongapo, P. I. and as usual we suffered another air raid. It was about 10:00 when a bomb hit the hold in which we were confined and as it hit it was in a group of American Field Officers numbering about 115. After the smoke cleared away there were approximately nine survivors of this explosion. Immediately the Japanese, under orders of TOSHINO, started throwing hand grenades into the hold, started firing with their rifles and some used their pistols on the injured and uninjured Americans who attempted to crawl out of the burning hold. I saw one man who was attempting to crawl out of the hold get shot in the chest by one Japanese up on deck. Some of the prisoners claim to have seen TOSHINO firing his pistol into the hold with the intent of killing as many of us as possible. Finally I reached the deck and looking around I found a life belt. Immediately after putting it on, I jumped overboard as did a great many other prisoners. No attempt was made by the Japanese to rescue the dying and wounded from the burning ship and I would estimate that about 230 men were left to burn in the hold of the ship. Altogether about 305 men died aboard the ship from suffocation and from the actual bombing.

All of the survivors were soon re-captured by the Japanese and placed in confinement inside a tennis court on shore. After we were herded inside we found that there was just enough room to lie down. We received no food that day which was 15 December 1944. On about 20 December 1944 one man in our group had his leg amputated on the floor of the tennis court which resulted in his death. At San Fernando, La Union, there was an abundant amount of water that could be had but no amount of pleading helped convince TOSHINO that we needed it. On 27 December 1944 we were placed aboard an empty freighter at dawn and soon got under way once again. We were given one meal which consisted of about one-third cup of rice and one-half pint of tea. There was one soldier in the group, named D. C. Brown, who was shot and killed when he attempted to jump overboard and escape. During this trip we were made to lie in horse manure and urine. No attempts were made by the Japanese to clean the ship after it had taken a cavalry unit to Luzon. On 31 December 1944 we arrived in the Port of Takao on Formosa. We remained here until 13 January 1945 at which time we were moved to another ship but still no food or water. On the ninth of January 1945 we suffered another bombing attack by our planes which resulted in the death of Captain Whaley. The bombed ship was repaired by placing wooden plugs in the small holes. This day we received two meals. All during the time we were in the port, the Japanese made no attempt at all to remove the dead Americans from the hold of the ships. It was not until 13 January 1945 that the odor of the dead bodies became so bad that the Japanese guards removed them. On 14 January 1945 we moved out in convoy en route to some northern point. Still at this point men were dying of old wounds which had gone unattended by the Japanese. All during this time we were pleading with TOSHINO for assistance, but it was all to no avail. We remained aboard this ship until 30 January 1945 and was sent to Fukuoka Camp #3 and, to my delight, the treatment received here was excellent. It seemed that the officer in charge of the camp was as liberal and as good to us as anyone could be.

Q. Do you feel that the deaths of the men which occurred on this trip was from neglect on the part of TOSHINO?

A. Yes, I do, inasmuch as he refused to give us more food, water, and medical supplies with which we could aid the sick and the wounded. Above all, I don't feel that it was necessary to crowd all the men in the small area in which he had us placed.

Q. Of the original number of American prisoners who started this trip, approximately how many reached the port of debarkation?

A. Of the original 1,619 Americans who started we estimated that approximately 303 survived. Of course these figures are only estimates because we had no possible means of an exact count.

Q. Were you confined at Fukuoka #3 at the time of your liberation?

A. No, I was not. On 25 April 1945 we were moved to the Hoten prison camp at Mukden, Manchuria, where we remained until our liberation.

Q. Were you associated with TOSHINO or WADA while you were in the camps named above?

A. I do not know for sure but I do not believe they came with us on our last two moves. The last I saw of them was on 30 January 1945 when we were taken from aboard ship at Moji, Japan.

Q. Is there further information which you can furnish pertaining the affidavit above?

A. To the best of my knowledge this is all that I can remember inasmuch as a period of about two years has elapsed since that time.

Q. Can you name others who might be able to furnish further information pertaining the statements above?

A. Yes, there was one that I doubled with all of this time and he is Lt. Col. R. J. Lawlor, 314-1 3rd Street, Ft. Levenworth, Kansas. There were also these officers aboard this ship in that same group: Major George Moore, Ft. Sheridan; and Lt. Col. A. J. van Oosten, Executive Officer, Separation Center #32, Ft. Sheridan.

ROTC, 1939
Bloomington, IN

William Miner, 1941
Before leaving the States

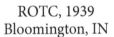

On the S.S. *President Pierce* (*center*) somewhere in the Pacific (June 1941) heading for the Philippines

Christmas 1945

Miner (*upper left*) with a Marine sergeant teaching Filipinos how to operate a machine gun. (U.S. Army photo, 1941)

Hoten POW Camp, August 1945

Miner *(front, wearing hat)*,
weighing approximately 60 lbs.

Oryoku Maru

Oryoku Maru prison ship being sunk off Olongapo
Dec. 15, 1944 (Naval Historical Foundation)

Hoten POW Camp Mukden, Manchuria

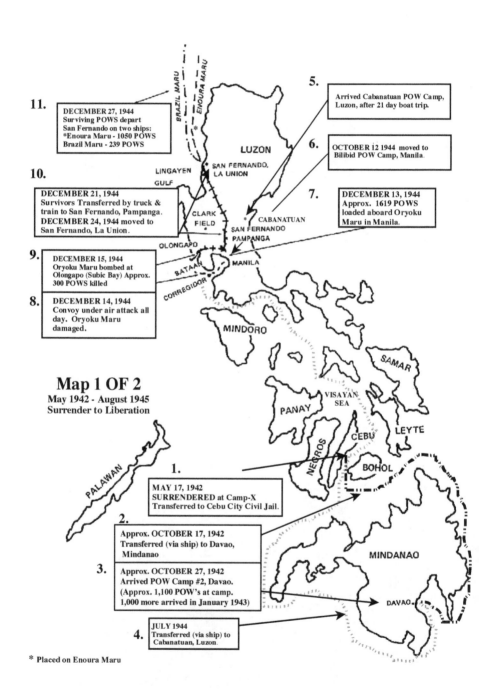

11.

DECEMBER 27, 1944
Surviving POWS depart
San Fernando on two ships:
*Enoura Maru - 1050 POWS
Brazil Maru - 239 POWS

5.

Arrived Cabanatuan POW Camp,
Luzon, after 21 day boat trip.

6.

OCTOBER 12 1944 moved to
Bilibid POW Camp, Manila.

10.

DECEMBER 21, 1944
Survivors Transferred by truck &
train to San Fernando, Pampanga.
DECEMBER 24, 1944 moved to
San Fernando, La Union.

7.

DECEMBER 13, 1944
Approx. 1619 POWS
loaded aboard Oryoku
Maru in Manila.

9.

DECEMBER 15, 1944
Oryoku Maru bombed at
Olongapo (Subic Bay) Approx.
300 POWS killed

8.

DECEMBER 14, 1944
Convoy under air attack all
day. Oryoku Maru
damaged.

Map 1 OF 2
May 1942 - August 1945
Surrender to Liberation

1.

MAY 17, 1942
SURRENDERED at Camp-X
Transferred to Cebu City Civil Jail.

2.

Approx. OCTOBER 17, 1942
Transferred (via ship) to Davao,
Mindanao

3.

Approx. OCTOBER 27, 1942
Arrived POW Camp #2, Davao.
(Approx. 1,100 POW's at camp.
1,000 more arrived in January 1943)

4.

JULY 1944
Transferred (via ship) to
Cabanatuan, Luzon.

* Placed on Enoura Maru

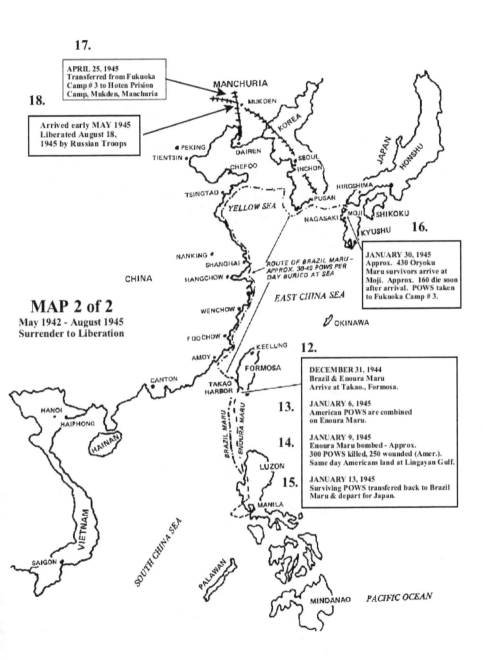

17.

APRIL 25, 1945
Transferred from Fukuoka
Camp #3 to Hoten Prision
Camp, Mukden, Manchuria

18.

Arrived early MAY 1945
Liberated August 18,
1945 by Russian Troops

MANCHURIA

MUKDEN

KOREA

PEKING

TIENTSIN

DAIREN

CHEFOO

SEOUL

INCHON

JAPAN

HONSHU

HIROSHIMA

TSINGTAO

YELLOW SEA

PUSAN

NAGASAKI

MOJI

SHIKOKU

KYUSHU

16.

NANKING

SHANGHAI

CHINA

HANGCHOW

ROUTE OF BRAZIL MARU -
APPROX. 30-40 POWS PER
DAY BURIED AT SEA

EAST CHINA SEA

JANUARY 30, 1945
Approx. 430 Oryoku
Maru survivors arrive at
Moji. Approx. 160 die soon
after arrival. POWS taken
to Fukuoka Camp # 3.

MAP 2 of 2

May 1942 - August 1945
Surrender to Liberation

WENCHOW

OKINAWA

FOOCHOW

AMOY

KEELUNG

12.

FORMOSA

TAKAO
HARBOR

CANTON

13.

14.

15.

HANOI

HAIPHONG

HAINAN

BRAZIL MARU

ENOURA MARU

LUZON

DECEMBER 31, 1944
Brazil & Enoura Maru
Arrive at Takao., Formosa.

JANUARY 6, 1945
American POWS are combined
on Enoura Maru.

JANUARY 9, 1945
Enoura Maru bombed - Approx.
300 POWS killed, 250 wounded (Amer.).
Same day Americans land at Lingayan Gulf.

JANUARY 13, 1945
Surviving POWS transfered back to Brazil
Maru & depart for Japan.

MANILA

VIETNAM

SAIGON

SOUTH CHINA SEA

PALAWAN

MINDANAO

PACIFIC OCEAN

28. Hoten-Japanese officers (Matsuda)

Hoten-Japanese officers

Matsuda (*center*), Hoten POW Camp Commander

Mr. Wada

Lt. Toshino

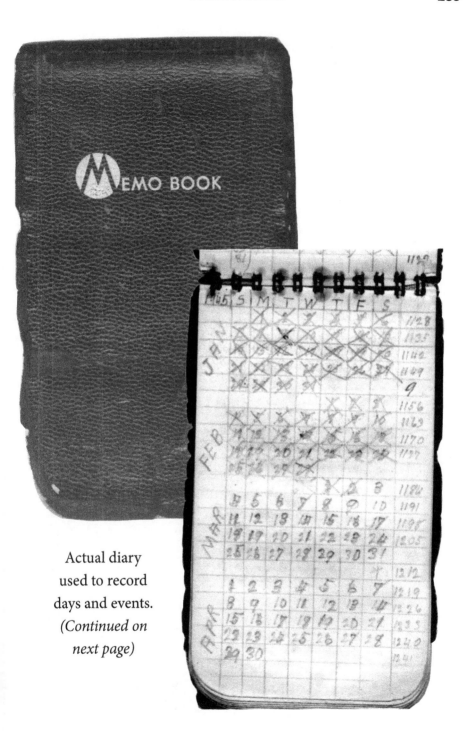

Actual diary used to record days and events. *(Continued on next page)*

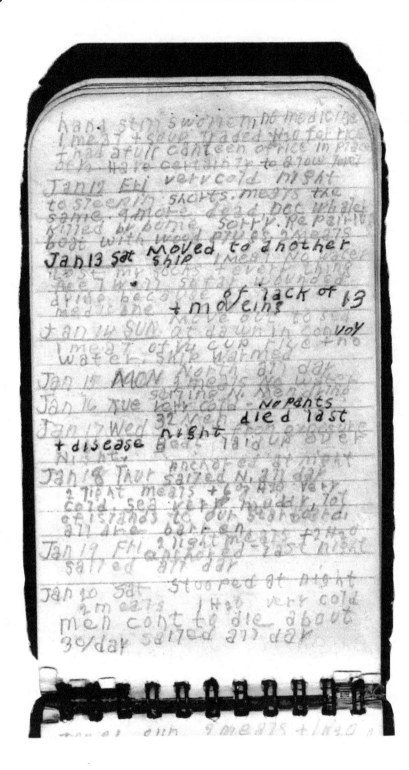

hand still swollen, no medicine
1 meal + soup traded two for rice
I had a full canteen of rice in P[..]
[...] Hole certainly to grow [...]

Jan 12 Fri very cold night
to steer in shorts. meals the
same. 1 more dead Dec whaler
killed by bomb. sorry. repair[..]
boat with wood pins. 2 meals

Jan 13 Sat Moved to another
ship 1 meal No water
lost my books + everything
died w[..]? so far. wounded
dying because of lack of 13
medicine + moving move boat to sea
+ an w sun at dawn in convoy
1 meal of w cup rice + no
water. Ship warned North all day

Jan 15 Mon 1 meal N. no water
serving N. no medicine

Jan 16 Tue very cold - No pants
32 men died last
Jan 17 Wed night [...]
+ disease Boats laid up over
Night. anchored at night

Jan 18 Thur sailed N. all day
2 light meals + soup Also very
cold. sea very muddy. Yoi
or islands to our starboard.
all the bark on

Jan 19 Fri 2 light meals + soup
sailed all day

Jan 20 Sat stooped at night
2 meals 1 H2o very cold
men cont to die about
30/day sailed all day

ans June 2-'42

1110 Indiana Ave.
New Castle, Ind.
April 26, 1942

Dear Mrs. Miner:
I was so glad to hear
of the radiogram you had
received from Bill. Mrs
Ingersoll called me a
few days later saying
that they had also
received one.
Since the invasion of
Sabu, however, I have
thought of Bill so very
often and hoped that
by some divine act he
has been spared injury
or capture.
You being his mother,
I am sure, feel the thing
which I have expressed
so poorly. My heart goes
out to you, for I can
understand the pain
and anxiety that you
must feel all of the

time. I will say to you what I would like to say to him, "Be strong and of good courage." His friends never get together here that they do not speak of him, and wonder about his safety, so any news you may receive will be appreciated by all of us.

Most sincerely,
Clara Charles

CLEAR CHANNEL · 50,000 WATTS · 890 KILOCYCLES
1230 WASHINGTON BLVD. TELEPHONE-MONROE 9700

Burridge D. Butler PRESIDENT
Glenn Snyder MANAGER

The Prairie Farmer Station

CHICAGO

April 16, 1942

Mr. A. B. Miner
Table Grove,
Illinois

Dear friend:

    I can readily realize your concern over the news from the Philippines. You may rest assured that Ervin Lewis and I will broadcast every available bit of information regarding Cebu. I sincerely hope that you have good news from your son shortly.

        Sincerely yours,

        Julian Bentley

        Julian T. Bentley
        News Editor

JTB:EMc

WLS

JULIAN T. BENTLEY
NEWS EDITOR

Aug 10, 1942.

Mrs Anna Miner
Table Grove
Illinois

Dear Friend:
Please find enclosed a sheet from the Chinese Information Service,
relaying a story short-waved from Chungking.
Erv and I are both glad you were in communication with your son.
And I sincerely hope that today's news from the Solomons is the start
of an offensive which will eventually bring him home. I noticed in a
"Knox Student" that Lee Blessing ('29) was interned at Manila. News
from or concerning Cebu is practically non-existent on the wires these
days but we'll see that you are informed of anything that is available.

Sincerely yours,

Julian Bentley

WLS

Mrs Anna Miner
Box 663
Table Grove
Illinois

WLS

JULIAN T. BENTLEY
NEWS EDITOR

Sept 10, 1943.

Mr and Mrs A Burns Miner
Table Grove, Illinois

Dear Friends:
Ervin and I are very happy to learn that the Captain
is safe. I had looked for some word of him in the last
issue of the Alumnus but did not find it. Recently I read
something which should encourage you. The State Department
has some evidence that the Japanese have begun to give better
treatment to Allied prisoners in general. As the certainty
of defeat dawns on them, it said, they are beginning to live up
to the Geneva Convention regarding prisoners.
If all goes well, I expect to be talking to you from
England in the near future. Unless something untoward occurs
I should be there in two or three weeks.

Sincerely yours,

Julian Bentley

CLASS OF SERVICE		WESTERN	1364	SYMBOLS

CLASS OF SERVICE

This is a full-rate Telegram or Cablegram unless its deferred character is indicated by a suitable symbol above or preceding the address.

WESTERN UNION

SYMBOLS

DL = Day Letter
NT = Overnight Telegram
LC = Deferred Cable
NLT = Cable Night Letter
Ship Radiogram

A. N. WILLIAMS   NEWCOMB CARLTON   J. C. WILLEVER
PRESIDENT   CHAIRMAN OF THE BOARD   FIRST VICE-PRESIDENT

The filing time shown in the date line on telegrams and day letters is STANDARD TIME at point of origin. Time of receipt is STANDARD TIME at point of destination

CK 33 GOVT WASHINGTON DC 1241 PM MAY 20TH 1943
MRS A B MINER
ROUTE ONE
TABLE GROVE ILLS

REPORT JUST RECEIVED THROUGH THE INTERNATIONAL RED CROSS STATES THAT

YOUR SON CAPTAIN WILLIAM D MINER IS A PRISONER OF WAR OF THE JAPANSE ·

GOVERNMENT LETTER OF INFORMATION FOLLOWS FROM PROVOST MARSHALL GENERAL

THE ADJUTANT GENERAL

THE COMPANY WILL APPRECIATE SUGGESTIONS FROM ITS PATRONS CONCERNING ITS SERVICE

WESTERN UNION TELEGRAM

(Acknowledgment of POW status came one year after surrender.)

WAR DEPARTMENT
ARMY SERVICE FORCES

OFFICE OF THE PROVOST MARSHAL GENERAL

WASHINGTON

May 22, 1943

RE: Captain William D. Miner

Mrs. A. B. Miner,
    Rural Route Number One,
        Table Grove, Illinois.

Dear Mrs. Miner:

The Provost Marshal General directs me
to inform you that by following the inclosed
instructions you may communicate, postage free,
with the above-named prisoner of war.

It is believed that the accompanying
circular #10 contains all information available
at this time.

Rest assured that any and all information received will be promptly forwarded to you.

Sincerely yours,

Howard F. Bresee

Howard F. Bresee,
Colonel, C.M.P.,
Chief, Information Branch.

2 Incls.
    Infor. Cirs. Nos. 1 and 10.

24-25544

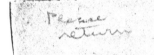

LOCAL NEWS

GREETINGS FROM PRISON IN JAPAN

Efforts in Progress to Have Captains Whaley and Miner Exchanged

Word received from Philippine Military Prison Camp No. 2 from Captain Milton Whaley via Imperial Japanese army post card to E. E. Morris indicates that "Doc" seems to be his old congenial self and that he is in excellent health. He indicates under No. 5 to tell his wife to learn to cook rice. He states that he is an experienced RR Tie man at the writing and hopes for a reunion about Christmas.

Mr. Morris is to notify the captain's wife at Petros, Tenn., and regards are sent to Mrs. Morris and daughter, Whipple, Knox college, Mr. Lahr, Punch and love to all in Galesburg.

Prison Camp No. 2 is identified by Mr. Morris as at Davos at the south tip of Mindanao Island and further word received in answer to request to a high officer in the area to release Captains Miner and Whaley is that the job will be accomplished and that it may be accomplished sometime in the not too distant future with the island hopping getting within striking distance with the safety margin.

Captain Miner's home is at Table Grove. He is also a graduate of Knox college.

A Soldier's Creed.

To the Editor: As a soldier in the United States Army let me thank you for your stand against isolationism and isolationists. We realize that the road ahead is still rocky and difficult and that we are fighting a war due mainly to their pigheadedness and disinterest in the national welfare. Many of our comrades have given their lives and unfortunately many more will follow in their hallowed footsteps before we can once again return to a civilian way of life. Yet these same people are still endeavoring to split the nation and set the stage for another world conflict in which we may really be there with 'too little and too late."

* * *

I, and most of my buddies, am only out of high school a few years and we realize that it will be our duty to reconstruct the world after the war. We all want to go back home with the knowledge that we have done a complete and final job. But we want to come back to a country united in a defined peace. We don't want to fight another war in 20 years or have our children fight it for us. We all love this nation and its ideals more than words can express. We're doing our job and are willing to give our all for it. You've got to see to it that the people back home—all the people —are willing to do the same. If politics can mean more to a man than America, then America has little need for his "contribution" to democracy. Believe me, there were no atheists on Bataan and I assure you there were no isolationists either.

PVT. M. B. MILLER.
Camp Ellis, Ill.

Table Grove Man Is Prisoner Of Japs

Mr. and Mrs. A. B. Miner of Table Grove received a message Thursday from the U. S. government stating that their son, Captain William Miner, is held prisoner by the Japanese. He was reported missing in action following the fall of the Philippines a year ago.

The last word that has been received from him was last year on Easter Sunday when his parents received a cablegram from him.

Captain Miner is a graduate of Knox college and was a student at the Indiana state university when he was called into active service.

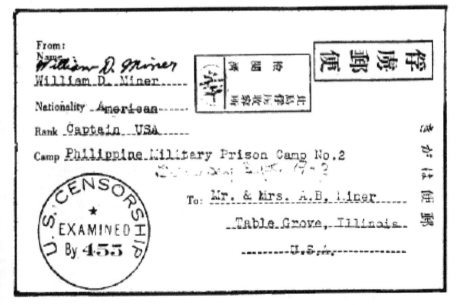

IMPERIAL JAPANESE ARMY

1. I am interned at _Phil. Mil. Prison Camp No.2_

2. My health is — ~~excellent~~; good; fair; poor.

3. I am—~~uninjured~~; sick in hospital; under treatment; not under treatment.

4. I am — improving; not improving; better; _well_.

5. Please see that _hunderd dollar per month allotment ends_ _May Forty Four. Invest Most of it_ is taken care of.

6. (Re: Family): _Love to Grand mother, Aunt Bessie and_ _food. Love to Martha._ _You all. Received Welcome Br. and Can. Red Cross_

7. Please give my best regards to _Herbert Heller, New Castle._ _Ind._

From:
Name _William D. Miner_
Nationality _American_
Rank _Captain USA_
Camp _Philippine Military Prison Camp No.2_

To: _Mr. & Mrs. A.B. Miner_
Table Grove, Illinois.
_U.S.A._

U.S. CENSORSHIP ★ EXAMINED By 455

OFFICE OF

THE VICE PRESIDENT OF THE PHILIPPINES

1617 MASSACHUSETTS AVENUE, N. W.

WASHINGTON, D. C.

January 5, 1944.

Mr. A. B. Miner,
P. O. Box 663,
Table Grove, Ill.

Dear Mr. Miner:

I acknowledge receipt of your letter of
January 2, 1944. I am pleased and share with
you the relief for hearing good news from your
son, Captain William D. Miner.

My understanding is that Camp No. 2 is
within a few miles to the North of the town of
Davao, the capital of the Province of Davao,
Mindanao, where the Davao Penal Colony used
to be during the pre-war time. I was also
informed that there are quite a few United
States Officers in that camp but the number
is not known.

Information received recently with regard
to Mr. Camilo Osias was that he was in good
health and living in Manila together with his
family.

If I could be of further service to you,
please let me know.

Sincerely yours,

S. OSMEÑA.

Mr. A. B. Miner,
P. O. Box # 663,
Table Grove, Ill.

From:
Name

William D. Miner

Nationality American

Rank Captain

Camp Philippine Military
Prison Camp No. 2

To: Mr. & Mrs. A. Miner
Table Grove
Illinois, USA

CENSORSHIP
EXAMINED
By 588

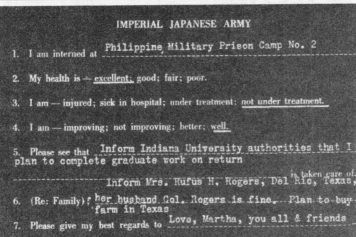

IMPERIAL JAPANESE ARMY

1. I am interned at Philippine Military Prison Camp No. 2

2. My health is — excellent; good; fair; poor.

3. I am — injured; sick in hospital; under treatment; not under treatment.

4. I am — improving; not improving; better; well.

5. Please see that Inform Indiana University authorities that I plan to complete graduate work on return

is taken care of.
Inform Mrs. Rufus H. Rogers, Del Rio, Texas,

6. (Re: Family): her husband Col. Rogers is fine. Plan to buy farm in Texas

7. Please give my best regards to Love, Martha, you all & friends

POW Card

Miss Ruth Miner
5778 Dorchester
Chicago 37, Illinois

HEADQUARTERS ARMY SERVICE FORCES
Office of The Provost Marshal General
Washington 25, D. C.   **15 June 1945**

RE: Captain William D. Miner
United States Prisoner of War
Fukuoka Prison Camp
Island of Honshu, Japan
Via: New York, New York

Mrs. A. B. Miner
Box 107
Vermont, Illinois

Dear Mrs. Miner:

        The Provost Marshal General has directed me
to inform you of the transfer of the above-named
prisoner of war to the camp indicated.

        You may communicate with him by following the
inclosed mailing instructions.

        Further information will be forwarded as soon
as it is received.

                        Sincerely yours,

                        Howard F. Bresee

                        Howard F. Bresee,
                        Colonel, C.M.P.,
        Assistant Director, Prisoners of War Division.

1 Incl.
  Mailing Circular.

24-63094ABCD

Copy of letter from William
Written at Hoten Prisoner of War Camp
Mukden, Manchuria. Sunday, August 19, 1945.
(Retype and edited)

Dear Dad and Mother:

The age of miracles is not yet over- the war has come to an armistice - it is seems unbelievable!! Now that I have a chance to send you a letter I don't know what to say. I am stumped - I have even forgotten how to spell and write. For the last 39 months I, with many other Am, Br, Dutch, Indian and Australian prisoners have existed in many and various camps. We are all Rip Van Winkles, and we have no idea what has gone on out in the world.

It has been the policy of the Japanese to keep us concentrated in camps without any kind of contact from the outside. For months they let our mail lie around in their warehouses, giving it to us in small batches as it suited them. Their attitude has been - "you are a prisoner of war therefore you do not deserve anything. You are indebted to the Imperial Japanese for being permitted to live and you should be grateful to them for that favor no matter how much they maltreat, torture or starve us."

As a POW I received about a total of 66 letters and practically no Red Cross. Fortunately by the grace of God, a background of clean living and help of friends I am coming out of this war in good shape. The educational value of this experience is beyond power of description, but I wouldn't go thru it again for anything - it's indescribable and if I ever describe some events to the fullness of their reality most people will not believe me. At the present I shall waste no more time in that line.

I am looking forward to the future - if I have good fortune I'll be home shortly after this arrives - the diplomats will have to argue and it may cause dely... I am bursting to get some news of things outside.

During the war prior to the surrender out here I was a Special Staff Officer for General Bradford G. Chynoweth in Cebu. I helped in the surrender arrangements there. General Chynoweth is here in camp with me now. We have quite a liking for each other. Without present knowledge I am the only officer left of all his command except for his Chief of Staff who is a full Colonel and has been with him all thru his imprisonment. There may be others, but all that we have any knowledge of died on the Oryoka Maru bombing when we were shipped to Japan last Dec.

That was a fearful trip- it is indescribable. I was slightly wounded in each bombing, but nothing to speak of. The conditions of that trip were unspeakable so I won't speak of it here. Just know we are waiting for our planes to come in, bring food, medicine, and clothing. Soon we can have more communication so I will stop now.

Love,
Wm.

WESTERN UNION

1204

DR CK 44 GOVT WASHINGTON DC 711PM 12

MRS A B MINER
RR I
TABLE GROVE ILL

THE SECRATARY OF WAR HAS ASKED ME TO INFORM YOU THAT YOUR SON

CAPT MINER WILLIAM D RETURNED TO MILITARY CONTROL 10 SEPT 45 AND IS

BEING RETURNED TO THE UNITED STATES IN THE NEAR FUTURE PERIOD

FURTHER INFORMATION WILL BE FURNISHED WHEN RECEIVED

E F WITSELL ACTING THE ADJUTANT GENERAL

705PM

Two Released From Japanese Prison Camps

Sgt. Leo Harmon of Bardolph and Capt. Wm. D. Minerf of Table Grove, prisoners of the Japs for more than three years, have been released from Jap prison camps, according to messages received by their parents, Mrs. Mary Harmon of Jacksonville, and Mr. and Mrs. A. B. Miner of Vermont.

Both were taken prisoner following the fall of the Philippines in the spring of 1942.

The government message to Mrs. Harmon which she received last night was the first word that she has had concerning the safety of Sgt. Harmon since victory over Japan was announced.

By coincidence, a letter which he had written October 7, 1944, was also delivered to Mrs. Harmon yesterday. The letter was written in a Jap prison camp. It is believed it was written about the time he was being transferred from the Philippines to Osaka.

Sgt. Harmon was the third man from the Macomb area to be reported missing in action following the fall of Corregidor. He was not reported officially as a prisoner until May, 1943.

The government message which Mrs. Harmon received was as follows:

"The secretary of war has asked me to inform you that your son, Sgt. Leo Harmon, returned to military control Sept. 11 and is being returned to the United States within the near future and will be given an opportunity to communicate with you upon arrival."

Mr. and Mrs. A. B. Miner, former residents of Table Grove, learned that their son, Capt. Miner is on his way home. The message stated that he was fine but gave no other details.

Earlier in the week the Miners received a letter from Capt. Miner, dated August 19, in which he stated that the men were awaiting planes to bring them food, medicine and other supplies. On the back of the letter he wrote, "Hello to all my friends and relatives in and around Table Grove."

Their last previous message from him was a card dated July 10, 1944, when he was a prisoner on Luzon. About two weeks following victory over Japan, the Miners were informed by the government that their son's name had appeared on a list of prisoners at Camp Hoten, Mukden, Manchuria, and it is from this camp that they presume he was released.

WITH THE U. S.

Miners Hear From Imprisoned Son

Mr. and Mrs. A. B. Miner of Table Grove have received two post cards this week from their son, Capt. William D. Miner, who is interned in the Philippine Islands prison camp No. 2.

He stated that he was well and uninjured and had received welcome food from the British and Canadian Red Cross. He would like to be remembered to relatives and friends. He reported that his Knox college friend, Capt. Milton (Doc) Whaley, is safe.

Mr. and Mrs. Miner had last heard from their son on Easter Sunday, 1942.

—God Bless America—

FIRST NEWS FROM CAPT. WM. MINER SINCE APRIL 5, 1942

Mr. and Mrs. Burns Miner received two cards Monday afternoon from their son William. This is the first news they have received from him since April 5, 1942.

On the cards, which were typewritten, but bearing his signature was the following: "Love to relatives Hello to Hazel Green neighborhood. Am uninjured and well. Received welcome food from British and Canadian Red Cross."

Capt. Miner is in Military Prison Camp No. 2, Philippines.

Words cannot express how joyous Mr. and Mrs. Miner are over receiving the news.

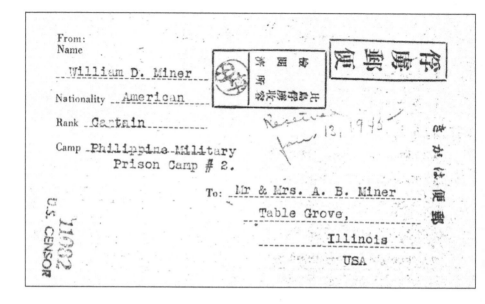

From:
Name

__William D. Miner__

Nationality __American__

Rank __Captain__

Camp __Philippine Military__
__Prison Camp # 2.__

U.S. CENSOR 11032

Received Jan, 13, 1943

To: __Mr & Mrs. A. B. Miner__

__Table Grove,__

__Illinois__

__USA__

IMPERIAL JAPANESE ARMY

1. I am interned at __Philippine Military Prison Camp # 2.__

2. My health is — excellent; good; fair; poor.

3. I am — injured; sick in hospital; under treatment; not under treatment.

4. I am — improving; not improving; better; well.

5. Please see that __last pay drawn included Nov, 1941. Wish__ __you to consider farm in Texas with me__ is taken care of.

6. (Re: Family); __inform uncle Charley that Knox colle a__ __Buddy, Doc Whaler is here with me and is doing fine__

7. Please give my best regards to __love to Martha, you all &__ __friends.__

Area lost a proud American this week

I'm so glad that Charleston's Red, White and Blue Days Committee honored World War II veterans in 1994 and 1995.

And I'm equally glad that the Times-Courier and Journal Gazette produced a 70–page section on the 50th anniversary of the end of WWII in September 1995.

Because we are running out of time to hear from those men and women who experienced the worldwide catastrophe that continues to shape our world.

We lost another veteran this week when Bill Miner died at the Odd Fellow-Rebekah Home at the age of 83.

Writing in our WWII section, Harry Read said it best about Bill Miner:

Bill Miner's odyssey in hell began on May 17, 1942, when he was taken by the Japanese on Cebu Island (Philippines), and ended, officially, 39 months later when he was liberated by soldiers of the Russian Army at a POW camp in Manchuria.

"Officially," because Dr. William D. Miner, professor emeritus of history, Eastern Illinois University, probably will never be freed from the physical and emotional ordeal of those 39 months. This gentlemanly, soft-spoken and frail man suffered more than most persons can envision in their most demonic nightmares.

Gentlemanly and soft-spoken is how I remember Bill Miner. We were neighbors on a west side Charleston street.

On balmy spring and summer nights, he and his wife, Mary Ellen, liked to sit in front of their garage, in the driveway, and watch the traffic and people go by. They always spoke to Cheryl and me on our walks.

I knew Bill Miner had been a Japanese prisoner during World War II. But it was Harry Read's story in our commemorative section that described it so graphically.

Miner had been in the ROTC program at Knox College in Galesburg and was a reserve officer until 1941, when he reported for duty in the Philippines.

Bill Lair

Lair is managing editor of the Times-Courier and Journal Gazette.

Bill Miner spent 3 years in captivity during WWII.

He spent most of the war in the capture of the Japanese, and barely survived.

From his diary, Dec. 25, 1944: "This is the lowest Christmas I ever had; we are without hope almost. Waiting to be put on ship again to sail to Japan. 2 meals, total one cup of rice."

And Jan. 1, 1945: "Still on ship in harbor, flies horrible, men dying. No water. Not a nice new year's beginning."

After his freedom:

"I have lost every close friend I had out here — I have been through filth, destruction, near death many times, and lived under conditions that warp men's souls. I haven't come through unscathed in the latter.

"I go home to a land of memories and hope, leaving behind a land of memories — memories of love, hate, fear, heroism, sacrifice, atrocities, destruction, torture, death, and of living friends.

"When I boil it all down, all I want out of life is 'quiet happiness.' All the glory, riches, power, pomp and splendor I have ever had or ever seen I would throw away for happiness and a healthy physical body. Such is life — it's a pretty empty affair at times."

Bill Miner always considered himself fortunate to have survived his ordeal.

"I am lucky. People fell beside me and people were blown apart beside me. Anywhere I went as a prisoner (Miner was in six POW camps) I tried to be aware of the situation and use it the best I could so that I could survive.

"Despite the controversy in recent years over President Truman's decision to authorize dropping A-Bombs on Hiroshima and Nagasaki, I believe it should have been done. I believe it for the tens of thousands of young Americans who would have died on the Japanese homeland. I also believe it for me. Had the war lasted only a few weeks more I could not have survived. My weight was down to 60-some pounds and I could barely stand."

And Bill Miner again said "I am lucky."

During his missions behind enemy lines, Miner earned the Silver Star for valor and the Purple Heart. Other decorations included the American Defense Ribbon with Battle Star, Philippine Liberation Ribbon with Battle Star, Philippine Liberation Ribbon with Battle Star, and a Presidential Unit Citation with two Oak Leaf Clusters).

Bill Miner was one of the WWII veterans who was featured in the July 4, 1995, parade and selected to ring the Liberty Bell.

"I've enjoyed it," he said of the festivities.

But mostly, Bill Miner told our reporter, "I'm proud to be an American."

LT. WILLIAM D. MINER
1914–1998

William D. Miner, a native of Table Grove, IL, received a Bachelor of Arts degree and ROTC, 2nd Lieutenant commission in 1936, from Knox College.

On May 22, 1941, Miner was ordered to active duty and immediately sent to the Philippine Islands and assigned to the 31st Infantry. Beginning in September 1941 he was made commander of the Philippine Army in Calape, Bohol. As hostilities developed, he was designated force communications officer on the special staff of Gen. B. G. Chynoweth, commanding general of the Visayan Forces in defense of the Visayan Islands. During part of the defense of the Visayans, Miner operated behind enemy lines and was awarded the Silver Star for this dangerous duty.

After the forces under Gen. Chynoweth surrendered on May 17, 1942, the Visayan POWs were sent to the Davao Penal Colony where Miner served 21 months as a slave laborer in the rice paddies. All told, he was in six different POW camps and on six Japanese "Hell Ships," including the notorious *Oryoku Maru*. Miner was rescued while at the Hoten POW Camp in Mukden, Manchuria, by the Russian forces on August 18, 1945.

Upon returning home, William Miner finished his Ph.D. in history at Indiana University and as a lieutenant colonel was active in USAR units in Bloomington, IN, and commanding officer of the Charleston/Mattoon, IL, USAR unit. He was professor of history, assistant dean of students, and director of Veteran Services at Eastern Illinois University at Charleston, IL. He also devoted much of his time to community service.

LEWIS A. MINER

Lewis Miner has been a Project Management Professional for over 25 years. He holds a Bachelor's degree in Physics from Eastern Illinois University with a minor in Business Management. He earned his Project Management Certification from Southern Polytechnic State University. His writing credits include contributions to *Permian Basin Oil & Gas Magazine*, *Astronomy Magazine*, *Tracing the Infinite*, *The International Who's Who in Poetry*, and the books *The Astronomy of One Constellation*, *Surrender on Cebu*, and *In the Shadow of the Rising Sun*.

"I have worked as a Senior Level Project Manager," Miner offers, "in various multifaceted industries; both private industry and government. However, I consider writing *Surviving Hell* to be my greatest project-related accomplishment. Preparing this third edition for publication was truly daunting! All told, it has taken more than 13 years to complete. For each edition, I grabbed for snips and slices of writing time, juggling between being a father to four and an employee with 60-hour workweeks and frequent job travel. There were days where I wanted to give up. . . . Fortunately, the opportunity to contribute to posterity and history, as well as pay honor and tribute to my heroic father, kept me going.

"In 1998, I started compiling information for the first edition of this book, *Surrender on Cebu*. For months I immersed myself in my father's documents, diaries, and notes (some written on Japanese toilet paper). I interviewed family members to glean remembrances of any war experiences my father had shared with them; and I researched and blended in historical fact. The book is dedicated to my father, LTC William D. Miner. It details his many, often-horrific experiences as a POW during World War II. During his 39-month internment/odyssey at the hands of the Japanese, he was imprisoned at six different prison camps and was a traveling captive on six different prison ships. He endured unspeakable suffering and was surrounded by death, facing his own mortality daily. Miraculously, his skeleton and spirit survived, and downstream he healed and thrived. It was with fond memories of, and gratitude for, the man he became that I took on this project . . . and completed the third edition."